DISCIPLINES IN TRANSFORMATION

A Guide to Theology and the Behavioral Sciences

William W. Everett
T. J. Bachmeyer

UNIVERSITY
PRESS OF
AMERICA

LANHAM • NEW YORK • LONDON

Copyright © 1979 by

University Press of America, ™ **Inc.**

4720 Boston Way
Lanham, MD 20706

3 Henrietta Street
London WC2E 8LU England

ISBN: 0-8191-0692-5

All University Press of America books are produced on acid-free
paper which exceeds the minimum standards set by the National
Historical Publications and Records Commission.

Library of Congress Catalog Card Number: 78-68570

To our mentors
Kenneth W. Underwood
and
Arthur Brandenburg,
in gratitude.

ACKNOWLEDGMENTS

This book arises out of an ongoing effort to relate theology and ministry to the behavioral sciences. Many colleagues and students have helped us to modify and refine this book. We especially want to acknowledge the encouragement and help we have received from Fr. Martin Pable, OFM Cap. He worked closely with us in developing the program in theology and behavioral sciences at St. Francis Seminary. The seminary student body and faculty have been indispensable in bringing our thoughts and methods to their present form.

Other institutions have also nourished our work along the way. The major direction and form emerged from working together at the Institute for Ecumenical and Cultural Research in Collegeville, Minnesota. Since then various members of the Lutheran World Federation, Department of Studies, in Geneva, Switzerland, have provided very helpful support and critique. Finally, colleagues in the Forschungstätte der Evangelischen Studiengemeinschaft, Heidelberg, and the Fachbereich, Religionswissenschaften, Johann-Wolfgang Goethe Universität, Frankfurt, have supported and critiqued the drafts of the manuscript.

To all of these individuals and groups we give our thanks. We hope that this document gives further impetus and clarity to their work.

For their good will and clerical efficiency, we thank Joyce Marcussen and Bette Draeger. For their interest as well as their help we thank Michael Witczak, Michael Krecji, and Ellen Rau.

Milwaukee
November 1978
William W. Everett
T. J. Bachmeyer

iii

PREFACE

Ministers and theologians have turned to the behavioral sciences in recent years both to carry out and to critique their own work. The rising psychotherapeutic professions have contributed new practices to pastoral care and Christian education. Sociological methods of planning, surveying, organizing and institutional change have found an eager audience in the churches, and have stimulated sophisticated Christian ethical reflection.

The interchange between the church professionals and behavioral scientists goes far beyond the bounds of ecclesiastical practice. It includes the task of theological construction as well. Freud and Marx have exerted enormous influence on theologians and ethicists. The challenges they raised have continued in dialogue with other figures in the personality and social sciences--Jung, Erikson, Rogers, Maslow and Skinner as well as Parsons, Weber, Durkheim and Arendt. Specific religious disciplines have their favorite partners in the behavioral sciences. Biblicists and liturgists, for instance, are especially open to structural-functional analyses of society, while pastoral counselors have been drawn particularly to Carl Rogers' work.

Handling the richness and complexity of theology-behavioral science exchanges (and we have not even mentioned the approach to religion by behavioral scientists) leads to a number of problems. First of all, there is no clear or systematic way to introduce students to this interdisciplinary field. Secondly, most contributions in the field do not reflect a critical methodology. Thirdly, all too often the interchange does not proceed in a comparative way that reflects important value issues present in the dialogue. Finally, theologians and ministers often converse with either the personality or the societal partners but not with both. This neglect leads to the impoverishment of their own thought and action. These difficulties have led us to develop a book with a two-fold purpose.

Our first aim is to order the field of theology and behavioral sciences to introduce people to it. Our second aim is to provide the basis for a critical and practical participation in these interchanges. While we seek to introduce people to the basic approaches of the sociological

and psychological sciences, our effort is not merely intro-
ductory, since we strive to order vast amounts of data
encountered in preliminary exposure to a number of disciplines. These disciplines represent the means by which
people try to grasp the realities of personality, society,
and Christianity. Therefore we are primarily concerned with
relationships among the three disciplines of theology,
psychology, and sociology. Half the book takes up questions
of method and criticism that stand at the heart of the
interplay among them.

This book is divided into five parts. Part I introduces the reader to the scope of the interdisciplinary
interchange. We use two typical cases that will be familiar
to many readers--the use of Carl Rogers' work in pastoral
counseling, and the use of Saul Alinsky's work in church-
sponsored social action.

In Part II we introduce a typological description of
the disciplines of theology, psychology, and sociology. We
order the disciplines in terms of their approaches and their
respective practices, theories and loyalties.

In Part III we begin to interrelate elements of the
three disciplines systematically. We believe each discipline has affinities with the other two. Indeed, we align
particular approaches in each discipline with approaches in
the other two. These alignments, or "triads" as we call
them, form the basis of critical interdisciplinary thinking.
In this part we also align certain dimensions of theory,
practice, and loyalty among the disciplines. We examine
these alignments in terms of both historical and contemporary theological figures who have developed their own syntheses of theological, personality, and societal considerations.

In Part IV we detail the decisions and commitments participants face in interdisciplinary dialogue. We analyze
Thomas C. Oden's engagement with psychotherapy and Gustavo
Gutierrez' engagement with sociology. Each figure has encountered the behavioral sciences in depth, and as a result
has made significant theological reformulations.

Finally, in Part V we look at the values and commitments behind the theology-behavioral science interchange
itself. We sketch our own notion of the enterprise of interdisciplinary, or "trilateral" theology.

The thread which weaves our interdisciplinary effort
together is what we call trilateral analysis. Essentially
this involves three separate steps of interdisciplinary
exchange. The first is making distinctions among the disciplines (Part II), the second is drawing relations among

vi

them (Part III), and the third is introducing changes in them (Part IV). In practice, participants engage in all three steps simultaneously in their interdisciplinary endeavors. We separate the steps to clarify the nature of the interchange and to look at it critically.

We originally developed our trilateral schema as an aid to teaching students in theology and behavioral science courses. We have since used it in consulting ministers, social workers, therapists, and community organizers to facilitate their own professional decision-making and their awareness of the critical dimensions of their work. In addition, our schema has proved helpful in organizing interdisciplinary curricula, in guiding research concerns, as well as in opening a novel path to important literature in the field. The book itself could be utilized in a large number of settings, ranging from seminaries, colleges, universities and professional schools of social work and psychotherapy, to churches and voluntary and professional associations.

CONTENTS

The disciplines of theology, psychology,
and sociology are ways of getting at the
realities of Christianity, personality,
and society. Approaches within the disciplines vary. Each approach has dimensions
of practice and loyalty as well as of
theory. The three disciplines can affect
each other in a variety of ways. Trilateral
analysis pursues three steps for identifying
issues in this complex interchange--making
distinctions, drawing relations, and
introducing changes.

Many pastoral counselors adopt client-
centered therapy. Some do not see how it
conflicts with their own theological
beliefs. Others do not see the societal
implications of Rogers' work.

Many priests and ministers use Alinsky's
style of community organizing. Some adapt
their own religious commitments to do so.
Others miss the tension between their
beliefs about religion and the social practices they engage in.

PART I

RAISING THE ISSUES

We begin this book by introducing the reader to the
encounter among the disciplines dealing with Christianity,
personality, and society. This encounter involves practices
and loyalties as well as theories. Theologians and ministers have engaged in frequent and intense dialogue with
psychologists or sociologists. In this book we want to move
these encounters from a bilateral to a trilateral interchange. Many of these interchanges have been intuitive and
pre-critical. A trilateral analysis seeks to move the
engagement to a more critical level.

In Chapter One we point out the three steps of making
distinctions, drawing relations, and introducing changes.
Each step exposes certain key issues in the interdisciplinary interchange. The rest of the book explores the meaning
of these three steps.

In Chapter Two we point out how some of these issues
have arisen in the encounter of the pastoral care movement
with the work of Carl Rogers.

In Chapter Three we explore the issues Saul Alinsky's
community-organizing work has raised for ministers, theologians, and churches. Both chapters raise problems and
issues that take us to the heart of the critical method
we call trilateral analysis.

1

CHAPTER ONE

STEPS IN TRILATERAL ANALYSIS

A. The Scope of Our Interest

This is a book on interdisciplinary thinking. Its
scope is framed by one particular interdisciplinary field,
theology and the behavioral sciences. Our goal in writing
is to stimulate new ways of approaching the disciplines of
theology, psychology, and sociology. Though our point of
departure is theological, our thinking is already imbued
with methods and concepts from the behavioral sciences.
Thus this is not strictly a book on theology, nor one
strictly on psychology or sociology. We will be looking
at the interchange among these three disciplines from a
perspective that itself is already interdisciplinary.

In the theology-behavioral science interchange, there
are many starting points and numerous directions one can
take. One might start from any of the disciplines and take
up the other two in any order. This requires that we
approach theology and the behavioral sciences in a comparative way. We are more interested in the fruits and pitfalls
of diverse approaches to issues than in the advantages of
any single approach. We contrast and compare alternative
possibilities and seek the truth within each.

We also see the behavioral sciences as essential partners for contemporary theology. Psychology and sociology
in particular and the behavioral sciences in general offer
fresh avenues for theological exploration. Some people see
the behavioral sciences providing a new philosophical base
for contemporary theology, much as Plato's and Aristotle's
thought have done in the past. The behavioral sciences themselves, however, are also shaped by philosophical constructs.
So while our aim is not to substitute the behavioral sciences for philosophy, we do see them as partners of importance
equal to philosophy. The implications of this dialectical
partnership lead us to most of the methodological issues in
our work.

B. A Brief History of the Theology-
Behavioral Science Interchange

Theology has always had implicit or explicit concerns

3

with self and society. Augustine, for instance, did not
have a "psychology" or a "sociology" as we would use the
terms today. Yet his thinking on the nature of the soul
and on heavenly and earthly kingdoms continues to influence
the thinking of behavioral scientists, philosophers, and
theologians to this day. Until the last century the Western
legacy of reflection about self and society has generally
been transmitted by theologians and philosophers.

In the last century psychology and sociology have become autonomous disciplines in themselves, independent in
thought and method from theology and philosophy. The result
has been a new relation between theology and the sciences
of self and society. Moreover, the new relationship has
many facets. On the extremes, Marx and Freud directly
attacked traditional theological claims. And theologian,
Karl Barth, defended theology against the pretensions of
these rising sciences. In a very different way the churches
in America have actively used behavioral sciences as instruments of ministry and of church and societal reform. Accommodation, rejection, and adoption have all marked the
theology-behavioral science interchange.

The behavioral sciences have an enormous impact on our
everyday lives. Their mode of thought shapes the way we
think about ourselves, others, our God, even the way we
think about our past and our futures. This is one reason
theology can be so helpful to the behavioral sciences.
Theological tradition carries modes of thinking and acting
from the past by which our current thought and practice--
so influenced by the behavioral sciences--can be assessed.
Actually, the most creative assessment is a mutual one, and
we will be using the theological sciences to look at the
behavioral sciences in a new light and the behavioral
sciences to see theology in a new way.

Theologians and behavioral scientists have been carry-
ing on this mutual interchange most intensely in the last
twenty-five years. From the theological side the result
has been transformations in church practice, in theology,
and in religious self-understanding. Churches have adopted
practices of counseling, group work and community organizing.
Theologians have grappled with issues of divine immanence,
the relation of love to justice, and the meaning of the
Incarnation in light of concerns raised by the behavioral
sciences. In an area of difficult definition, church people
have struggled with their own confessional, denominational,
and faith-understandings in a pluralistic and fast-changing
world in which the behavioral sciences have become a new form
of faith.

The overall dialogue between theology and the behavioral sciences in the last several decades has been

essentially intuitive and unsystematic. Theologians and ministers have adopted behavioral science ideas, practices, and even values, often in an uncritical way. Ironically enough, some behavioral scientists have treated religion in the same way. We call this the "precritical" level of interdisciplinary conversation.

We believe the theology-behavioral science dialogue is ready to move to a more critical level of thinking. The foundation for this has been laid in the theological camp by earlier figures like Seward Hiltner, Paul Tillich, and Reinhold Niebuhr and by more recent writers like Don Browning, Gustavo Gutierrez, and Max Stackhouse. Our method of trilateral analysis clarifies the methodological issues they have raised and indicates how the encounter should proceed.

C. Steps in Trilateral Analysis

People involved in the Church and the behavioral sciences are looking for ways to reflect critically on their work. They are aware not only of alternatives and tensions within their own field but also of implications their work bears for other disciplines. Theologians are aware that they deal with theories of self and society. Therapists know there are social and religious dimensions of counseling. Community organizers deal with religious and psychological factors in any program of community action.

We believe that such critical reflection involves making distinctions, drawing relations, and introducing changes. Our process of critical thinking can be stimulated in many ways. For example, we may experience conflicts when we introduce changes in our ministry under the impact of societal theories and practices. We may be unable to sort out the source of disagreements among professionals or between them and their clients or parishioners. In this chapter we want to describe briefly the three steps which can guide our process of reflection and show how problems arise when we do not observe them. Parts II, III, and IV of this book will then be devoted to filling out the substance of these three steps.

1. Making Distinctions

First we turn to the matter of making interdisciplinary distinctions. Our program involves three kinds of distinctions--that among the disciplines themselves, that among various approaches within a given discipline, and that among the dimensions of theory, practice, and loyalty.

a. Distinctions among Disciplines

When professionals with interdisciplinary interests become interested in another disciplinary area, they may fail to make distinctions among the disciplines. They often transfer concepts from one discipline to another without recognizing that the concepts come from two quite different frames of reference. As the philosopher Ludwig Wittgenstein pointed out, people confuse the different "language games" that arise from different "modes of life." This means they act as if there were no difference among the institutions and organizations through which ideas find expression. They erect new syntheses with no regard to longstanding traditions of verifiability, logic and practicability. We believe disciplinary distinctions are important boundaries. While not absolute, they help us define personal, social, and spiritual realities.

b. Distinctions among Approaches

Every discipline contains considerably different approaches to its subject. What disciplines may hold in common is a shared subject matter, codes of professional conduct, and some basic presuppositions. Apart from this, people within a discipline often proceed along quite different paths. It is thus important not to ignore these different perspectives or to try to meld them into a single harmonious approach.

For instance, in appropriating sociology, many Christian liturgists and sacramental theologians have spoken only with cultural anthropologists. Most, if not all, of these share a common societal perspective we call "systemic." They focus on the unity of society and the process of integrating individuals into it. Thus they are surprised when theologians adopt other perspectives, such as Marxist ones, which emphasize societal tension and the constructive value of conflict.[1]* Similarly many religious believers are drawn to psychologist Abraham Maslow's portrait of peak experiences as unitary, flowing, and loving.[2] These same people are often surprised when they confront a different psychology or a different religious approach that emphasizes personal conflict. It will be hard for them to understand psychoanalytic psychology or Calvinist theology, both of which stress personal and societal tension. Thus while people may prefer a particular approach in a discipline, it is important not to deny that other approaches see the same subject matter in a very different and perhaps contradictory fashion.

---

*Notes for this chapter begin on page 231.

6

c. Distinctions among Dimensions

Thirdly, participants in interdisciplinary dialogue
need to make distinctions among the three dimensions of any
discipline. Each discipline, as well as any distinct approach within it, contains dimensions of theory, practice,
and loyalty.

Theory is the rational clarification of our ideas.
Theory enables us to order our thought, action, and values
in a logical, consistent, and complete manner. It helps us
spell out the relationships among our various concepts and
how our various models of the world work in order to interpret reality. Theory helps us build connections between
our loyalties and our practices. It helps us describe the
way the world is as well as how it ought to be.

Our practice is the whole set of regular actions we
engage in. It includes the institutional patterns within
which we work, the various techniques we use, and the habits
by which we try to embody our theories and loyalties. Practices both shape our thought and loyalties as well as give
body to them.

Loyalties are the primary values at work in our thought
and action. They are the basic commitments and orientations
which guide us in the selection and use of our theories and
practices. They are often manifested in the symbols that
grasp us at a deep emotional level. They may exist as commitments to our present theories or practices or they may
drive us to change them and to change the world we live in.

Frequently, a theologian, sociologist, or psychologist
will account for one or two of the dimensions. However, in
ignoring or dismissing the third, often the value component,
a person does not account for something that could radically
change the character of his or her work. Operation Camelot
is a famous example of this neglect. A social-science
research venture in South America in the 1960's, Operation
Camelot was ostensibly a "value-free" and practice-free study
of certain features of several countries. In reality the
research was enmeshed with covert U.S. intelligence and
military operations. The expose of this venture did much
to raise the question of the values and practices of behavioral sciences in subsequent years.[3]

Along a different vein we find an emphasis on practice
to the detriment of theory and value in many church-
sponsored social surveys. The recent Sociological Study of
American Priests pursued very sophisticated opinion gathering
practices, with almost complete inattention to the problem
of theoretical or value contexts of the survey.[4] By only
sampling opinion, the survey avoided looking at wider

7

societal causes of those opinions, such as the conflicts between the middle class and the working class in the church.

A third example illustrates the failure to distinguish between value and theory dimensions--in this case in developmental psychology. Many developmental psychologists seem to presume that a later developmental stage is "higher" or "better" than an earlier stage. Lawrence Kohlberg's work stands at the center of this contemporary discussion. Kohlberg envisages people's capacity for moral judgment in a hierarchy of six sequential stages. In practice Kohlberg seeks to use Socratic moral dialogue to move individuals' moral judgment stage by stage toward the sixth. Yet Kohlberg does not squarely face the elitist implications of his hierarchy. Clearly a stage six person is better than a stage three person in his scheme. Kohlberg probably would not accept this value commitment stated so boldly. Yet, this value-assumption underlies both his developmental theory and his practice of moral education.[5]

Effective participation in church and professional life involves distinguishing all three dimensions--loyalty, theory, and practice. Ministry, for instance, involves the utilization of diverse practices, the transmission and development of values and ultimate loyalties, and the maintenance and revision of theology. The behavioral sciences are also gaining a fuller vision of the three dimensions, particularly with the reintroduction of the role of values into their self-understanding. Any adequate engagement within these fiel , not to mention drawing relations among them demands recognition of the three dimensions present in them all.

This completes our overview of the first step in trilateral analysis--that of making interdisciplinary distinctions. It is essential to differentiate disciplines, approaches, and dimensions. While this may seem obvious to some, many accomplished professionals ignore or bypass these basic distinctions at some point, as we have just shown.

2. Drawing Relations

Once we have discerned and clarified the distinctions among disciplines, approaches, and dimensions, we are ready to take the second step in critical thinking. We now begin to draw relationships among these components. Here we will examine and evaluate the way people have drawn these relations. We will first look at how they have related theory, practice, and loyalty; secondly, how they have related different approaches in a discipline; and finally, the relative position they assign various disciplines in the interchange.

8

a. Relations among Disciplines

The most frequent problem in drawing relationships among disciplines has been bilateralism--dealing with only two of the disciplines within the interchange. This kind of approach has been aggravated by the existence in many universities and seminaries of bilateral programs in either religion and personality or religion and society. In other cases authors may give a charitable nod toward a third partner, thus acknowledging it, yet not deal with it in a relational fashion.

Max Stackhouse, for instance, a leading figure in sociology and theology, remains in a bilateral exchange in his study, Ethics and the Urban Ethos.[6] He establishes the importance of transformed personality in his Trinitarian approach to a theology for urban life. However, he does not develop the personality aspects of his thought. In personal conversations Stackhouse has professed a preference for Erik Erikson's psychology. Yet he does not incorporate that into any systematic relationship with theology and sociology.

Many pastoral theologians face a parallel issue. They adopt psychology in order to understand the God-man relationship. Yet they neglect the ways social and institutional forces affect man's encounter with the divine. Roman Catholic authors like Adrian van Kaam, C.S.Sp., and Charles Curran write about human spirituality as if the believer existed apart from the institutional Church. They see interpersonal relations as the basic milieu for spiritual growth. They do not account for ways administrative and political structures hinder as well as foster creative and potent selfhood.[7] The same is true of Protestants. Seward Hiltner makes an attempt to deal with "community," yet also does not treat how culture and institutions shape personality.[8] Indeed, culture and personality shape one another, and pastoral theologians need to account for both in their attempts to offer vital alternatives for faith and spirituality.

b. Relations among Approaches

In every discipline there are a number of differing approaches. From within a discipline we can see the approaches as a harmony of perspectives, as a plurality of coexisting alternatives, or as claimants battling for supremacy. In the discipline of psychology, for instance, psychoanalysis and behaviorism often rival one another as exclusive interpreters of personality.

It is also possible to draw relations between approaches drawn from two or three different disciplines.

9

For instance, prophetically-oriented theologians frequently use the Marxist idea of alienation to speak about the Christian notion of sin. Yet not all social theorists listen to Marx nor are all theologians attuned to the prophets. Certainly Marx and the prophets have affinities for one another. We are interested in questions such as: How far do we push these affinities? How deep can they be carried into theory, loyalty, and even practice? What are the natural antagonisms as well as the natural compatibilities between these schools? Exploring such relationships among approaches can provide solid rationales for intuitive interdisciplinary connections.

One of the popular marriages theologians have explored in the behavioral sciences has been that between Marx and Freud. Reinhold Niebuhr used Freud to lessen the utopian revolutionary implications of Marx. Niebuhr drove the problem of social conflict so deep into the psyche that it could be resolved only beyond history. Gregory Baum seems to have followed much the same move. Both authors seem to depend on Marx and Freud for their basic portrait of self and society. However, Marx and Freud are not necessarily compatible approaches to self and society. They can be joined only in a very careful fashion. Freud sees the self in conflict, Marx the society. Joining the two leaves no realm for conflict resolution, unless one moves like Niebuhr to a cosmic arena beyond self and society. This leaves unanswered immediate questions about responding to or resolving worldly conflict.

In a similar manner, pastoral theologians have used psychological concepts to clarify the meaning of "salvation." Some equate salvation with Rogers' notion of the fully functioning person. Others identify salvation with Freud's notion of conflict management. Still others see salvation in terms of certain moral behavior. In using psychology to define a theological term, theologians of necessity select from very different psychologies. Fully-functioning religion stresses fulfillment on the individual's own terms. Behavioral religion rewards action the environment defines as fulfilling. A conflict management approach to salvation stresses the needs of both the individual and the environment. Thus the selection of "psychology" does not itself clarify what one means by salvation, or even identify one's "inner" or "outer" religious orientation. Which approach people choose affects the religion they will advocate.

c. Relations among Dimensions

Theory, practice, and loyalty necessarily imply each other. Theory is implicit in practice. Wherever a psychologist, community organizer or minister makes an intervention into the system he participates in, there is an

10

implicit reason or rationale for that action. He or she may
or may not be aware of a rationale at the time, yet reflection often yields reasons for action. This is one of the
tensions in professional education in America--bringing
together reason and action, theory and practice.

At the same time theory is implicit in value schemes.
Simply put, for every "should," a "why" is logically available. People who effectively communicate or transmit their
values have reasons for them. There are reasons some therapists believe in personal autonomy for clients while others
emphasize adaptation to culture. There are reasons for
believing in revolutionary change just as there are reasons
for holding to the value of the survival of the system. And
there are reasons for believing divine authority is passed
through apostolic succession as well as through charismatic
experience.

Given the interrelation of theory, practice, and value,
action and valuation are implied within theory too. Theories are not mere abstractions, but have direct implications
for practice. Some psychological theories of human development imply treatments in which patients "go back" and re-
learn what they failed to incorporate at a given stage. In
Christianity the idea of priestly power can lead to the
practice of the believer's receiving the communion host
directly on the tongue rather than taking it in the hand.
Durkheim's sociological notion of organic solidarity
implies that social problems can be alleviated by developing more comprehensive occupational groupings to integrate
deviant individuals into the society. These are but a few
examples of how theories have inevitable implications for
practices.

Likewise, within any theory there are implicit or
explicit values. The clearest example today is the controversy surrounding the sexist implications of Freud's "penis
envy" theory of female psychology. Alinsky's theory of
community organizing has explicit values about who should
have power and how power should be used--values often not
shared by those having a monopoly on societal or political
power. And finally, the doctrine of the Virgin Birth has
numerous implicit values about the ideal mother, non-sexual
yet procreative.

Thus we see theory, practice, and loyalty naturally form
an interlocking circle. Moreover, we generally try to draw
our loyalties, theories, and practices into some kind of
fitting congruence. We seek to adjust our models and concepts so that they accurately depict what we are doing. We
try to engage in practices that will further our loyalties.
In short, we strive for congruence among the three dimensions.
When we fail to relate them successfully we fall into

11

incongruence.

One of the most important forms of incongruence is
that between theory and loyalty. This is generally called
ideology. Here a theory or a conceptual description functions as a set of loyalties, or prescriptions. This glosses
over the distinction between "is" and "ought." This may
occur, for instance, when theologians describe the Church
as a "fellowship of believers." This description subtly
masks the dissension and unbelief of everyday church life.
It is important to know when a theory is disguised as a
loyalty or when a loyalty parades as a theory.

The relation between theory and practice can also be
tenuous. Theologians have encountered problems in trying
to move from a radical, Marxist description of society to
some adoption of practices for reform. On theological bases
they may accept Marx's description of oppressive societal
dynamics, and yet reject the revolutionary practices that
attend that analysis. When they adopt social goals that are
more pluralistic, open, free, or even communitarian, then
they are left invoking the practice of reform, not revolution.
Their practice or prescription does not flow from their
original analysis.

Thirdly, there is the disjunction between loyalty and
practice. In recent years psychological testing has become
a very important part of many seminary programs in evaluating readiness for ministry or candidacy for ministerial
education. Psychological tests are used to identify personality characteristics which may be quite unsuitable for
ministerial roles. The question then arises: to what degree
are these testing practices in line with theological values
in ministry? Is the testing practice only legitimating
personality values of middle class culture in the clergy?
Is this process of "identification" congruent with the kinds
of direction planned in traditional programs of spiritual
formation? Is the testing subordinate to the seminary's
goals or is it producing a new configuration of values?

3. Introducing Changes

As we get involved in drawing relations among elements
within any theology-behavioral science exchange, we almost
inevitably introduce some change into our original positions.
Our commitments to practices, loyalties, or theories in
other disciplines do not necessarily fit with those in our
own disciplinary homeland, or with the commitments we
believed we held originally. At this point we might
reassess the position we had assigned each discipline when
we first entered the interchange. In doing so we may discover the reasons we entered interdisciplinary conversation
in the first place. Or we may reach a point of disciplinary

change and only then realize where our path has taken us.

Interdisciplinary encounter involves interest in, contact with, and exchange among other disciplines. When we do make some disciplinary change as a result of the conversation, it is not always our own discipline that we change. There are both "domestic" and "foreign" disciplines. We see six possible outcomes in the last step of critical thinking. Each involves domestic and/or foreign disciplinary change.

The six outcomes are rejection of other disciplines, the addition of parts of a discipline(s) to one's own. the reduction of another discipline to one's own, the corroboration of one's discipline by others, the translation of one discipline into the terms of another, and the transformation of the disciplines at stake. Each outcome describes a distinctive way of approaching interdisciplinary change.

Each outcome also strikes a balance between substantive and formal commitments. Substantive commitments are the particular loyalties we hold. They are our "vested interests" in interdisciplinary negotiation. For example, we may believe that the Sacraments are the prime vehicle of the sacred, or that the Scriptures are literally true. We may believe people can always change, or that some people choose not to change. We may believe war is a necessary evil, or that it is never justifiable. These are examples of substantive commitments the participants might bring to interdisciplinary dialogue.

Formal commitments involve systematic, critical thinking involving all three disciplines. Formal considerations account for the distinction, relations, and changes that are a part of critical thinking. Substantive commitments are dearly held, but always in some way parochial. Formal commitments open our interests to their implications and alternatives.

Each of the six outcomes takes into account some blend of substantive and formal considerations. Rejection, reduction, and corroboration weigh substantive considerations more heavily. Addition, translation, and transformation put increasing weight in the direction of formal thinking. Whatever formula for making interdisciplinary changes we eventually decide upon, it will necessarily account for both our interests and for their systematic elaboration.

Our preferred outcome is reciprocal transformation. In this pattern of interrelation, each discipline is changed under the impact of the conversation. Through reciprocal transformation the disciplines respect one another's integrity and yet demand that each partner's contribution be

13

taken into account as well. Substantive commitments are the basis of any interdisciplinary change, yet in reciprocal transformation systematic, trilateral relations are fully considered as well. To engage in interdisciplinary encounter at all is to risk some kind of disciplinary transformation.

D. Summary

Our program of trilateral analysis is a program of action as well as thought. We have identified issues that face interdisciplinary professionals when they begin to talk with one another, when they become committed to one another's ideas or values, or use one another's practices. The current cross-fertilization among theology, sociology, and psychology is stimulating and rewarding. It can also be frustrating and confusing. By using our three steps of analysis, participants can reduce the disadvantages and increase the rewards of interdisciplinary work.

These three steps--making distinctions, drawing relations, and introducing changes--are also tools for identifying issues, problems, and possibilities in an interdisciplinary interchange. To illustrate these issues we shall now analyse two practitioners who have had a great impact on the Church and ministry. First, we shall treat psychologist Carl Rogers and second, community organizer Saul Alinsky.

CHAPTER TWO

CARL ROGERS AND PASTORAL CARE

We have just cited many ways theologians and behavioral scientists converse with one another. In the next two chapters we wish to deal with two cases in depth. We will take a representative of a particular approach to personality--Carl Rogers--and to society--Saul Alinsky.

We have picked Rogers and Alinsky for several reasons. First of all, each is a practitioner who is well known and who has had tremendous impact in his own field. Secondly, both offer excellent examples in their work of the interrelation of practice, theory, and loyalty. Finally, theologians, ministers, and church professionals have drawn heavily on all three dimensions of their work.

Many church professionals who have engaged Rogers and Alinsky in dialogue have done so on an intuitive basis. While much of this work has been stimulating and become widely popular, we wish to go beyond it to systematic considerations. Thus, Chapters Two and Three will lay the foundations for later trilateral considerations in Chapters Ten and Eleven. There Thomas Olden uses Rogers' work and Gustavo Gutierrez Marx's work in a systematic fashion. At this point we turn to the beginning of trilateral thinking by looking at Rogers' work and his overtures for interdisciplinary dialogue.

A. Client-Centered Therapy

Carl Ransom Rogers has influenced several generations of psychologists, ministers, and mental health professionals. We will be dealing particularly with Rogers' early work, since it has had such an impact on the pastoral counseling movement. Rogers' influence began in Clinical Pastoral Education where practice is the focus. His impact later spread to pastoral psychology departments in seminaries, and has affected diverse aspects of seminary education including liturgy, scripture, and theology.

We first will trace Rogers' work, dimension by dimension--his loyalties, practices, and theories. We then will move on to church professionals' encounter with each,

15

concluding with an overall evaluation of Rogers' contribution and of the dialogue itself.

1. Therapeutic Loyalties

In 1951 Carl Rogers opened his second book, Client-Centered Therapy, with a rather startling focus--the "faith" of the counselor. For Rogers, the essence of the therapeutic relation is the people in a situation--never any intellectual or therapeutic system transcending counselor and client. In Rogers' eyes, successful therapy requires the therapist to believe deeply that each individual has worth and significance. Two implications flow from this central conviction of the client's worth. The first is that clients have the capacity for, and the right to, self-direction. The second is that clients are responsible for their own growth. These convictions stand in contrast to other more directive therapies which assume that because of greater skill and knowledge the therapist is entitled to guide or direct clients in healthy directions. Rogers' belief in people's capacity for self-direction, however, includes even the area of potential suicide, the point at which other would-be believers start throwing in the non-directive towel. This strong belief in the client's capacity for self-direction might seem to be extreme, yet it is firmly grounded in theoretical and clinical considerations.

Rogers' approach makes the client, not the therapist, the central focus of psychotherapy. Yet Rogers also values certain qualities in the therapist. The good therapist exhibits congruence, unconditional positive regard, and empathic understanding. By congruence, Rogers means integrity, genuineness, and the capacity to be in touch with the deepest levels of one's own being. The opposite of this is feeling or acting in conformity with the expectations of others rather than with one's true self. Therefore, the Rogerian therapist does not diagnose his clients, because he does not wish to foist his individual feelings or perceptions on them. By this reserve, he permits clients to explore their own feelings and thus establish their own congruence.

By unconditional postive regard Rogers means that the therapist regards clients positively regardless of what they say, feel, think, or imagine. Nothing sordid, weird, or immoral should qualify the therapist's valuing clients as people of worth. This does not mean the therapist will agree with them but it does mean they will be unable to shake the therapist's conviction that they are worthwhile and important human beings. The opposite attitude is conveyed when the therapist accepts only part of the client's reported experience, or puts a subtle value on that experience. The effect is to limit the extent to which clients

16

are willing to explore the hidden and unacceptable parts of themselves--aspects which are often the source of their dilemma.

By empathic understanding Rogers means that the therapist makes clear in his responses to clients that he empathizes with and understands what they experience during the therapy session itself. Clients often believe they are the only ones in the universe with their particular affliction. They experience great relief when they meet someone who accepts them in spite of their problems. From the client's point of view, unconditional positive regard and empathic understanding are obviously closely related. Yet the latter carries the important quality of "being with" that the former does not.

Rogers notes that of the three attributes of the therapist, congruence is the most fundamental. If the therapist expresses positive regard toward clients but inwardly is afraid of them, they will pick up double signals and will not trust the positive regard they are sensing. Thus if the non-directive therapist finds that his feelings toward clients obstruct his positive or unconditional regard for them, he will report his experience directly to them at the time. The clients will then know that they can trust the therapist, even if he reports "negative" or problematic feelings. This congruence in the therapist promotes a credibility with clients that enables the therapist's empathy and positive regard to have a real impact. Thus Rogers' therapy is much more than a way of being nice to clients. It requires therapists to draw themselves into the deepest layers and furthest reaches of their own experience and that of their clients, whether these by joy, suffering, suspicion, rage, or fear.

2. Therapeutic Practices

In implementing his non-directive conviction, Rogers makes clear that there are no non-directive therapeutic techniques per se. By looking for techniques or tools, therapists lose touch with their clients' inner experience. Without this sensitivity, they may introduce some therapeutic deus ex machina inappropriate to their client's experiential fields. Just as Rogers keeps a wary eye out for therapists who believe in client-autonomy but behave in terms of client-inadequacy, so he is careful to pinpoint any therapeutic practices whose use will deny that autonomy. Therapists should avoid interpretations which say in effect, "Trust me. Really I know what's best for you."

Technically, then, we should say that the only true client-centered practice is empathic listening and non-directive verbal responses. In fact, however, non-directive

17

therapy has come to be typified by a technique called
mirroring of feeling. In this the therapist mirrors or
reflects back to clients their innermost feelings and perceptions, especially those on the periphery of their awareness. A client's anxiety could be reflected with the remark,
"You're so scared, you're tied up in knots." Such mirroring
can become a cold technique which Rogers would abhor. It can
be inappropriate, or heavy-handed, or just plain wrong.
The best use of the mirroring technique is by those in whose
hands it becomes the true recognition of client worth and
capability that Rogers upholds.

If therapists are truly to mirror client feelings and
perceptions without judging them they must bracket their own
self-concerns and take on those of the client. This absence
of self-concern is neither passivity or non-commitment. It
is an active, careful listening which exhibits positive regard for a client's total life expression at a given moment.
Furthermore, mirroring has great therapeutic power, for when
done skillfully it conveys to clients that the therapist
truly cares about them and truly believes in them. This is
the therapeutic payoff. It only occurs when therapists effectively implement their belief in the client's capacity
to actualize themselves. When the therapist fully cares for
them, clients realize that the therapist will not give them
a diagnosis and will not solve their problems. The therapist cares enough to let them suffer through their anxiety
and also to reap the rewards of reaching their own solutions.

3.   Therapeutic Theory

Rogers' commitment to respect the autonomy of his
clients becomes more understandable when we look at the theory that underlies his therapeutic practice. Rogers moves
consistently from the value of client autonomy to the
implementation of that value in the mirroring of feeling
to the theoretical concept of congruence. His therapy systematically intertwines loyalty, practice, and theory.

From his counseling experience Rogers has developed
both a theory of effective therapy and a theory of personality. Among his most important personality concepts are
the self-actualizing tendency, the organismic valuing process, incongruence, the self-concept, introjected conditions
of worth, and the fully functioning person. Together these
describe the therapeutic journey from fearful attachment to
an imagined past to open commitment to an emerging selfhood.

The self-actualizing tendency.   The cornerstone of
Rogers' personality theory is his concept of the self-
actualizing tendency. Rogers sees people basically as organisms striving to actualize themselves. Self-actualization
is the most fundamental human motive. It is prior to

18

motives of sex or aggression (Freud), of love (William
Glasser) or competence (Robert H. White). Regardless of
their inhumane social conditions or irrational motives,
Rogers sees people continually striving to maximize their
potential in a positive direction. If successful, they will
develop into what Rogers calls fully functioning persons.
If human organisms meet significant obstacles, the self-
actualizing tendency will become bent and twisted. Yet
it will not thereby cease striving. This conception
opens Rogers to the criticism of being a naive optimist.
In fact he is not.

> It disturbs me to be thought of as an
> optimist. My whole professional exper-
> ience has been with the dark and often
> sordid side of life, and I know, better
> than most, the incredibly destructive
> behavior of which man is capable. Yet
> that same professional experience has
> forced upon me the realization that man,
> when you know him deeply, in his worst
> and most troubled states, is not evil
> or demonic.[1]*

The notion of the self-actualizing tendency does not blind
Rogers to the reality of conflict, suffering, or even self-
destruction in life. He denies the pessimistic view that
classical psychoanalysis takes of human instincts and he
stands on a positive theoretical foundation instead--the
concept of the self-actualizing tendency.

The organismic valuing process. Every person possesses an organismic valuing process. This means that at some
level of awareness each person experiences what for him or
her is the ongoing striving of their organism. This inner
striving takes the form of a value-seeking process which
gradually unfolds in each individual. Each person has unique values, preferences, and strivings which are essential
reality for the individual. Rogers aims to protect these
from outer manipulation or exploitation. The prime dilemma
of those who come to therapy is that they have lost touch
with their inner valuing processes and are operating on
desires that are not truly their own. This leads to psychic
pain and tension. Incongruence is the experience of being
out of touch with oneself as well as it is the self-
consciousness and anxiety that accompany this dilemma.

Incongruence and the self-concept. As infants, Rogers
theorized, we are in touch with our organismic experiencing.

---

*Notes for this chapter begin on page 232.

19

We readily and spontaneously experience bodily sensation and feelings, and perceive a great variety of phenomena. Gradually in the "world" of infant and young experience, we begin to differentiate a part of that experience as our organismic selves. We discover the boundary between the "me" and the "not me." Because we are born into families, however, sooner or later we find that it is better not to experience certain parts of ourselves. Rogers calls this failure to integrate aspects of ourselves the failure to "own" our experience. For example, if our parents cannot handle the anger and frustration we experience in being a small person in a giant-sized world, then we may learn our expression of anger will get us punished. We may learn, on the other hand, that our expression of anger is accepted, but that sadness is not. In time we begin to form a picture of the acceptable parts of ourselves, i.e., a self-concept. The self-concept then functions as a filter determining which aspects of our organismic experience we may acknowledge and what parts we must deny. Whatever we must deny in ourselves at one level, however, still is part of our organismic experience at a different level. This disjunction between the self-concept and the actual organism is the state of incongruence.

Introjected conditions of worth. Once as infants we differentiate ourselves from others, we need positive regard for our environment in order to maintain and actualize our unique sense of self. As infants we are unable to supply our own positive regard. We are dependent on our parents or surrogate parents to provide it. As children we know we are worthwhile if others say so. Thus we are greatly affected by the attitudes with which our parents regard us. Parents often give a child positive regard only for certain things, only on certain occasions, or only for certain behavior. These conditions Rogers calls conditions of worth. We learn that if we are to get the positive regard we need, then we must meet certain conditions--not hit our sister, not speak back to parents, or not be angry. In order to get that regard, we then internalize the value-laden conditions that will get us parental approval. Should these values be congruent with our own inner valuing system, then we will be congruent. If in order to supply the positive regard we need, we will internalize parental values that are in conflict with our own, in so doing, we become incongruent. By denying qualities or values that are deeply a part of ourselves, we experience tension between our self-concept and our organismic valuing experience. The greater the conflict between our introjected self (the self-concept) and our inner organism, the greater tension we experience. Everyone experiences some psychic tension. Those who are unable to manage the tension or who want to change the balance may seek therapy.

Individuals who come to therapy often have a rigid

self-concept. They have denied or distorted so much of
their own inner experience that they have difficulty in
everyday life. Their perceptions may be so distorted that
they misread the verbal, gestural, and behavioral cues of
fellow workers. They may be denying sexual or angry feelings so strongly that they are having marital difficulty.
Such people live under great psychic tension. Their present
life demands that they change in order to function better.
Yet by changing they risk losing the values that gained
positive regard in the past, as conditional as that regard
may have been. Rogers believes that people will risk change
only in a non-threatening climate. Clients will not change
if they experience any further conditions of worth or if
they experience the conditions of worth they have taken from
their parents. This is the bind of every incongruent person.

The concepts of incongruence and conditions of worth
are Rogers' theoretical rationale for the desirability of
unconditional positive regard, empathic understanding, and
congruence--the three therapeutic qualities necessary for
growth. The therapist needs to provide the unconditional
positive regard that the client's parents did not supply.
She needs to let the client know that whatever the client
feels and experiences is permissible and acceptable. The
therapist should also provide an empathic understanding
that communicates acceptance and permission to change. This
is not license for immoral behavior, but permission to give
up oppressive bonds that the client no longer needs. The
third therapeutic quality, congruence, is essential as well.
The therapist must herself be in touch with the kinds of
feelings the client has denied in order to detect these
glimmers within the client. This is important because the
client is not able to own them. In detecting and reporting
these experiences back to clients, the therapist becomes a
mirror through which clients can see the parts of themselves
they have long avoided, and can come to own them.

The recovery of the forbidden and threatening aspects
of experience in a warm, accepting climate enables clients
to change their rigid self-concept and to accept wider and
wider aspects of themselves. In so doing, they claim more
and more of their own organismic valuing process. They
begin to change from the static, stagnant selves they had
been to more flexible selves in process. They become fully
functioning persons.

The fully functioning person. Self-actualizing people
are characterized by self-acceptance, flexible perception of
others, tolerance and prizing of others. The fully functioning people accept themselves in that they are open to
the wide variety of feelings they experience. They accept
them as no more and no less than feelings. They are able to
accept feelings of loneliness, anger, frustration as clues

21

to action they need to take, instead of condemning themselves for having the feelings. Self-acceptant people are
able to manage their feelings rather than be managed by
them. Consequently they are able to perceive the experiences of others more accurately and objectively. Thus, says
Rogers, the fully functioning person is both tolerant and
prizing of others. Just as internalization of conditions
of worth leads to self-rejection and self-distortion, so in
reverse the recovery of self-worth leads to the valuing of
others without placing unrealistic expectations or rigid
demands upon them.

Now we can see that Rogers' basic personality theory
is closely intertwined with the values he espouses and
with his therapeutic practices. Unconditional positive
regard, empathic understanding, and congruence are important
therapeutic qualities because they respectively reverse the
stultifying effects of conditions of worth, introjected
values, and incongruence. The technique of mirroring is
important in a climate of acceptance because it promotes the
congruence clients previously had lost. The therapist's
belief in clients' capacities for self-direction implies an
unconditional and radical acknowledgment of their worth.
It demands that the therapist provide a climate which pre-
cludes the imposition of new conditions of worth.

B. Theological and Ministerial Appropriation
of Client-Centered Therapy

Carl Rogers' work has received a warm welcome in the
pastoral care field, his theories of therapy and personality
have been the source of creative theological reflection, and
his compassionate words about the struggles of human beings
toward authenticity have captured the hearts of many in
ministry and other caring professions. We now turn to ways
that Rogers' work has attracted theologians and ministers.
First, we will look at Christian loyalties that parallel
his notions of empathic acceptance and unconditional positive
regard. Second, we will describe the work of several theologians who have used Rogerian theory in creative ways.
Third, we will examine the practical aspects of client-
centered therapy that have made Rogers so influential in the
pastoral counseling movement.

1. Christian Parallels to Rogerian Loyalties

Rogers' theories of personality is often called a
"self" theory. This is due to his emphasis on clients'
self-esteem and capacity for self-actualization. Also by
taking the client's inner experience seriously, Rogers departs from classical psychoanalytic and behavioristic perspectives, particularly those prevailing in the 1940's and
1950's. At that time most psychoanalytic diagnosticians

saw personal experience as representing something other than the client reported (Oedipal fixations, transference relations, etc.) and most behaviorist theorists avoided any notion of the self by describing learning in terms of relfex arcs and stimulus-response associations. Rogers, along with others like Gordon Allport, became a champion of the "self" in the world of psychological theory. His work has come to represent a special concern for persons.

Rogers' writings have drawn extensive attention from ministers, theologians, and lay Christians. They often find within Rogers' writings dim beckonings of images and symbols that have long been a part of their religious traditions. First of all, many find Rogers' emphasis on the self and inner experience an inviting version of a belief they deeply hold--the sacredness of persons. Secondly, Rogers' optimism about human potential fits well with the Christian hope expressed by St. Paul--that though sin abounds, grace abounds even more. Third, the freedom of clients to make their own decisions and their responsibility for growth fit in well with the faith assumption that people are created in the image of God.

Perhaps most enticing to Christians reading Rogers are the parallels between his notion of empathic understanding and the Christian idea of "agape" or selfless love. This is what Rogers says about empathic understanding:

> The counselor says in effect, "To be of assis-
> tance to you I will put aside myself--the
> self or ordinary interaction--and enter
> into your world of perception as com-
> pletely as I am able. I will become, in
> a sense, another self for you--an alter
> ego of your own attitudes and feelings--
> a safe opportunity for you to discern
> yourself more clearly, to experience your-
> self more truly and deeply, to choose more
> significantly.[2]

In light of the Christian value of self-sacrifice, Rogers' words depict the charitable selflessness that abounds in Christian devotional writings. Putting oneself aside, enter-ing into another's world, becoming another self for the client--these are concrete parallels to what God has done for humanity through the Incarnation, and what through love Christians do for their neighbors.

Charles A. Curran has applied these interesting simil-arities to a theory of what constitutes creative communica-tion.[3] He cites the need for a special form of listening called incarnate-redemptive communication. Curran sees all understanding and redemption grounded in the second person

23

of the Trinity. Christ is both Logos and Redeemer. Creative communication involves redemption because it affirms
the worth of those conversing. By being truly listened to,
Curran believes, a person feels worthwhile and appreciated.
This is redemption.

     Creative communication also involves incarnation.
This occurs when persons genuinely invest themselves in what
they say. They become "incarnate" as their words embody
their feelings, and even their whole being. As their words
become "flesh," people gain power to convey worth to others.
This is incarnate-redemptive communication. Clearly,
Curran presupposes the notion of congruence in referring
to the genuineness of the incarnate communicator. Redemptive listening occurs when the listener is empathically
mirroring the inner concerns of the communicator. Rogers
claims these produce self-acceptance and prizing of others.
Curran believes that through understanding and redemption,
God generates perfect love.

     Others have applied Rogers' quality of unconditional
positive regard to the Christian notion of covenant. God's
covenantal commitment to Israel is similar to the therapeutic commitment to a client. Just as through his covenants
God took Israel to be His people and promised they would
always be His people, so Rogerian therapists are similarly
committed to standing by the worth of their clients. The
therapist is steadfast in a way that God was steadfast in
His covenant relations in the Old Testament. God refused
to withdraw His covenant with Israel in spite of her
idolatries and propensity to sin. Client-centered therapists likewise remain steadfast in never compromising their
unconditional positive regard for their clients. Regardless of how clients feel, in spite of what they say, and
even in spite of their subtle attempts to get therapists
to judge them or to solve their problems, therapists must
remain committed to the conviction that clients are worthwhile and capable. Unconditional positive regard thus
provides a compelling analogy for illuminating the meaning
of unrelenting divine steadfastness.

     Though Rogers himself had a background of conserva-
tive Protestantism and attended Union Theological Seminary
in New York City, he had not initially conceived the rather
self-evident parallels between Christian values and his
therapeutic interests. Ministers and theologians who hear
Judeo-Christian motifs of anguish and transformation in
Rogers' description of the self have made the connections.[4]
It is not surprising that with the value Rogers places on
the self, on its potential for actualization, and on the
importance of empathy and caring, he draws an extensive
Christian readership.

2. Theological Reconstruction

On first reading, the notions of empathic understanding and unconditional positive regard seem to parallel the Christian values of selfless charity and steadfast love. Two Protestant theologians have taken these intuitions a step further and systematically examined Rogers' work in order to clarify the parallels between psychotherapy and theology. Thomas C. Oden's book, Kerygma and Counseling,[5] contends that Rogerian psychotherapy implicitly assumes that God is radically for us. This is the full meaning, Oden says, of Rogers' commitment to the worth of persons Don S. Browning's book, Atonement and Psychotherapy,[6] uses Rogers to construct a theory of Christ's atonement that is relevant to contemporary life. Browning sees Christ's crucifixion and resurrection in the context of God's empathic acceptance of the human condition.

Both Oden and Browning see a basic structure in the counselor-client relationship that has great affinities to evangelical Christian views of the God-man relationship. They see Rogers' theory of the stages of therapeutic progress bearing many similarities to the Christian drama of the individual's salvation. In Christian terms the self begins in a basic state of goodness (creation in the image of God) which is lost or distorted (the fall) and which leads to pain and despair (sin). God's love moves the self from selfish pride to loving selflessness.

Rogers also portrays the self in transformation. However, he does not attribute to divine initiative the move from preoccupation with self to self-acceptance and the prizing of others. Rather, it is the persons in the therapeutic relation who ultimately effect personal growth. Therapists enable clients to get in touch with their own organismic valuing process by creating an atmosphere of acceptance and permission. Both Browning and Oden respect this difference between theological and psychotherapeutic claims. They do not identify Rogers' notions as Christian, but instead use them as natural analogies for religious experience.

Browning and Oden then move in very different directions. Oden uses Rogerian constructs to critique psychotherapy itself. Browning uses Rogers to reconstruct theology. Oden claims that psychotherapy is really a secularized version of the Christian kerygma, and that therapists should recognize the implicit kerygmatic basis of their profession. Browning develops a notion of God as unconditionally caring for the world. God deeply feels the sin of the world, yet does not let evil diminish His capacity to care redemptively for the world. This contrasts with classical notions that God is "a se," an immovable and

unfeeling Being who needs no relationship with humanity.
Theologians other than Browning and Oden have widely used
Rogers' model of therapy and personality, but none have
been as systematic or careful in their efforts. They
both exhibit the third level of critical thinking we have
identified--making disciplinary change under the impact
of interdisciplinary dialogue.

3. Pastoral Counseling

Rogers' writings have attracted Christians interested
not only in spiritual values and systematic theology, but
also in the practice of pastoral counseling. William E.
Hulme refers to Rogers' <u>Counseling and Psychotherapy</u> (1942)
as the bible of the early pastoral care movement.[7] Ian F.
McIntosh says Rogers' influence was dominant if not
overwhelming.[8] In fact Rogers' practices have many advantages for counseling in a pastoral setting.

First, the practice of mirroring and of bringing
warmth and empathic understanding does not require the extensive technical training demanded by other depth therapies.
Second, many claim that client-centered therapy takes less
time than other therapies which report lengthy case histories. This is an obvious advantage for pastors with limited
time for counseling. Third, client-centered therapy is free
of technical jargon, and ministers can use it without
adopting a language foreign to the pastoral context. Moreover, the qualities demanded of therapists by client-
centered therapy are very similar to the moral and spiritual
character expected of the spiritual counselor in many
Christian traditions.

Most of the figures influential in pastoral care today
have relied on Rogers' work. Some have used it directly,
others have modified it for their own purposes. Charles A.
Curran, the grandfather of Roman Catholic pastoral counseling, uses Rogers extensively if not exclusively. European
Catholics like Andre Godin, S.J., and Raymond Hostie, S.J.,
have also incorporated significant amounts of Rogerian theory and practice.[9] Almost all the major figures in Protestant pastoral counseling have been influenced by Rogers. [10]
Two in particular are Seward Hiltner and Paul E. Johnson.
Both have had continuing and popular influence in the field.
Though pastoral counselors have used other psychologies than
Rogers', his remains the dominant influence.

C. Critical Evaluation of the Dialogue

Carl Rogers has greatly affected Christian spirituality,
theology, and ministry. His affirmation of self has fos-
tered recovery of the importance of individual spirituality
in an age of church upheaval and change. His careful

thinking about how people change has gained the attention of theologians interested in human motivation. His own personal congruence and his therapeutic consistency have made him a model for pastoral genuineness and practical effectiveness. His work is a model par excellence of how behavioral science can have a positive impact on church life and practice.

For many years Carl Rogers and Sigmund Freud formed the only formal psychological legacy for pastoral trainers and educators. In most Clinical Pastoral Education programs and seminary departments, the influence of both men is declining. Numerous other psychologies have gained popularity in recent years. These include the humanistic therapies of Eric Berne (Transactional Analysis) and Fritz Perls (Gestalt Therapy), the modern behavioral psychologies of O. Hobart Mowrer and William Glasser, the developmental psychologies of Erik Erikson and Lawrence Kohlberg, and even the older depth psychologies of Carl Jung and Alfred Adler.

Criticisms of Rogers' work (and Freud's) have followed in the wake of these new psychologies. Howard Clinebell claims that while client-centered therapy is valuable for pastoral listening, its dominance in pastoral counseling should end.[11] Pastors need other tools when they function as teacher, exercise ecclesiastical authority, or treat emotional needs in counseling. He suggests numerous kinds of counseling for which client-centered practices are not appropriate, including spiritual, marriage, and crisis counseling. Clinebell's critique is essentially one of practice, and implicitly one about the limits of a single approach to counseling. Thus his criticism comes at the first level of trilateral analysis—making distinctions among approaches in a discipline.

Others have challenged the effectiveness of the non-directive practice of counseling. Rogers himself acknowledges that not all people can benefit from his approach. Ian McIntosh questions whether the approach has even short-term effectiveness. He believes that in the long run Rogerians themselves are unable to be consistently warm, empathic, and non-directive. McIntosh agrees with Clinebell that the pastoral counselor must have diverse resources, techniques, and practices.[12]

Our perspective does not involve an examination of Rogers per se, but of the way church professionals have used his work. We will look at several issues in practice, theory and loyalty that arise in this psychology-theology dialogue. We will show how trilateral thinking can increase one's appreciation of Rogers as well as his contribution to pastoral care.

27

1. Distinguishing Practices

Proponents of both client-centered therapy and of pastoral counseling have been tempted to reduce one to the other. Reductionism from the psychological side would claim that all good pastoral counseling should follow Rogerian non-directive lines. Theological reductionism would claim that Rogers' work is really Christian at root and differs in no basic way from centuries old Christian spiritual guidance. Either form of reductionism obscures some important differences between non-directive and pastoral counseling.

First of all, the moral setting of pastoral counseling alters what otherwise might be a non-directive therapeutic process. The priest or minister is an agent of a moral tradition which often has specific positions on issues like suicide, abortion, and adultery. Rogerian therapy represents no such moral tradition. Thus, Don Browning says the Church's moral context should be the basis on which Rogerian practices are adopted.[13]

Secondly, a pastoral counselor represents a system of spiritual authority. Ministers and priests are familiar with the difficulties of playing a double role with their parishioners. It is hard to be directive authority and compassionate friend simultaneously. Client-centered therapists have no obligation to spiritual authority per se, though they are accountable to secular authority for responsible counseling practice. Making such distinctions between psychological and pastoral counseling helps clarify the similar roles within separate disciplines. Those who reduce one to the other have no conceptual way of handling the tension between fostering individual autonomy and cultivating creative compliance to ecclesial authority and morality.

2. Distinguishing Theories

We also must distinguish between Christian theology and Rogers' theory of the self. In one of the earliest and yet best dialogues between Rogers and Christian theologians, several of the latter compared his notion of self-actualization with Reinhold Niebuhr's idea of sin as self-love.[14] Some of these and other theologians have felt that the self-actualized person has no consideration for others. This would exemplify Pelagian efforts at salvation through one's own means. They believed Rogers has no concept of sin or of the "Fall" of humanity. Others like Thomas C. Oden see Rogers' idea of incongruence as a doctrine of sin. Then the human predicament would be lack of self-assertion or self-love, not the existence of self-love as Reinhold Niebuhr has claimed.

28

Part of the difference betewen theological and psychological perspectives on the nature of man stem from different ontologies. Psychologists deal with empirical and observable concerns, or what theologians would call an "immanent" perspective on man. Many theologians, however, stress the sovereignty, power, and transcendence of God. Thus they see psychological claims for human autonomy as blasphemous and striving against God. For them the ultimately real exists in the realm of the transcendent, not in the direct "here and now" of human interaction.

When it comes to basic issues like the notion of sin, it is important not to make a psychological claim into a theological one, or vice versa. Rogers is not a theologian, however many may have used him that way. Reinhold Niebuhr is not a psychologist, though he does have a theory of the self. In comparing the disciplines of theology and psychology, our goal is to respect the integrity of each discipline. This means keeping distinctions while we converse among the disciplines. This will also mean recognizing the diversity of approaches within one's own discipline as well as in the other. The debate on "Rogers' notion of sin" is really an intramural theological debate about the nature and extent of sin, a dialogue that is centuries old, and not one that has emerged on the horizon of Western thought with client-centered therapy.

There are also other reasons for distinguishing Rogers' or any other psychological theory from theology. For one, Rogerian and other psychological theories lack reference points for several notions essential to theology. Because of Rogers' concentration on the interpersonal milieu, theologians have difficulty utilizing his thought to develop their own ideas of church and eschatology. This is a limit of many theology-psychology dialogues, what we call "bilateralism." This in turn would imply some system of ethics for Christians, an area on which Rogers is silent. William C. Bier, S.J., finds Rogers' thinking aligned with situation-ethics, and thus unusable for longer range decisions Christians need to make. Oden points out that Rogers' theory has an implicit antinomian bias and avoids what classical Protestantism has called the dialectic between Gospel and Law.

Theologians who have changed their theories and practices under the impact of Carl Rogers' work frequently have also reduced one discipline to the other. In so doing they miss the richness of theological perspectives on the nature of man that exists within their own discipline, though perhaps beyond their own denominational confines. At the same time they are not perceiving two special contributions of Rogers' thought. First, Christians' moral behavior and sense of self-worth is closely related to the conditional patterns of worth they received as children. A doctrine of

sin needs to account for the way human development affects
Christian freedom and responsibility. Second, static or
rigidly internalized values, though they be religious,
prevent persons from growing as human beings and from
responding to God's grace. Theologians need, consequently,
to incorporate an element of self-criticism into their conception of religion. This is what we call "reciprocal
transformation," changing one's own discipline through the
impact of interdisciplinary dialogue.

3. Distinguishing Loyalties

Finally, we will look at the importance of distinguishing psychological from religious values. First of all, the
selflessness of the authentic, non-directive counselor is not
synonymous with Christian charity. The same selfless love
that led Jesus to have compassion for people also led him
to drive the Pharisees from the temple. Furthermore, the
counselor's empathic participation in the internal frame of
reference of the client is not identical with the meaning
of Christ's Incarnation. In the Incarnation God was present
and ministered to people. The danger of seeing empathic
participation as an example of this love is not that the
empathy is neither healing nor redemptive. Rather the pit-
fall is that the arena of salvation can be reduced to the
souls of individuals instead of including all of salvation
history. While this might seem quite proper within the
confines of an existentialist philosophy of the individual,
it is not appropriate to the biblical witness which finds
nations (Israel, Syria, Egypt), officers (monarchs, priests,
prophets, judges), and individuals all participants in the
Christian drama of salvation.

We end our consideration of the relation of theology
to psychotherapy by summarizing the significant influence
Carl Rogers has had on the invigoration of ministerial training and practice, on theological thought, and on new
understandings of Christian life and symbols. Our goal is
to put this dialogue between theology and psychotherapy
under close scrutiny. In this way those who wish to reduce
Rogers' work to old time religion or baptize him as a new
Christian prophet can begin to see his uniqueness and
integrity as a psychotherapist.

CHAPTER THREE

SAUL ALINSKY AND SOCIETAL MINISTRY

Churches have always been involved in attempts to remedy social problems, whether through acts of charity to bind up the wounded or through direct influence on government or economic organizations. Even within churches that profess to be uninvolved in "worldly matters" we find many arrangements for helping people secure the basic necessities for living. Moreover, many of these "withdrawing churches" greatly affect society through their very existence by posing fundamental criticisms of its structures and policies. The question therefore is not whether to have social ministries. The question is which approach to choose.

In recent years churches have employed numerous strategies for tackling social evils. Some have thrown their weight behind particular popular causes, such as the national mobilizations to stop United States war policies in Vietnam. Others have tried to influence decision-making elites through high level conferences on foreign or national policy. Many denominations operate large social service agencies dealing with family problems and mental health. Others campaign to change laws affecting basic moral concerns. Among these many forms of societal ministry we will examine closely the practice of community organizing--a controversial but very influential approach to social problems.

A. Alinsky-Style Community Organizing

In recent years many ministers have been attracted to the community organizing practices of Saul Alinsky and his colleagues at the Industrial Areas Foundation in Chicago.[1*] While Alinsky offered a distinctive approach to community organizing, many people associate his name with a wider variety of approaches to community problems.[2]

The interchange between Alinsky and the churches raises a number of issues characterizing the general encounter between the churches and the behavioral sciences.

---

*Notes for this chapter begin on page 233.

While neither Alinsky nor his school offer us a systematic
theory of society, their encounter with an appropriation
by ministers bears careful scrutiny for a number of reasons.
First, the encounter has been a popular one that has made
a wide impact over a period of at least fifteen years. Thus
a discussion and evaluation of it could prove helpful for
many people. Second, the sometimes bitter controversy which
has met ministerial appropriation of Alinsky indicates that
significant issues and interest are at stake.[3] Third, the
Alinsky method, both as theory and practice, is simple
enough to be grasped in an immediate way and related to
obvious counterparts and loyalties in Judaism and Christianity. In this chapter we will set out briefly the dominant
ways the churches have engaged Alinsky's approach to community organizing.

1. Community Organizing Theory

     Alinsky's analysis of social problems clusters around
five basic concepts--self-determination, power, self-interest, organization and conflict.[4] A "social problem" exists
when people are unable, whether as individuals or as groups,
to participate effectively in the major decisions affecting
their lives. This marginal position affects them more
deeply than any absence of goods and services. They become
apathetic and disoriented. This powerlessness is at the
root of the deterioration of their neighborhoods and their
inability to secure the goods and services enjoyed by the
wider society.

     People can determine their lives only when they have
power. Power is the capacity to participate in decisions.
It is the capacity to act. What happens in human affairs
is always a matter of power. It not only determines who
will make decisions but who will carry them out and who will
formulate issues for debate. The distribution of power
even affects mental life and culture. Our rhetoric, symbols, rituals, and philosophy become governed by our self-
interests in the pursuit or defense of power. The privileged
speak in terms of due process and working through the system, while the dispossessed march under direct appeals to
liberty, justice, and equality.

     For Alinsky, society itself is a series of conflicts
among at least three groups of people--the Haves, the
Have-nots, and the Have-a-little-want-a-little-mores. The
effective struggles arise between the first and the third
groups. It is here that the balance of justice is struck
in society. This conflict is not merely an economic one.
Power cannot be reduced to economic relations. It can arise
in the conflict over prestige, institutional control, education or customs.

All this is to say, thirdly, that human affairs are governed by <u>self-interest</u>. Self-interest indicates not only the more objectively describable defense of money, property, family, and country. It also refers to people's perceptions of their interests. A few people are motivated by perceptions of longer-run interest--preservation of just legal procedures, ecological constraint, or changing the society's basic ideas about race, sex, or acquisition. But most people operate according to their perceptions of their interests in the short run--preservation of their immediate neighborhoods, securing a decent job, or paying their bills. In either case self-interest is the motor of history, whether for good or for ill. The pursuit of self-interest by the powerful gives rise to injustice and exploitation. The self-interested struggle of the oppressed yields reform and betterment--at least until they too become powerful.

All stable relationships are built on the foundation of mutual self-interest. Self-interest can be transformed into power through <u>organization</u>. Without organization people may receive certain benefits from time to time--the garbage from the banquet of the rich--but they will never be able to secure benefits on a regular basis. With organization people can consistently compete with other groups in the struggle for goods. People can determine their lives only if they are organized on the basis of an accurate perception of their self-interests and the interests of their regular opposition. In that sense, the kind of organization which Alinsky strives to create is basically political. It takes its shape from American political parties and voluntary associations, in which self-interests can be mobilized effectively without denying the integrity of the members.

The purpose of any organization is power--the power to engage in <u>conflict</u>. Organizations create conflict and are built in conflict. To elicit participation they must cut issues in decisive ways so that people can pit "us" against "them." Conflict is not only the purpose of organization but also the means to build and sustain it. Conflict, rather than being a disease to cure, is the lifeblood of society and organization. People come to trust and support one another when they face common enemies discerned in open conflict. Battles yield the commitment, courage, and self-sacrifice that makes organization possible.

Conflict pervades and sustains life. It decides what people will think about and what they will deal with. Because power is complex and people's self-interests are manifold, the lines of conflict are constantly shifting. The struggle for power flows along many lines, demanding a mental and political agility even a Machiavelli would applaud.

2. Community Organizing Values

Alinsky's values and goals are already implied by his
analysis of social problems and social process. Though some
of these values appear both as instrumental values and as
ends in themselves, their chief end seems to be that of
empowerment. Gathered around this value are more traditional
general values of justice, equality, and dignity. In Alinsky's words, "we are concerned with how to create mass organizations to seize power and give it to the people; to realize
the democratic dream of equality, justice, peace, coopera-
tion, equal and full opportunities for education, full and
useful employment, health, and the creation of those circumstances in which man can have the chance to live by values
that give meaning to life."[5]

While Alinsky's talk of conflict, class opposition,
power, and radicalism leads many observers to call him a
Marxist, he is a distinctly American product. Some might
call him an urban populist. Moreover, while class analysis
finds frequent utilization among organizers, the goal of
organizing is much more that of group advancement than of
class overthrow. Moreover, while Alinsky frequently sounds
atheistic, it is the atheism of the prophet who attacks
false religion in the name of God's justice. He draws
freely on biblical concepts and language as well as liberal,
democratic values to sustain his arguments. Borrowing from
classical and contemporary political theoreticians he pursues a pragmatic activism. If he has any theological dogma,
it is that activity is divinity. If he has any sociological
dogma, it is that power is captive to no man or group. In
short, Alinsky is the thorough activist.

3. Community Organizing Practices

Alinsky's practices, like his values, also flow from
his analysis of society. Any practice which builds lasting
organization can be brought under the Alinsky tent. However,
some techniques and skills stand at the core of the "Alinsky
method," a term he would have professedly abhorred. At the
center of his preferred practices stands a certain kind of
person--The Organizer. In Alinsky's description of the
organizer we find the key to his practices: The organizer

1. arrives in a community at the request of a group
which represents that community or its real interests in
some effective way,

2. surveys the community by listening to a wide
number of people and identifies their definition of the
basic issues in that community,

3. locates the people who have a following in that

34

community. These leaders are the foundation stones for building a community organization,

    4. assists interested persons and leaders in defining their interests and issues more precisely,

    5. helps them engage an issue that will enable them to build an organization and gain power through establishing a postive image as a winner, and

    6. withdraws when formal organization has been established, enabling the organization to become self-sufficient and independent of all outside funding or control.

Organizers are always enablers and do not seek power on their own. They organize because they gain intrinsic satisfaction from seeing people become self-determining, engage in conflict, and emerge from apathetic powerlessness. They are extremely adaptable, becoming all things to all people in order to bring them together. They are workers to the workers, hippies to the hippies, elders to the elderly, without losing their own sense of identity and realism about their own prejudices, values, or worldview. They can adopt any strategy that seems likely to work and change strategies without nostalgia when they fail. Finally, they have a sense of humor to preserve a sober realism about people and society. Clearly the organizer is an extraordinary person. Alinsky made no claim to have cultivated more than a handful in his lifetime.

B. The Ministerial Response to Alinsky

Churches and ministers have responded to Alinsky in three ways: a pragmatic adoption of his methods and practices, a re-ordering of theological priorities and understandings, and a redefinition of the ministerial role in terms of organizing.

1. Practical Appropriations

Adoption of Alinsky's practices has been strongest among those churches grounded in geographical parishes. For them, what is good for the neighborhood is good for the church. Without a stable neighborhood there can be no stable parish. Conversely, organizers turn frequently to the churches for community leadership, meeting space, and funding. The symbiotic relationship is purely pragmatic and practical from both sides. Some people claim that the presence of community organizing efforts will directly revitalize churches, but others contend that experience in organizing may create clergy-laity tensions as new lay leaders arise in previously patriarchal ecclesiastical settings.[6] Regardless of the merit of these opposed claims

Alinsky has been popular with churches on additional, more theological grounds.

2.   Theological Reconstruction

Ministers and theologians have drawn on Alinsky to revitalize the concepts of God's power, of sin, grace and salvation. In most churches the attribute of love has taken precedence over God's power, judgment or wrath. But organizing brings the attribute of power to the fore. Power lies at the heart of the active life, just as it lies in the essence of God. The essence of God is action. And action is simply the manifestation of power. Power is central to community organizing just as it is to God. To say that God is all-power (omnipotence) is not to deprive people of power. It is to legitimate their search for power.

Power enables us to define both sin and salvation. Sin is powerlessness. As James Luther Adams has put it, "powerlessness tends to corrupt, absolute powerlessness corrupts absolutely."[7]   In order to make sense of this approach to sin we need to change our understanding of sin's context. Sin does not point to personal and psychological matters first of all. It is not merely a matter of intent and disposition. It refers primarily to social structures of injustice. It is a faulty arrangement of power in society. It is unbalanced relationships among groups, between businessmen and consumers, bureaucracies and neighborhood organizations, between banks and homeowners. The fundamental cause of this injustice is an imbalance of power. The only way to repair the injustice is to redress the balance of power.

Sin is the condition of a social system of unequal power relationships. This systemic evil affects even the deepest inner recesses of people's self-esteem and emotions. Salvation from sin means empowerment. Salvation is an Exodus from slavery--an act of power against oppressors. Here all the prophetic and biblical themes from Israel's hope and pilgrimage find a point of contact with contemporary experience. Alinsky's own free use of these themes demonstrates that these affinities are due to direct inheritance rather than mere coincidence.

Grace is the sign of the presence of power. It is the new freedom found in power as well as the new strength that enables people to work for power. Moreover, because power is found in organization, grace is always something that occurs in organization. It creates organization and is conferred within the context of organization. This can even be taken as a new way of saying, as does Max Stackhouse, that "outside the church there is no salvation." From a societal and organizational perspective, the Church comes to mean "those who are called out of ordinary existence to actualize a vision of life as transformed under the conscious influence of the ultimate and most worthy power of existence."[8]

3. Redefining the Ministerial Role

Within this theological formulation Jesus emerges as a leader but not as an organizer. Though He led the disciples and in that sense "founded" the Church, he certainly did not organize it. Alinsky claims that Jesus was a miserable organizer. It was Paul who knew how to organize. Jesus may have provided the inspiration, but it was Paul who knew how to blend competing interests into a network of mutually supportive organizations.

By offering new interpretations of Jesus, Paul, or the saints, Alinsky's theological disciples have affected many minister's definition of their role in the Church and in society. The minister need not be an imitation of Jesus--an example for others of higher ideals. He or she can be an organizer of people to attain the power which God intends for them. The minister works behind the scenes to enable people to organize themselves. Since the nature of sin and salvation has been defined firstly in terms of group conflicts, the object of the Church is not to provide a place where individuals can be cured of sin by ministers. The Church is an organization on the march against principalities and powers. Thus, the prime concern of the minister is not the individuals in the parish but the creation of organization. The Church as an institution is the minister's first concern.

This priority is not a callous disregard for individuals scarred and brutalized by the warfare of life. The organization minister, believing that organization conveys grace, must tend primarily to building that organization. The direct "cure of souls" must be left to others in the organization. Ministers are organizers, not healers. They heal only through organization.

Ministers have great difficulty, however, being pure organizers. Their status in the community usually impels them to assume a leadership position. Indeed, organizers often turn to ministers to legitimate their work and to perform the leadership task in the neighborhood. But their traditional leadership role is altered under the impact of the organizer role. This further complicates the tension they already face between their personal counseling and community roles.

But even in this conflict between therapeutic and organizational roles we find not a destructive opposition but a mutual transformation. In their relations with individuals organizers must first of all listen. Like the counselor, the organizer must believe that healing begins with listening.[9] Moreover, organizers must listen with the psychologist's third ear to detect underlying goals, motivations and self-interests--the solid foundations for viable organizations. We will not construct a whole counseling, psychological or therapeutic theory out of these scant leads here. We only want to note that Alinsky provides significant possibilities for entering into this task.

C. The Demand for Critical Evaluation

So far we have described the positive form of the encounter between community organizing and the Church. But this engagement has not been without its critics. Critiques against Alinsky have been marshalled on the grounds of practical achievement, theology, and ecclesiology.

1. Practical Criticisms

First, does it work? Numerous sociological studies have analyzed the success of such efforts in a number of cities.[10] In terms of the goal of greater local participation in major decisions the record is uneven. Organizing works well in working class neighborhoods still possessing a number of homeowners. But it achieves, at least in its standard form, lesser success among people outside the job system. People without homes, jobs, status, or belongings have little self-interest in the normal sense. Among these people methods other than community organizing must be pursued.

Moreover, radical critics claim that Alinsky is really a parochial conservative. He does not take on the suprametropolitan structures that affect local community life. He deals with cities as closed systems and thus leads people into ineffective limited strategies. In short, Alinsky is not radical.

In terms of the concepts we introduced in Chapter One these critics are faulting Alinsky for an inadequate relationship between his theory and loyalties on the one hand and his practices on the other. He seems to analyze society in a way that calls for polarization and revolutionary overthrow but in reality settles for much more modest achievements.

In response to such charges organizers argue that organizing is a continual process and not a state to be achieved. Today's powerless European immigrant is tomorrow's white racist. The liberating union of today is tomorrow's oppressor. At this point in the argument success begins to be measured in terms other than that of achieving community power. It is measured against the value of making it possible, even sporadically, for people to participate in genuine action and power. Their lives have been touched by profound meaning, by actions that produce stories and inspiring memories. They have really lived.

To make that kind of shift in the process of evaluation is to introduce the nagging question of "success in terms of what value?" We not only encounter the difficulties of measuring power, participation, or self-determination. We also must clarify the goals that organizing really pursues. What is power? What is real participation? What are the goals of human life? What makes life worth living? In pressing these questions we break through into theological domains, where we are greeted with critical questions from theologians.

2. Theological Critiques

Many theologians criticise Alinsky's exclusive focus on an ethics of ends and means--whether they call it a utilitarian or simply a consequentialist ethic.[11] Christian ethics, they argue, is an absolute ethic which does not concern itself with achieving ends. It calls for the immediate realization of certain virtues or dispositions, such as the ideals of perfection presented by Jesus in the Sermon on the Mount. Any calculation of means and ends, especially the justification of acts purely on the basis of their intended ends, radically conflicts with the Christian ethical stance.

Secondly, Alinsky's means almost always involve conflict. Conflict, the critics argue, is intrinsically unloving. It is an unloving means and can never be justified even by the claim that it is a means to love the oppressed. Moreover, it works more frequently to destroy people and organizations than to build them up. While conflict makes reconciliation necessary, it does not reconcile in itself. The Church has to exist apart from conflict in order to provide the basis for adjudicating it.

Thirdly, Alinsky's dependence on self-interest as the basis for organizing is a gross underestimation of the persistence of sin. The Church completely abandons its theological message when it begins to think of itself exclusively as a coalition of self-interested groups and individuals. The Church must try to be an altruistic community of love and uphold that ideal for all people. Moreover, it must try to show that genuine community and justice ultimately depend on love and self-sacrifice. In short, Jesus' death and resurrection are not only the path to a new life, but the real hidden foundation of all existing life. Participation in community organizing and proclamation of its rhetoric can only corrupt the Church's message if not its life.

All of these theological claims urge a greater respect for the integrity of theology and Christian life over against any efforts to reduce or translate it into community organizing terms. Each one of these critiques also employs some alternative approach in society or personality to bolster its critique. For instance, the claim that conflict is intrinsically unloving is a psychological claim that needs to be assessed against psychological categories. Alinsky, however, would contest that he is not making a psychological claim and that any attempt to interpret him in this way is to misconstrue the nature of his societal framework of meaning.

Each of the theological claims, moreover, can be faulted for having paid inadequate attention to other approaches in Christianity which would embrace a different hierarchy of values and different approaches to society and personality. The stance of the critics is itself uncritical of the differences among theological schools.

3. Ecclesiological Questions

These theological criticisms also include criticism of the way organizing affects the ministerial role. Critics of the organizing model of the minister's role stress the centrality of the liturgical or counseling roles of the minister. The minister, priest, or pastor is basically a liturgical leader. He or she is primarily a priest who cares for the cult, by which the Church remembers its commitments and truly encounters God and receives His grace.

As a person of culture the priestly minister is concerned with preserving these ideals in their purity, detached from tactics and interest groups. By preserving these transcendent symbols the priesthood nourishes an embracing sense of ultimate authority for church and society. In so doing it cultivates the common elements in the culture which can be the basis for reconciliation.

When this liturgical critique takes on a more sociological form it argues that as a cultic leader the minister is primarily concerned with culture, not with society, with authority, not with power. With regard to culture and authority Alinsky is far from conservative. While he appeals to the principles of constitutional democracy his emphasis on the importance of power leads to a neglect of the need to conserve the constitutional authority that makes it possible to resolve conflicts in a public realm or court. By seeing the political and legal process as a product of conflict he fails to attend to what needs to be done to preserve the authority that leads people to respect that process. The short-range strategies flowing from Alinsky's rhetoric undermine attainment of the ideals he professes in his more reflective moments.

Ministerial critics also draw on psychology to assess these proposed changes. Though rarely expressed openly in recent days, they believe that pastoral counselors must be entirely neutral, lest they contaminate the counseling or therapeutic transaction. To be a public figure with definite moral and political commitments will only infect the client's mind with distracting material that prevents dealing with that client's unique dynamics. The counselor must not only avoid expressing value judgments but shun political involvements as well.

The appropriation or rejection of Alinsky's method, in whole or in part, is not a simple matter. It involves not only sociological but theological and psychological analysis as well. It is not a neutral matter of ministers picking up some effective practices, but of contests among loyalties, values, and views of human affairs. This brief survey of some central aspects of the encounter between community organizing and the churches has attempted to show that the interchange between theology and social science is manifested in widely-known practical affairs as well as in theoretical conversations. Any evaluations of this interchange, whether at the theoretical or practical level, leads us into a thicket of complex and difficult questions.

This rich interchange challenges us to sort out the ways people engage and criticize Alinsky's method and thought. Critical issues emerge in the discernment of distinctions within and among disciplines, in drawing adequate relations between theory, loyalty, and practice, and in the creation of theological and sociological changes in this process. In this chapter we have raised the question of discerning the real differences between ministry and community organizing. We have shown how Alinsky's theory and practice may undermine the very constitutional, legal, and democratic loyalties which he espouses so dearly. Finally, we have called attention to the ways that theologians have changed their theories, practices, and even loyalties under the impact of Alinsky-type organizing.

Our next step is to penetrate more deeply into the process of trilateral analysis. We first examine the distinctions within and among the disciplines dealing with Christianity, personality, and society.

PART II

MAKING DISTINCTIONS

Making distinction is the first step in trilateral
analysis. It involves separately examining the three disciplines of theology, psychology, and sociology. Famil-
iarization with each partner is the foundation of interdisciplinary dialogue. We will therefore look at the
respective dimensions (theories, practices, and loyalties)
and approaches in each.

We entitle the following chapters according to the
field of action, thought and commitment in which each discipline operates. By saying "Christianity," "personality,"
or "society," we emphasize that each discipline operates
within a wider context of loyalties and practices.

In showing the variety of approaches in the three
fields, we lay the groundwork for understanding the complex
relationships they can form. The distinctions among the
dimensions underlies our later discussion of incongruence.

CHAPTER FOUR

CHRISTIANITY

Our interdisciplinary point of departure is Christianity. The term "Christian" embraces the manifold theories, practices and loyalties found among Christians past and present. The label "theology" might have constricted our attention unduly to theory, while that of "ministry" or "church" might have narrowed our concerns to practice. We are not using the broader label of "religion," because we will deal only with Christian actors and thinkers. We believe our general method is relevant to the interplay between the behavioral sciences and other religious groupings such as Judaism and Islam, but our purpose in this book must be more limited.

According to our analysis Christianity can be understood as a realm consisting of three dimensions--practice, theory, and loyalty. In the loyalty dimension appear the basic symbols of Christianity--words and images such as God, Body of Christ, the Cross, or the Dove. The term "symbol" originally depicted the simple creed affirmed by believers in Baptism. It has since come to mean any representation which goes beyond simple designation of fact and which evokes a wide range of deep repsonses in people-- responses that already begin to produce that to which the symbol seems to point. Thus, the Crucifix is not merely a reminder of a person called Jesus who died on a cross during the Roman rule of Israel. It generates a vivid sense of identification with all suffering that is undergone to redeem humanity. Symbols combine deep feeling, conviction, commitment, and meaning. They give form vitality, and direction to the loyalties of people.[1]*

In Christianity theory is generally known as theology. Theology is a rational attempt to understand faith and the object of faith. Theologians seek to conceptualize religious events, symbols, and experience so that they can be related logically or systematically. Theologians do this so that preachers can formulate a coherent and persuasive message,

---

*Notes for this chapter begin on page 234.

and so church people can think about relationships in some consistent way. Theology tries to order the basic practices of Christianity as well as its basic symbols. Theology therefore embraces pastoral or practical theology as well as dogma and doctrine. It attempts to describe the phenomenon of Christianity as well as the objects of its faith, trust, and belief.[2]

Christians generally call their practices "ministry," "mission," or "church." By practices we mean the observable patterns of action undertaken by Christians, whether as members or as leaders and officers in the Church. They include prayer as well as worship services, denominational organization as well as social behavior. The various ways the churches secure and train their professional personnel stand together with practices of spiritual direction and pastoral counseling. In speaking of these practices we will of course have to use concepts, just as we have to use concepts to talk about symbols. Whether theological terms offer the best description of these practices rests on the results of consultation with theories in the behavioral sciences--a task which lies ahead of us.

A.   The Christian Approaches

We look to the three different approaches that give us access to Christianity. Here any attempt at typology confronts enormous difficulties. Christian history spans two millenia and millions of lives. Moreover, the Church has taken on many structures and practices within various cultures. Therefore our efforts are provisional means to engage in critical inquiry and action. The distinctions among approaches should help us engage in critical interchange among alternatives.

Our categories should also give us an idea of the consequences different choices entail within Christianity. Thus, we will make these distinctions in the tradition of "ideal-type" thinking. Each approach is a pure alternative which almost no one follows through in total systematic clarity. Each represents dominant tendencies and possibilities. Historically each has existed in a dynamic tension with other ideal types. Ideal-type thinking helps us see sources of change and stability as well as chart possible consequences of a situation.

In this typology we have tried to hold together the basic patterns in ecclesiology, ministerial practice, historical traditions, and theology by directing our attention to the grounds by which Christian bodies or individuals legitimate their practices and thought. What is their distinctive final appeal? What seem to be the basic alternatives for legitimating the historically significant variety

46

of Christian life? Our threefold distinction of Christian approaches attempts to respond to these questions in a way that is true to the integrity of the Christian phenomenon. On this basis we find it helpful to distinguish among three approaches to Christianity--the prophetic, the cultic, and the ecstatic.[3]

1. The Prophetic Approach

The prophetic approach is characterized by its unique attention to the Word of God. Here every Christian concern must be grounded in God's Word as it is revealed in Israel's history. This Word of God is known through understanding the written record--the Bible. The Bible is the Word of God. We could call this the biblical perspective as well, except that "prophetic" resonates with more appropriate connotations for our purposes. In using this term, however, we assume something substantive about the content of the Bible--namely, that it is basically a "prophetic" theology. Ethics and proper behavior occupy its central focus--from covenant and Torah to Sermon on the Mount and apocalyptic judgment.

a. Prophetic Loyalties

Prophetic guides lead us to values and loyalties clustered around this central loyalty to the Bible and its prophetic demands. We ought to read and understand this Word. We need to be literate in order to grasp and expound its message. We should strive to interpret its consequences systematically for our thought and action. But mere understanding is not enough. We must obey God's commands and conform to God's will as revealed in the scriptures. The Bible is an adequate rule for our lives because it is not a hodge-podge of insights or commands, but a logical and rationally understandable communication from God to His people. The classic Lutheran cry, "sola scriptura" epitomizes this attitude.

These values and commitments are vividly expressed in the symbols Bible and Word of God, as well as Torah, Covenant, Commandment and Kingdom of God. God encounters humanity through a particular covenant with a particular people. The promises of the covenant find their meaning if not their complete fulfillment in human history. The Commandments are not merely a cause for our humiliation but also express God's promise to realize a perfect human community. Wherever we find such symbols as these we have probably taken on a prophetic approach to Christianity.

b. Prophetic Theory

The theology of the Word of God flows from these loyalties. The Reformation traditions set in motion by Martin

47

Luther and John Calvin have produced a host of prophetic theorists of the Christian faith--from John Knox to P. T. Forsyth. Its wider bonds embrace New England Puritans like Cotton Mather as well as Mennonite contemporaries like John H. Yoder. Most Evangelical theologians, such as Carl F. H. Henry in the United States, share the prophetic orientation in our sense. While Karl Barth may be best known as a theologian of the Word of God, his writing is also heavily infused with themes discerned by cultic guides. His emphasis on the vast gap between humanity and God, a heavily prophetic theme, is modified by his vision of Christ as the eternal reality of God's presence in Creation. In recent years this prophetic stream has surged forth in the work of Gustavo Gutierrez, James Cone and Mary Daly.[4]

Prophetic theology usually tries to order Scriptural revelation into some kind of logical focus that brings together the central Scriptural themes. This is not at all to say that such an effort is missing in the other two approaches to Christian thought. However, each of them adds something distinctive to it--the cultic introducing the thought arising from the priestly tradition and the ecstatic certain kinds of personal and communal experience. The prophetic theologian tries to present the Word of God as a "pure" message to be heard and understood. In reality this means placing the minds of Biblical experts--the rabbi and scholars--at the fore.

Generally, this interpretive effort has employed theories of covenant, history, law, and sin, and of imminent judgment and Kingdom of God. The Church is treated as an eschatological assembly of the elect. It emphasizes God's awesome transcendence rather than His immanence, the infinite gap between our wills and His rather than our harmonious partnership. His grace lies more in the divine decision to look on sinners favorably than in the specific strengths he gives them in order to attain to His presence.[5] Because of the boundless freedom of God the Church is construed more as a respondent to God than as a transmitter or occasion of His work. The bond between God and the Christian Church often appears as tenuous as that between God and the world in general. Indeed, in some recent "secular" versions of the prophetic approach we find the latter connection severed altogether in favor of a "world come of age."[6]

Prophetic theologians tend to approach Jesus as <u>rabbi</u> and <u>prophet</u>, the fulfillment of Messianic prophecy, and the first fruit of the coming Kingdom of God. Jesus' historical ministry of teaching, healing and prophecy is more important than His resurrection presence in Eucharist and preaching (kerygma). Since the Bible is the Word of God directly present for the contemporary reader, the prophetic theologian must attend more closely to the historical matters presented there than to an explication of certain of its dimensions that undergird a subsequent tradition or specific kind of experience. Readers must be brought into a direct relationship of obedience to the teachings of Jesus and imitation of His life.

This obligation to what is primarily a historical record of events does not mean that prophetic theology is any more difficult as an intellectual effort than that found in the other two approaches. Certainly ecstatic experience and sacramental mystery pose equally formidable problems for human intellectualization! However, it does present theologians with the peculiar problems of finding connections and an orderly message in a wide range of events and historically conditioned interpretations.

c. Prophetic Practice

As is obvious by now a great many Protestants adopt a prophetic orientation, at least in the dimensions of loyalty and theory. These kinds of symbols and concepts have been borne historically by Presbyterians, Congregationalists, and Calvinistic Baptists. We find sects such as Jehovah's Witnesses as well as large numbers of Lutherans, Methodists and Evangelicals on the prophetic itinerary. Prophetic orientations also arise as distinct minorities within Roman Catholicism and Pentecostal movements as well.

The ministerial practices emphasized by this approach seek first of all to preach, teach, and interpret the Word of God. Preachers are trained in rhetorical skill as well as scriptural exegesis. Since believers must have a direct relationship with the Scriptures, prophetic churches spend a great deal of time on educational efforts. Sunday school, vacation Bible schools, Bible study groups and the support of Bible colleges often prevail over practices of devotionalism, personal meditation, liturgy, and even worship that we find elsewhere in Christianity.

Because of the Bible's ethical demands, prophetic churches often tend to be rather sectarian--either withdrawing from the society or aggressively trying to transform it. They are more likely to engage in social criticism, including the support of stricter codes of personal conduct, than are other churches. Sometimes prophetic Christians, in order to give adequate witness to the Kingdom of God, draw aside in small communities governed by rules based on the Bible.

The creation of a tight-knit community of the righteous over against a corrupt world leads to rather exclusivistic membership practices. Coupled with the emphases on biblical literacy and study of Scripture, this sectarian orientation demands that church members first attain a way of life and thought that sets them apart from the world--they can be clearly seen to have been "called out." While they have been tormented by the same internal struggles as other people they have overcome them to the extent that they are new people. The community continually assists them in maintaining their new discipline.

This organization of the elect has been maintained to various degrees of purity. Sometimes it is modified by allowing the presence of "half-way" Christians in the Church under the strict control and tutelage of an elite of the righteous, as in many Calvinist churches. Other times the Church becomes a loose, often intinerant following of a biblical prophet whose whirlwind presence puts under judgment the tasteful moderation of settled Christians.

Prophetic Christians try never to lose sight of the Scriptures. They are the sole and sufficient revelation of the will of a mighty Lord whose righteousness is both judgment and salvation. But there are many Christians who contend that they thereby present too constricted a view of Christianity's terrain. It is not enough, they say, to make the Bible the sole loyalty without discriminating among the many practices, theories, and secondary loyalties within it. When the prophet directs our attention to the substance of covenant, conflict, sin, and prophetic judgment, others remind us of the passages of sweet comfort, affirmation of human goodness, and of the authority attributed to the Church founded by Jesus. As we inspect more carefully these themes of Church, of Christ's sacrificial presence, and of God's fatherly embrace of all His children we find ourselves on a different approach altogether--led by a cultic guide.

2. The Cultic Approach

People pursuing a cultic approach never stray far from a vision of Church, cult, and Sacrament. In them all the other elements of Christianity find their appropriate context and meaning. Matters of such importance can never be interpreted narrowly. "Church" is the historical bearer of the true worship of God. The cult constitutes all those actions which "cultivate" the Christian life, leading it through all of life's experiences with a wide range of symbols and rites. "Sacrament" embraces all kinds of efficacious symbolic action. It means the effective and tangible presence of God in Christ. Because of the importance of ritual action in cult we might have called this a ritual or liturgical approach. On the other hand, since most cultic traditions require a priesthood to care for the purity of these activities, we might have called this a priestly as distinguished from a prophetic orientation. However,

50

"cultic" seems to balance the general reference to ritual action with the specific reference to historical bearers of a cultic approach to Christian faith and life.

   a. Cultic Loyalties

   Through the center of cultic Christianity runs the desire for communion with God through participation in efficacious symbolic actions. This goal is not the absorption connoted by "union with God." It is a structured communion best symbolized in the family or brotherhood gathered for Eucharist.[7] The image of parental care this gathering evokes can be picked up not only in loyalty to Father figures in the Church, but to Mother figures as well. Underlying these vivid symbols and persistent loyalties stands a fundamental affirmation of an unbreakable relationship between God and His creatures--a relationship established by Jesus and made available to all through the Church's sacramental actions.[8]

   This relationship has been established above all through Jesus' sacrifice. Through sacrifice of Himself He became fully obedient to the Father. Through sacrifice of Himself He became fully open to all of humanity. He became the fulfillment of Israel's sacrificial tradition. The value of sacrifice finds vivid expression in the symbol of the crucifix. Through such suffering comes eternal life. Moreover the suffering presented in crucifix is an eternal moment which is constantly manifested in the sacrifice of the Eucharist. Here are gathered together the essential elements of communion, parental presence through priest and family, and Christ's eternal sacrifice in body and blood. All other sacraments find their ground or purpose in this efficacious meal of resurrection. Through these actions and mysteries Christians come to participate in the divine life. Communion with God is a goal already present in the cultic acts ordained by Christ. Through them He is present with us for all time. Their preservation and purity tower above all other Christian concerns. Loyalty to Christ cannot be separated from loyalty to the priesthood and Church which represent Him for us.

   b. Cultic Theory

   In recent time these cultic commitments have received a number of varied theological interpretations. Some of these result from ecumenical encounters with other Christians and others from the introduction of new philosophical or behavioral science concepts. Karl Rahner is the foremost sacramental theologian utilizing philosophical concepts, while Edward Schillebeeckx has found increasing help in the behavioral sciences.[9] More traditional approaches can be found in the work of the late French theologian Emile

51

Mersch, and Anglican theologians like E. L. Mascall.[10]

Cultic theology works out the rational grounds and implications of the belief that God is present in certain actions of the Church today just as He was present in Jesus Christ. The Church is the Body of Christ and through the sacraments the presence of God in the world.

Cultic theologies in the medieval period stressed the concept of transubstantiation in order to elucidate the mystery of God's presence in sacrament. Transubstantiation was a way of discussing how Christ could be fully and efficaciously present in bread and wine. These alone were chosen by God. These alone embodied the Christ. The Church might present these elements in various ways but they themselves were hallowed by God.

In our time cultic theologians, often influenced by anthropology and other behavioral sciences, emphasize the need for symbolic action in order to generate and reveal human fullness. These theologians ground cultic action in human nature itself, whether they speak of the psychology of individuals or the ritual and symbolic needs of groups and nations. The symbolic structure of human existence and the nature of cult are two points on a vector pointing directly to God. They describe humanity's basic thrust toward God and His goodness rather than to the Devil or to sheer chaos.[11]

Moreover, God reciprocates His creatures' desire for communion with Him. God finds a kind of completeness in communion with man. Whereas from the human side cultics articulate an anthropology focused on ritual action, from the divine side they usually rely on a metaphysical philosophy to show how God has a disposition toward His self-presentation in symbol and liturgy. We find the former effort in the sophisticated work of the English theologian, B. R. Brinkman.[12] Karl Rahner and Bernard Lonergan exemplify modern efforts to give metaphysical grounds for God's presence. Both of these theoretical moves seek to express the belief that in the Sacraments instituted by Christ and preserved in His body, the Church, believers encounter God in the mystery of salvation.

The cultic vision of Christianity does not at all overlook the Scriptures but finds in them God's efforts to prepare the world for His efficacious presence in Christ. It finds in Christ the founder of the Church and the institutor of the cult and Sacraments which continue His ministry until He comes again in glory. The Bible is continued in the history of the Church. The Church and its sacraments (some would even say the Church is sacrament) are the fulfillment of the Bible.

52

Because of its openness to the richness of human art
and thought cultic theology can assume many shapes and
patterns. However, all this richness can never take it
beyond Church and cult. It can encompass almost any point
found in other approaches to Christianity as long as these
features tower over the landscape.

c. Cultic Practices

We have already indicated that Roman Catholics,
Orthodox, and Anglicans are the foremost representatives
of a cultic conception of Christian faith. In addition
we find strong cultic tendencies in Lutheranism, popular
religious movements and among some American Black churches.
Thus, to equate the cultic approach with the Roman and
Anglican churches would be an excessive constriction.

To avoid this narrow view we need to observe the
practices peculiar to this orientation; namely, its concentration on acts of celebration, liturgy, and sacramental
rite. In this context the minister is first of all a cultic leader. Since participation in these ritual events is
the primary task of the Christian life, priests must strive
to involve everyone in appropriate ways and thereby affect
them at their deepest levels of thought and motivation.
These rituals can depart quite far from any forms they may
exhibit in the Bible or the early Church. All kinds of art
and action can be used to lead people to the efficacious
heart of the liturgy.

This concern to sanctify individuals, mediate divine
forgiveness and grace, and to rehearse the drama of human
redemption also determines the cultic approach to church
relations with society. As Ernst Troeltsch and H. Richard
Niebuhr have shown in considerable detail, cultics are more
concerned with making the society safe for the cultic life
of the Church than with transforming the society according
to some ideal will of God.[13] Where social critique arises
it tends to judge the society for not meeting the human
needs of church members rather than for its disobedience
to God's will. If they base their judgments on a vision of
a societal ideal, critical cultics have generally found it
in a law of human nature more than in a revelation from a
transcendent God. Moreover, social critique finds its practical manifestation in reforms through the present social
structures. Those with a cultic orientation tend to rely
much more on rulers, leaders, and elites to reform the
society than to produce whole new social microcosms or
counter-movements.

At the center of the Church's internal as well as
external relations stands the priesthood. Priests are the
product of intense training and personality formation.

Because they are charged with sacred things they are removed from customary patterns of life. Moreover, because the cult which they conserve in its integrity is the Church's whole reason for existence, they come to have general supervision over the whole life of the Church as well. It is in this sense that cultic churches tend to be "hierarchical." They are, as the origins of the word imply, ruled by priests. They do not have to be "bureaucratic" as the modern connotations of the word imply, so long as the priesthood has ultimate control.

Combined historically with priesthood but in many ways separate from it is the cultic practice of the religious life. As we have seen, the prophetic approach to Christianity sees God's calling to a purer life in terms of a new city or new society ruled by God--the Kingdom of God. Attempts to actualize it in this world have led either to highly sectarian critiques of the social order or to the establishment of whole cities and communes, usually withdrawn from the world. When this same higher call is encountered in the cultic approach it appears in terms of the religious orders, whose members live apart from the world and pursue a more rigorous ethical life. This impulse to the religious life differs in practice from its prophetic articulation in that it does not identify itself as the true Church in toto. It is only a part of the Church with a particular function of prayer, charity, or ecclesiastical service. Moreover, it does not try to be a pattern for the whole society. It is a company of people pursuing personal ideals of holiness who have banded together for mutual discipline and support. The prophetic sect, commune, or "saving remnant," though similar in many ways to this cultic practice, differs significantly from it.

While the vistas opened up by prophetic and cultic approaches seem to cover every aspect of Christianity, there have been Christians who have been dissatisfied with their inattention to the experiential side of cult and word, Church and God. Out of their struggle we can discern a whole different approach which we have called the ecstatic.

3. The Ecstatic Approach

Ecstasy is an experience of being outside oneself, of being taken up into some kind of rapture with a greater power, only to find one's true self. It exhibits a depth of vibrant feeling that goes beyond normal experience. This kind of phenomenon determines the loyalties, thought and action of many Christians. Certainly the centrality of experiencing the Spirit goes back to the early Church and before that to the bands of charismatic prophets--King Saul being perhaps the best remembered. In our own times we speak of experiential Christianity, Pentecostalism,

54

charismatic movements, mysticism and spiritual religion, all of which are successors in this ancient line.[14] We would have no great quarrel with using these common terms to describe our third ideal type. However they are also used to quite different effect in cultic contexts, so we have chosen the more distinctive term "ecstatic" to characterize this approach to Christianity.

a. Ecstatic Loyalties

Ecstatic Christianity finds its culmination in the personal experience of the Spirit. Worship, evangelism, and Christian witness prepare us to receive the Spirit of God as He gave it in Pentecost (Acts 2:1-21). Every Christian gathering ideally re-creates its own "upper room" where it can receive the Spirit. Christians are led by the Spirit rather than by human customs or reasoning. They are known by the freedom they have from bondage to law, etiquette, mores, and institutions. Feeling and disposition are far more important than exegesis or ritual, personal regeneration far more compelling than social criticism. Ecstatics can often be identified by their commitment to the symbols of Fire, Spirit, and Dove. The Fire expresses the intensity of experience generated in the hearts of believers by God. The Spirit symbolizes God's gracious and mysterious presence. The Dove manifests the gentle and elusive peace which God gives to people apart from their personal condition or social role.

Dance, song and spontaneous expression of the reborn Christian have a very high value for ecstatic Christians. They are visible signs that God's work has indeed been done among ordinary people. Certain gestures, shouts of joy or bodily movements can compress together a whole set of vital motivations. They are living symbols of the Spirit's effective presence.

The ecstatic is committed to feeling the Spirit in a thoroughgoing way that totally renews the self. Men and women receive through these experiences a new life in which they can have freedom and spontaneity--a liberation that goes beyond mere physical needs or conformity to a new law of God.

Ecstatics place great importance on the notion of love. God's love for us is infinite. Our capacity to return divine love knows no bounds. Understandably, love of neighbor is a prime ecstatic loyalty, which in turn legitimates many ecstatic practices. This illustrates how ecstatics quickly turn to practice to define their theology. Historically this has given rise to the charge of their being anti-intellectual or untheological.

b. Ecstatic Theory

Because of their very values, ecstatics have trouble
legitimating any reflection upon their position. Thus
their representation among theologians is always considerably less than among Christians as a whole. However they
have made a distinctive contribution to Christian thought.
We find many ecstatic themes in St. Paul's writings and
in Luke-Acts. We find similar ecstatic emphases in John's
Gospel, once again restrained by a basically cultic thrust.

In our own time the work of Paul Tillich can be understood as a defense of the ecstatic position, in which
the goal of life is an "ecstatic reunion with the es-
tranged."[15] Likewise, we find strong ecstatic impulses
in the mystical tradition, whether it is expressed by St.
Theresa of Avila or the American Quaker Rufus Jones.[16]
Many of the streams in Pietism can be appreciated best
from an ecstatic standpoint. Revivalist preaching tends
to be dominated by ecstatic strains from George Whitefield
to Billy Graham. Generally, as with Graham, this tradition is intertwined with prophetic orientations. In the
case of John Wesley, however, we see an ecstatic reformer
emerging from a cultic context.[17]

Because of its loyalty to personal experience
ecstatic theory often appears as autobiography.[18] The
Spirit's freedom and variety of impacts escapes rational
formulation. We can only speak for what it has done for
us individually or we can offer some basis for the possibility that life finds its fulfillment in the personal
experience of God's overwhelming and vibrant power. Even
given these strictures we can identify a few concepts
pervading ecstatic understandings of the Christian life.

Chief among them is the notion that our lives find
their ultimate meaning in the events in which we are
seized by a greater power. Under the impact of this
greater power we stand outside our normal selves while we
are led by another spirit. But in being taken over by
God's Spirit we are actually led into new depths of true
selfhood. We experience newly found feelings, newly
opened thoughts and visions, and a sense of well-being that
we never could have acquired on our own.

This fulfillment of the self is neither a result of
gradual growth (as in cultic practice) or simply of God's
call and justification (as in prophetic theories), rather
it is due to the radical invasion of the self by the power
of God. The growth and the fulfillment of His call may
emerge from this radical conversion, but this conversion
must be the foundation for all else. Conversion to the
Christian life is more than the performance of certain

public actions, such as baptism or confirmation. It is more than taking on a certain ethics of love or justice. It involves a total reintegration of the self around this personal event in which we are transformed by the Spirit of God. The Christian life is a deeply personal and individual articulation of a soul-shaking experience.[19]

c. Ecstatic Practices

The kinds of practices engaged by ecstatic Christians range from the quiet meditation of the Quakers and certain mystics to the shouting and seizures of some Pentecostal assemblies. In the contemporary Church we find a proliferation of experience-centered prayer groups, such as the charismatic-renewal movement in the Catholic Church, and personal growth groups of all kinds in mainline Protestant denominations. It is clear from this description that while the ecstatic form of Christianity is not prominent institutionally, it is extremely widespread among Christians and can have a great variety of manifestations. What holds them all together is their common appeal to experience and to cultivation of an experience of divine spirit.

By its very nature ecstatic Christianity is not amenable to large scale organization or the creation of a professional clergy. Since the fundamental ground for legitimating such organization is personal experience, there exists little space for group discipline which appeals to Scripture or Church tradition. Ecstatic Christians group together, break apart, and regroup in new combinations constantly. They constitute a movement or an underground stream rather than a stable institution.

Church leadership arises when a group of people recognize their common bond with the dynamic qualities of personality manifested in someone who seems to be led by the Spirit. Leadership is charismatic in this sense. Its consolidation rests on the leader's ability to provide a context and an inspiration which nurture the experience of the Spirit and growth in nourishing the fruits of the Spirit.

Stable ecstatic leadership has exercised its powers in intinerant revivalism, much of radio evangelism, faith healing and practices of divination and discernment. Ecstatic assemblies have also gathered around charismatic preachers on a fairly regular basis in "tabernacles" and store-front churches. Institutionally these are all practices of ecclesiastically independent ecstatic groups. We should not overlook the dependent forms of this orientation within both cultic and prophetic articulations of the Christian life--the cloistered and lay mystics, the faith healers, and approved evangelists, not to mention simple

57

lay devotionalism in many forms.

B. Relations among the Approaches

We have already indicated that each approach offers significantly different alternatives to Christians. Moreover, we can identify some customary ways in which they intersect each other. For instance, in defining ministerial roles we can either proceed by inspecting the Scriptures (prophetic), by spelling out the requirements posed by the need to provide for worship and the Sacraments (cultic), or by providing a way for enspirited Christians to lead other Christians (ecstatic). These three very different ways set forth the grounds and functions of Christian ministry.[20] Each will criticize the other from its own perspective. The prophetic asks of the cultic, Is your view of Communion or Eucharist really Scriptural? The cultic will in turn ask, Where do you find a norm for ministry in the diversity of scriptural records? What you need is some way of ordering those materials around the central religious reality, which is the festive banquet of the Eucharist. The ecstatic criticizes each for a sterile dogmatism which blocks out the Holy Spirit. They in turn demand of the ecstatics that they discern the difference between the Holy Spirit and the imaginations of our hearts or the works of the Devil.

In this brief example we can see evidence of a general pattern. Prophetics and ecstatics meet and often follow cultics when they touch upon matters pertaining to orderly, educative worship. At this point the cultic approach has the best access to a rich and exhaustive panorama of practices and theories. When, however, ecstatics and cultics come to the question of history, ethics, and human destiny, they yield to the prophetic approach. Finally, when prophetics and cultics reach the point of focusing on the personal appropriation of cultic act and divine command, they defer to the leadership of ecstatics.

At this point some readers might find our scheme oddly Trinitarian, not only in its tri-partite division but in its emphasis on the legitimacy of all three kinds of approaches to Christianity. Indeed, one might speculate that each approach represents a different person of the Trinity. The ecstatics are obviously responding to the Holy Spirit. The cultics seem to emphasize God the Father, the one who embraces all created life and draws it to Himself through the sacrificial intervention of His obedient Son. The prophetics focus on the Son Himself--His life, His teachings, His position in the long line of prophets and messianic expectations.

This analogy, however, would seem to be excessively

forced. While one can view the Trinitarian doctrine as an effort to hold together various theological thrusts, these do not necessarily appear in the shape we have identified. The prophetic approach can just as easily find legitimation in the person of the Father, while cultics frequently turn to the incarnate Son as the center of the cult.

Too close an analogy with the Trinity and its three-in-oneness might lead readers to infer that all the data of Christianity can be fitted into one or another approach in a mutually exclusive and yet harmonious way. The point of an ideal-type approach to these Christian alternatives is to emphasize the tensions and conflicts among them while also recognizing that almost every important form of Christianity is made up of varying proportions of these emphases. The ideal typology leads us to inquire after the degree to which a church, theologian, or believer is willing to take a particular emphasis. On what grounds do they curb its tendencies? Secondly, it helps us find out what a position needs in order to achieve a greater strength and cogency. What rough edge is sticking out, requiring us to explore elsewhere to make sense of the whole?

For example, ecstatics are people of the Spirit, but it is the Spirit of God the Father. What then do they mean by Father? Is Father the Creator Lord to whom sacrifice and worhsip are due or is He more the giver of justice from whom the righteous Kingdom will come? How, in short, are cultic and prophetic themes to be related to the principal commitment to a Christianity of the Spirit?

No matter what approach or combination of approaches we adopt we can be led to investigate other vistas in order to gain greater perspective on our religious values, practices, and theories. Ecstatics, with their concern for the self, tend to find the personality sciences very helpful, while prophetics, with their concern for the Kingdom of God, find societal perspectives important in filling out the practical implications of their vision. Cultics sometimes explore societal sciences to find out the Church's appropriate function in the whole social order, while they also turn to personality sciences to develop more effective cultic practices.

Therefore, the distinction among approaches within Christianity is not only important for discerning tensions and decisions within a position, it also begins to offer us clues for the kind of engagement that needs to be pursued with the behavioral sciences.

Our travels across such complex interdisciplinary terrain have led to the central interests of this book. We have approached Christianity with the intention of making connections with the behavioral disciplines, not with the intention of providing an exhaustive portrayal of Christian thought or history. We have taken up the essential we will need in order to begin a more critical inquiry into the relations among the disciplines of theology, psychology, and sociology. Our next step takes us to the domain of the personality sciences.

APPROACHES TO CHRISTIANITY

	Prophetic	Cultic	Ecstatic
T H E O R Y	Word of God Covenant Law Sin Judgment Kingdom of God Jesus, the Rabbi and Prophet	Divine Presence in cultic Action Sacraments effect Christian growth Communion Church as channel of grace Church as Body of Christ	Love Union with God Conversion Transformation Jesus, the New Man Church as the New Covenant
P R A C T I C E	Teaching Preaching Prophetic Judgment Sectarian Organization	Eucharist Rite Sacraments Priesthood Hierarchy Religious Life	Prayer Groups Meditation Conversion Experiences Faith Healing Revivalistic Preaching Charismatic Movements
L O Y A L T Y	Word of God Obedience Scriptures as Norm Understanding God's Will	Sacrament Communion Participation Sacrifice Crucifix Eucharist	Personal Experience of the Spirit Regeneration Fire Spirit Dove Freedom

CHAPTER FIVE

PERSONALITY

There are three basic approaches to personality within the behavioral sciences. We call them the conflict, fulfillment, and equilibrium approaches. In general these correspond to the schools of psychoanalysis, humanistic psychology, and behaviorism. Most options emerging in the last decade are different blends of these three historical schools. Eric Berne originated Transactional Analysis, for instance, as a blend of psychoanalysis and behaviorism. His followers have added their own humanistic interpretations. Many behavior modification theories are blends of behaviorism and psychoanalysis as well, but with an emphasis on the former. Assertiveness training, on the other hand, combines behaviorism with humanistic psychology.

Even the classic three psychologies are not pure types in themselves. Though psychoanalysis is a prime example of a conflict psychology, Freud and Erik Erikson softened original psychoanalytic theory in humanistic directions. Carl Rogers, on the other hand, an exemplar of humanistic psychology, has many conflict motifs in his theory that his followers often dismiss. And behaviorist B. F. Skinner has admitted the existence and importance of "private," internal psychological events, a move in the direction of the conflict and humanistic psychologies.

As with Christianity, we are ordering the different approaches to personality with an "ideal-type" typology. Conflict, fulfillment, and equilibrium orientations are pure types that never occur perfectly in history. The advantage of thinking in this way lies in seeing the tensions between the three types in any given psychological theory, practice, or loyalty. The pure typology highlights the options available when any theorist or practitioner concerned with personality begins his or her work.

Our typology is an interdisciplinary one. It arises in the context of interdisciplinary conversation among psychology, sociology, and theology. Thus it is not a strictly "psychological" typology. At the same time it parallels distinctions that many psychologists have made themselves.[1]*

We distinguish the three basic approaches to the self according to the distinctive dynamics they see in personality. Those with a conflict orientation see conflict as a typical state within the self, and between the self and others. The normative value for these people becomes personal management of conflict in a way that allows gratifying personal and social functioning. The equilibrium orientation conceives intrapsychic and personal relations in terms of a balance of forces. The ideal outcome of equilibrium practice is a new equilibrium in which psychic and interpersonal conflict is done away with. The fulfillment orientation judges personality relations in terms of the satisfaction individuals gain in them, and self-actualization is the goal of their work.

All approaches see elements of conflict, equilibrium, and fulfillment in the self, yet each understands them differently. Each approach constructs a unique pattern for weaving them together.

A. The Conflict Approach

The conflict approach sees the self continually involved in tension or conflict. This may be intra-psychic tension, interpersonal conflict, or conflict between an individual and his culture. In psychology itself we find the conflict orientation mainly in psychoanalysis and psychoanalytic ego psychology. Sigmund Freud originated the former, and Erik Erikson is his best known successor in ego psychology.[2]

For Freud, conflict arises between sexual and aggressive instincts in the personality and the restraints of society upon the instincts. Freud believed that babies at first freely express their psychic drives, and later as they grow find it necessary to control them. The watershed of conflict comes in the period of age three to five, the time of the Oedipal complex. At this age children express their love for the parent of the opposite sex. The presence of the same-sex spouse, however, intrudes on the infantile hope for gratification. This child-parent social conflict is the basis for later internalized conflict between superego and id.

In the overpowering presence of the spouse of their beloved, children are powerless. Instead of pursuing their instincts, they identify with the prohibitive parent of the

*Notes for this chapter begin on page 237.

same sex. This sexual identification leads to an internalization of parental restraint and to the child's choice of his or her own sexual identity. This includes repression of sexual desire for the parent of the opposite sex, and of aggression toward the parent of the same sex. By the end of the Oedipal period, parental prohibitions are ideally internalized in the form of the superego, or conscience. The superego contains the taboos, limits, and commandments of culture as transmitted by parents. It operates throughout life in the absence of a person's real parents, and continues to exert control and censorship over the instincts.

Freud believed the renunciation of instinct was necessary for individual and cultural survival. He also believed that the conscious self, the ego, could never eliminate intrapsychic conflict. It could only referee or occasionally manage the tension between the id and superego. This assessment of the pervasive conflict in personality and between individual and culture is distinctive of the conflict approach to the self.

Erik Erikson's conception of the ego's capacity for handling conflict differs from Freud's. Erikson sees culture supporting the ego as well as forcing it to restrain the instincts. For Erikson the ego is stronger than Freud first believed. Yet he agrees with Freud that the ego generally finds itself with the task of managing conflict. Erikson sees the human life-cycle from birth to old age constituted by eight distinct psycho-social crises. At each stage the ego exists between two inner opposing polarities. The task of the infant ego, for instance, is to resolve the tension between trust and mistrust. The infant needs to learn to trust others in order to receive nourishment and support. At the same time the infant needs to discern whom not to trust, lest it take in something detrimental to its health. Each stage of life confronts the person with a similar crisis to resolve.

As the individual enters subsequent stages, such as adolescence, he must also face conflicts not adequately resolved in previous stages. The adolescent may be plagued with unresolved issues of shame or inferiority from early childhood. For Erikson, this means that the individual is never immune from conflict in his life. Each stage brings new challenges to integrate one's past strengths and weaknesses with the demands of the present. No ego resolution is so permanent as to be exempt from tension at some other time. While other approaches to personality would agree to some extent about the existence of personality conflict, they hold for its resolution or control, rather than its management. This is because they have differing views of the fundamental dynamics of the

self, and of the relation of the self to its environment.
Before treating them we first will turn to the dimensions
of theory, practice, and loyalty in the conflict perspective.

1. Conflict Theory

     The conflict approach sees the self as an organism,
existing in a state of illness or health. The basic form
of conflict is neurosis. The neurotic person is one who
experiences unrealistic anxiety. Even though Freud dis-
tinguishes between "normal" and "abnormal" people, he
assumed that most people were neurotic to some degree.
Neurotic anxiety differs from normal anxiety in that the
latter is a response to some real danger, like being the
victim of an armed robbery. Neurotic anxiety is a response to a threat which is imagined but highly unlikely
in fact, for example being attacked when walking into a
cocktail party. Neurotic anxiety expresses itself in some
set of symptoms. Bodily pain, paralysis, sexual impotence,
depression, and insomnia are examples of symptoms. Symptoms
change from culture to culture and from one historical
era to another. Erikson has focused on the symptoms characteristic of youth in an advanced technological society.
He calls the search for fidelity and the difficulty in
committing oneself to others and social tasks "identity
diffusion."

     Symptoms are always evidence of an underlying psychic
conflict. They are not the cause of psychic illness. The
real conflict arises in the patient's attempts to gratify
basic human instincts, especially those of sexuality and
aggression. In order to live in civilization, people must
sacrifice some instinctual gratification. Sexual and
aggressive instincts cannot be totally gratified, or else
society would be brutal and anarchic. Each must learn
renunciation of some immediate gratification. Some people
learn this lesson too well, however, and become over-
restricted. The formation of conscience in the child then
becomes too rigid, and the conscience or superego demands
more renunciation of instinct than is necessary. This is
the essence of neurosis. Neurotic symptoms such as impotence or frigidity indicate underlying tension between
sexual desire and sexual restriction. The psychic balance
leans to an unhealthy degree on the side of restriction and
needs to be renegotiated. The adjustment of this balance
is the subject matter of therapy.

     It is possible to reconcile instinct and renunciation
through psychoanalytic therapy. The difficulty is that
people who come to therapy are not aware of their underlying psychic conflicts, but only of their symptoms. Part
of their renunciation of instinct has been the denial or
distortion of instinct itself. On the level of consciousness,

66

people with headaches are not aware that their problem
possibly has childhood roots in feelings of anger. They
may not even be feeling particularly angry. The perceptual
and emotional barriers to the recognition of these underlying causes of psychic distress are defenses.

Defenses are unconscious ways patients deny or ignore
tensions within them that are threatening. The prime
defense is repression. If a boy is continually punished by
his parents for the pleasure he receives out of playing with
his genitals, and yet he knows that he has no power to
resist the punishment, he may come to repress the pleasure
he feels in his body, and probably repress the anger he
feels at the continual punishment. Consciously, the child
may come to see himself as not particularly interested in
sex. Emotionally he may not experience his sexual and
bodily pleasure, and when he experiences impotence as an
adult, may come to a therapist having no idea of the real
cause of the problem which embarrasses him. Unconsciously
the sexual instincts have been repressed, but the energy
that motivated the instincts still remains in'the psyche
in some form and seeks an outlet. Thus the patient may
be able to involve himself in some sexual liaison that he
considers "immoral" but not in normal sexual relations.
Such behaviors become symptomatic of the unsatisfactory
adjustment between instinct and repression that was struck
in childhood. Defenses are attempts by the unconscious to
cope with this imbalance.

Repression is one defense. Others are intellectualization (talking about sexuality, for example, to avoid
facing one's sexual feelings), sublimation (unconsciously
channeling aggressive or sexual energy into culturally
approved activities), projection (condemning something in
another in order to avoid recognizing the same in oneself)
and denial (denying one has a problem). Because human
instincts are strong and essentially anti-social, every
individual knocks heads with social restrictions. Everyone
must make some renunciation. In the process, every person
will learn certain defenses to help the ego cope with
renunciation. There is no such thing as a defense-free
person by the very nature of the irreducible conflict
between individual gratification and cultural restriction.
The issue is whether an individual's defenses permit him to
function reasonably well and satisfactorily in society.
If defenses are won at a cost of crippling anxiety or
impaired psychological or social functioning, then a new
balance needs to be struck. This new balance will not
eliminate an individual's defenses entirely, but it should
make them more flexible and more satisfying.

Conflict theorists see the ideal outcome of their
psychotherapy in terms of cure. Cures take the form of

revision in or removal of symptoms. This is accomplished by getting to the roots of underlying psychic tension, examining the fundamental conflict that is the source of tension, and striking a new balance between instinctual satisfaction and personal restriction. Usually this will involve increased awareness of the underlying conflict and recognition and acceptance of the instinct at issue. Such acceptance would be seen in a less rigid behavior, more relaxed body tension, more inner comfort, and increased capacity for social functioning. Freud's dictum for the healthy personality was "Lieben und Arbeiten," the capacity to love and work. The test of cure for conflict theorists involves increased inner satisfaction and better social functioning.

2. Conflict Practices

Psychoanalysts seek to affect a patient's psychic balance through promoting insight. The patient reports to the therapist situations which have aroused her anxiety and the ways she has coped with them. The therapist listens objectively and then makes interpretations of what the patient has reported. Interpretation is the key to psycho-analytic therapy. Through interpretation the therapist and client retrace the path from the patient's symptoms to the underlying conflict which is causing them. In the pro-cess the patient begins to understand her emotions and behavior in a new light, and in so doing begins to see how her current behavior is an inappropriate or unrealistic response to anxieties experienced in the past. The patient may block this process with her own defenses.

Defenses involve distortions or denial of our own consciousness. We erect defenses to avoid facing under-lying tension or conflict. The aim of interpretative tech-niques in therapy is to uncover the anxiety-laden source of the conflict. As insight into underlying dynamics is gained, the conflict will be alleviated. This is because defenses play an important part in the balance between instinct gratification and renunciation. As emotional and perceptual defenses are changed with increasing insight, the balance of energy in the psyche is affected by a reduction of tension. This reduction of tension is then reflected in the lessening or removal of symptoms.

The insight pursued by psychoanalytic therapists is not merely intellectual. It involves the patient's emo-tions and perceptions as well as his intellect. If a therapist's interpretation is only cognitive, it can play into the patient's scheme of defenses, such as intellec-tualization. The achievement of genuine insight is not simple, because defenses form barriers to the restoration of insight. Defenses exist to reduce anxiety. When a

patient begins to look into herself and her past and gets
a glimmer of the conflict she has been avoiding, she will
re-experience the anxiety that caused the defenses in the
first place. Resurgence of anxiety often leads to resistance. The good therapist will recognize this resistance
as an indication that the patient is on the track of insight. The therapist's gentle interpretation of the resistance as itself symptomatic of anxious conflict can lead
to further uncovering and to eventual insight on the
patient's part.

Freud also described a special form of resistance
called transference. In transference the patient transfers
her unconscious feelings onto the analyst. These feelings
usually are warm and affectionate at first, and then later
turn hostile. The patient may become angered by small
gestures of the pscyhoanalyst, or by suggestions that the
patient had previously welcomed. The patient typically
becomes resistant to further therapy and will want to
terminate treatment.

The analyst's use of transference is instrumental
for curing the patient. It is a difficult and sensitive
area, because analysts are looking not at "objective"
therapy material like dreams or past family relations, but
at their own relation to the patient. The therapeutic
aim here is the same as with other symptoms of underlying
conflict--to help the patient see how instinctual energy
from the unconscious is affecting her everyday relations.
In making the unconscious conscious, as Freud said, the
patient transfers energy from id to ego, and thus is able
to see herself in a new light and relate with others more
freely. Psychic energy is no longer stored in conflicted
symptoms, but is available to the self for creative uses.

In addition to analysis of transference, two other
well known insight techniques in the conflict approach are
free association and dream analysis. Each is a means to
overcome resistance and to further insight. In free-
association the therapist invites the patient to say anything that comes to mind, not matter how irrelevant, strange,
or shameful it might seem. These self-revelations enable
the therapist to get underneath defenses to the level of
unconscious awareness. Free association is aided by the
patient lying on a couch and relaxing as she talks. The
therapist may stimulate the flow of association from time
to time, either by inserting cues for the patient to
respond to ("father," "childhood," "anger") or by assuring
the hesitant patient that it is permissible to utter
anything in therapy no matter how terrible one's thoughts
may seem. Freud assumed that blocks or hesitancies in free
association were clues to material the patient was avoiding, and he would focus in on this in order to uncover the

psychic issue underneath.

Another psychoanalytic technique is <u>dream</u> <u>analysis</u>. The patient reports her dream and the therapist analyzes or interprets its meaning in reference to the patient's symptoms and case history. Dreams are produced by underlying unconscious conflict. They are rich material for insight and understanding because they are not distorted by ego defenses. Dreams symbolize an unconscious understanding of the patient's problem. Through analysis of the dream this awareness arises to full consciousness.

The prime therapeutic practices for psychoanalytic therapists are interpretation, analysis of transference, free association, and dream analysis. Psychoanalysts may ply their trade in private practice. They may also work in an institutional setting such as a mental hospital, the psychiatric wing of a community hospital, or in mental health clinics. Psychoanalysts generally work with individuals on a one-to-one basis, though in recent years some have expanded their treatment to include simultaneously entire families or small groups of patients.

3. Conflict Loyalties

Psychotherapists in the conflict approach have values and commitments that relate directly to their professional theory and practice. These form the analyst's central concern of <u>curing</u> the patient. Conflict therapists have been accused of having inordinately lengthy cures, lasting for years and years in some cases. They spend this time getting to the childhood roots of underlying psychic conflict in order to ensure a genuine cure. This is due to their commitment to a particular vision of psychic health. Freud believed health meant the <u>capacity</u> to love and work. His criterion for cure was the <u>restored</u> <u>ability</u> <u>to function</u> <u>socially</u> <u>with</u> <u>manageable</u> <u>degrees</u> of <u>tension</u>. People he saw could not function "normally" (those with sexual deviations, or paralyzing phobias, for instance) or they could not constructively manage their inner tension (neurotics and psychotics). Conflict therapists who have defined health in terms of normal behavior have drawn the criticism of promoting social conformity. Though some assume rather unconventional behavior is also evidence of cure, most conflict therapists define health in terms of adjustment to prevailing cultural norms. In a time of rapid social change, "personal adjustment" has become a questionable norm for cure. This leaves conflict theorists searching for more definitive criteria.

The last loyalty issue we will treat before we leave the conflict approach is the assessment of basic human potential. Each approach to personality, has a different

70

notion of the potentials of the individual. These differing interpretations of human strength and virtue exist side by side even in the face of the same case histories and other similar evidence. This indicates that the conception of human nature held by each approach is not strictly "scientific" or "objective," but is a matter of loyalty that may have other grounds. The conflict assessment of human nature believes that we are never free of conflict. As such, there is no such thing as a conflict-free, "good life," or a conflict-free state of perfection in life. This is because human instincts (the id) are seen as powerful, cultural restrictions (the superego) as overbearing, and individual resources of reason (the ego) as weak or impotent. The best each individual can hope for is an adjustment to culture that is relatively satisfactory. Conflict theorists offer no utopian vision of person or society. Nor do they suggest fatalism, as some have charged. There is always the possibility of altering the balance of energy in the self or between the self and others to a more satisfactory position. Yet for conflict theorists, we are so limited by our past and our psychic structure, that a verdict of sober realism is cast upon any idealist pronouncements about human nature and society.

B. The Fulfillment Approach

The fulfillment approach to the self includes various schools of psychology--phenomenological and existential psychology, Daseinanalysis, humanistic psychology, and "third force" psychology.[3] The latter term refers to the emergence of a trend in the field dominated for years by the forces of psychoanalysis and behaviorism. The leaders here are many, including Gordon Allport, Analytic therapist Carl Jung, Logotherapist Victor Frankl, and Gestalt therapist Frederick Perls. We wish to focus on two humanistic psychologists--Carl Rogers and Abraham Maslow.[4]

The most important feature of the fulfillment approach is its concern with individual fulfillment. This is defined as intrapsychic harmony and self-acceptance. These criteria for the ideal personality differ from conflict and equilibrium perspectives in that the latter two believe adjustment to social conditions or environmental factors is an inescapable necessity for the well-functioning personality. Fulfillment psychologists, however, speak of transcending social conditions. Being true to oneself is more important than being true to the demands of society. This is not to say that they pay no attention to social environment nor that they reject its importance. Rather, culture and society are not the criteria by which they measure personal worth and satisfaction.

71

1. Fulfillment Theory

The fulfillment approach, like the conflict, sees
the self as an organism. Fulfillment theorists, however,
portray the human organism in terms of growth rather than
health. Growth is understood in terms of the central
concept of actualization. The human organism possesses
innate tendencies toward self-actualization. Carl Rogers
uses the term self-actualizing tendency, while Abraham
Maslow refers to a basic growth tendency.

Fulfillment theorists agree that the key to actualization is the fulfillment of basic psychological needs.
If these are not met, growth will not occur. For Rogers
the self-esteem need is crucial to growth. This is why
unconditional positive regard is so basic in his theory.
Maslow makes a distinction between survival and growth
needs. The former include physiological and safety needs.
As these are met, growth needs become activated. These
include needs for belongingness, cognition, aesthetic
appreciation, and even actualization itself. Fulfillment
psychologists agree that the human organism is fragile in
its early years and that a positive environment is necessary if basic needs are to be met, and if growth is to
occur.

When growth is stunted due to deficiencies in environmental supply, certain barriers to growth arise. Rogers
refers to these as introjected conditions of worth, Maslow
merely as defenses. In either case the self incorporates
deficiencies that result from unmet needs, and these in
turn become internalized blocks to further growth. The
notion of barriers to growth is similar to the conflict
perspective's concept of defense. The difference is that
conflict theorists tend to focus on the patient's role in
the erection of defenses. The choice of defences is a
clue to how the therapist will direct the therapy. In contrast fulfillment therapists emphasize the role of the depriving environment. The particular defenses a client uses
have little import for the conduct of therapy.

The ideal outcome of the human growth process is the
self-actualizing person. Rogers' notion of the fully
functioning person involves a congruence between inner
feelings and outward expression. This psychic integrity
is rooted in an acceptance of self and others. Fully
functioning people also have a realistic picture of themselves, possessing neither perfectionistic nor fatalistic
self-expectations. The authentic source of moral obligation for self-actualized people is their awareness of the
feelings and needs of others. Thus, relations with others
are motivated not by external pressure or demands, but by
concern for them as fellow human beings.

72

Maslow's conception of the self-actualized person
is very similar to Rogers'. Maslow includes self-
acceptance, a low degree of self-conflict (congruence),
openness to experience, unbiased understanding and unsel-
fish altruism. In addition Maslow includes capacities
for creative living and peak experiences. His notion of
creativity includes personal uniqueness, spontaneity,
playfulness, and vitality. Peak experiences are high
points of self-actualization. On occasions when they are
experienced, a person feels whole, at one with himself.
At the same time he experiences being one with another--
whether it be another person, one's work, or the universe.
In the peak experience the individual experiences freedom,
spontaneity, and self-transcendence. She may be particularly poetic or aesthetic in her communication. Finally,
she may feel especially graced or fortunate. Maslow
refers to growth as being-motivation. Growth is an ongoing
process, not a completed goal. His description of peak
experiences parallels mystical experience in many ways
(the sense of inner and outer unity for example). Maslow
draws a large following from religious and theological
readers for this very reason.

2. Fulfillment Practices

Fulfillment therapists use a diversity of therapeutic practices in their work. Because they believe that each
person has the inner resources to achieve fulfillment, they
are more oriented to whatever seems appropriate and helpful
than to predesigned techniques. Rogers basically uses the
reflection of feeling technique. The therapist reflects
back the client's innermost thoughts and feelings in a caring fashion. In addition, Maslow uses interpretive tech
niques of the conflict approach as well as some assertive
techniques found in equilibrium practice. With the latter
the therapist urges a client to overcome his anxiety in a
situation by asserting himself--perhaps talking more loudly
or more frequently, or by refusing to be shoved around. The
therapist may have the client actually role-play a situation
and practice self-assertion in the therapeutic hour.

Rogers, of course, uses the reflection of feeling
technique. He also has extended his work into the small
encounter group format. As a result he increasingly expresses his own feelings and confronts behavior that he
experiences as unauthentic. Maslow uses group as well as
one-to-one therapy formats. Both he and Rogers have been
involved in the use of sensitivity and T-groups in education
and business settings to stimulate person-centered alternatives to task-centered administrative and mangement
patterns.

Fulfillment therapists use another distinctive

practice, values-clarification. This can be done both with individuals and groups. They assume that personal incongruence is reflected in an incongruence of values. The counselor or educator helps a person locate the value dimension of his problem by asking him to specify the several values at stake in his problem. Then she asks the individual to sort these values into higher and lower importance. When this becomes difficult because two values conflict or have the same priority, the counselor asks the client to look for a variety of alternatives to solve the conflict. The counselor then helps the client to evaluate each alternative in terms of the client's own value system. She carefully avoids imposing her own values so that the client's intrinsic tendencies can reach their own unique fulfillment. The counselor must be aware of her own values to do this, and to make discriminating judgments about when or when not to convey her own value scheme.

Values-clarification is a technique for helping a person move through barriers to growth. Fulfillment theorists clearly recognize conflict in the self. Yet, psychic conflict here is conceived differently than in the conflict approach. Here conflict arises from a barrier which when eliminated unleashes the self-actualizing tendency. The aim is not merely to manage better, but really to resolve the conflict. In the conflict approach conflict is never fully resolved. It is always present and the client always requires certain defenses to handle his conflict. "Growth" means making defenses more flexible and efficient, not doing away with them altogether.

The rapid expansion of the human potentials movement in the last decade has brought an entire cafeteria of other techniques from fulfillment therapists. One is the Gestalt practice of dream work. The client tells her dream as if it were happening in the present, and then becomes objects in the dream, reporting how she feels, for instance as a tree (perhaps immobile and alone), or a swamp (sluggish and depressed). Working through the feelings she experiences in her dream, the client can resolve the psychic bind her dream symbolizes. Another technique is the Bioenergetic practice of hitting pillows and yelling. This is used in connection with feelings of anger. Hitting, kicking, and screaming are important for releasing body tension associated with anger. Yelling and screaming are also important for releasing inner tension, by expressing the words in which anger has been stored.

There are many other fulfillment practices prevalent today--meditation, guided fantasy, emotional education, and rebirthing, as well as interpretative practices like transactional analysis. The aim of many is to get a person in touch with bodily and sensory feelings that he has long ignored or denied. This fits into the fulfillment assumption that self-actualization is a basic human motive, and that once tapped, it will flower. There are differences among fulfillment therapists about how to handle defenses against growth. Some tend more toward the psychoanalytic position that defenses are very important and must be handled carefully. Others see defenses as obstacles to be readily set aside so inner potential can bloom. In either case, therapeutic practices are related to basic theories about human self-actualization and to values about personal growth. We turn now to the values that pertain to these therapeutic endeavors.

3. Fulfillment Loyalties

The prime fulfillment loyalty is the value of self-fulfillment. Fulfillment is defined in terms of individual, inner satisfaction. The self-actualized person is, to be sure, altruistic and self-transcendent. Yet this is possible only because the self's basic needs have already been provided for. This is in radical contrast to conflict theorists, who see adaptation to culture requiring some cost to, or compromise of, individual gratification.

Fulfillment psychologists are more optimistic about the possibility of self-fulfillment because of their view of basic human tendencies. Fulfillment proponents see our intrinsic motivation as essentially social and rational. Conflict advocates, on the other hand, see the basic human instincts, such as sexuality and aggression, to be irrational and asocial. Theorists like Rogers and Maslow acknowledge irrationality in human motivation, but attribute this to the failure of getting basic needs like self-esteem or safety met. This conflicting assessment of human instincts is the most crucial difference between the conflict and fulfillment approaches. It influences the choice of directive and non-directive practices, respectively. It also shapes the differing ideals of therapeutic outcome, conflict theorists working for a better adjustment to overbearing culture, fulfillment theorists for a transcendence of culture.

Individual autonomy is another important value in the loyalty dimension. Fulfillment theorists believe the self is initially fragile and at the mercy of a powerful environment. Since the environment is potentially more damaging than growth producing, gaining independence from and control over one's interpersonal environment is very important. This fits with Rogers' belief that the client is capable of self-direction, has a right to it, and that she, not the therapist, should decide the course and content of the therapy sessions. Furthermore, Rogers' choice of reflection of feeling provides minimum direction for the client and maximum opportunity for self-exploration by the client of her inner self. This reduces at the same time the possibility of the therapist's imposing his own conditions of worth on the client, thereby reduplicating the childhood dilemma that qualified a client's autonomy in the first place.

The fulfillment emphasis on individual autonomy in face of an overpowering familial or cultural milieu is deficient in one regard, however. Families can be sources of strength as well as conditions of worth. Moreover, social, political, and economic institutions affect a family's sense of well-being, and consequently the kind of regard they are able to offer one another. By emphasizing individual transcendence over culture, fulfillment practitioners often ignore institutional and cultural influence on self-worth that may promote or deflate self-esteem. A logical value for those concerned with self-worth would be an improvement of the broader social milieu that affects a family's capacity to communicate self-worth. From a fulfillment standpoint, however, cultural improvement happens every time an individual becomes more actualizing. Her increased openness, trusting and prizing of others affects the interpersonal environment of others, and thereby increases their opportunities for increased self-esteem as well.

Self-fulfillment and individual autonomy are values that contrast with Freud's personality values of work and love. Conflict therapists are more concerned with commitment and adjustment to culture, while fulfillment therapists more with transcendence over culture. This reflects the different responses to culture by the two perspectives. Freud sees culture as a necessary evil. It is evil in that it demands individual sacrifice; but it is necessary in that without the social cohesion that culture brings, life would be deadly competition for every individual. Fulfillment theorists believe that individuals do not have to be at the mercy of culture. They can avoid its evils through the cultivation of geniune selfhood. Self-actualization for fulfillment theorists is more advantageous for all than the conformity to culture that conflict theorists value.

C. The Equilibrium Approach

The equilibrium approach to the self is found in numerous behavioristic and cognitive psychologies. These range from learning theories to behaviorist and behavior modification theories. The best known among these is B. F. Skinner. Other figures of stature here include Albert Bandura, Joseph Wolpe, John Dollard and Neal E. Miller, O. Hobart Mowrer, Thomas Stampfl, and Albert Ellis. We also include Jean Piaget and Lawrence Kohlberg, theoreticians

76

of cognitive development.[5]

The basic feature of the equilibrium perspective is its conception of the self in terms of a balance or equilibrium of forces. Some see this as an intrapsychic balance (Dollard and Miller, Wolpe), some as a balance between the individual and his culture (Skinner). Others see the equilibrium involving both intrapsychic and interpersonal forces (Mowrer, Piaget, Kohlberg).

Conflict and fulfillment approaches also envisage some equilibrium in the personality. For them, the basic balance or equilibrium arises in the tension between individual satisfaction and cultural restriction. Conflict and fulfillment theorists also envision an intrapsychic balance between forces of growth and suppression. Equilibrium theorists, however, make no claim to achieve human ideals of health or personal growth. In the other two approaches, resolution of psychic tension leads to psychic advance (more satisfying adjustment) or to growth. But equilibrum theorists hold less of an organismic and more of a mechanistic view of the self. In the mechanical model, elimination of conflict leads simply to more efficient functioning.

A second feature of the equilibrium approach is the concentration on observable and quantifiable behavior. This is in contrast to the intangible feeling states of peak experiences, self-esteem, or unconscious attitudes that concern conflict and fulfillment practitioners. This means equilibriumists deal directly with behavior others call "symptoms." Equilibrium therapists do not focus on "underlying causes" of symptoms, nor do they deal in much detail with a client's past history. They see the client's past as a source of learning that is no longer socially helpful. Rather than recommending insight into the past, they seek to change behavioral or thinking patterns that are the source of current anxiety or discomfort. Equilibrium proponents are interested in fixing a patient's problem, not in creating fundamental personality transformation. Consequently, they generally are not occupied with debates between their conflict and fulfillment counterparts about what constitutes the ideal personality.

1. Equilibrium Theory

Equilibrium theory explains how people acquire new patterns of behavior. In general the concept of conditioning refers to the acquisition of any pattern of behavior. There are two different modes of conditioning that have developed over the last half-century--classical conditioning and operant conditioning. Ivan Pavlov discovered the first, and B. F. Skinner has developed many of the techniques of the second.

In _classical_ _conditioning_ the experimenter uses a reflex response and transfers it to a new stimulus. Pavlov used food to elicit a salivation response from a dog. Then by introducing a ringing bell just before he introduced the food, he found that gradually the dog salivated when it heard the bell, even if it did not receive food. Pavlov described this with the following formula: an _unconditioned_ _stimulus_ (food) which elicits an _unconditioned response_ (salivation) is replaced by a _conditioned stimulus_ (bell). Pavlov labelled the response to the bell a _conditioned response_, though it is the same physiological behavior (salivation) as the unconditioned response.

Operant conditioning differs from its classical predecessor in that subjects voluntarily exhibit the behavior to be conditioned. "Operant" conditioning means that subjects "operate" on or affect their environment rather than respond passively or involuntarily to it (as in the case of the dog salivating).

Since equilibrium theorists view all behavior as a _response_ to some antecedent _stimulus_, behavior patterns arise when certain responses are reinforced and others are not. There are two kinds of _reinforcement_ in behavioral theory. Positive reinforcement strengthens a behavior by rewarding it. Negative reinforcement reduces a behavior by punishing or ignoring it. _Schedules_ of reinforcement are used to plan behavioral change. Schedules arranges stimuli in a carefully programmed fashion. Teaching machines as well as slot machines have built-in schedules to reinforce specific behavioral goals. Token reward systems in classrooms, prisons, and other institutions also involve schedules of reinforcement for desired behavior. Thus reinforcement schedules can range from giving a single piece of candy upon completion of a task to arranging the routine of an entire day in an institution.

The notion of equilibrium pertains to any behavioral pattern. New behavior results from the balance (a new equilibrium) between an old response and a new stimulus.[6] Behavioral change occurs as people respond to stimuli in their environment. Planned behavioral change requires the structuring of an environment in a way that will optimally elicit desired behavior(s). Since all behavior is a collection of stimulus and response associations, behavioral management involves careful environmental management. Specifically how this is done involves therapeutic practice and the wide range of options equilibrium practioners use in their work.

2. Equilibrium Practices

Equilibrium practices involve the manipulation of

stimuli to achieve desired behavioral goals. Clients may
have a say in setting their own goals, as in individual
therapy. Or they may have no say in setting the goals, as
in learning settings or in settings which treat severely
disturbed children and adults. There the individual's
choice is limited to how to respond to the given stimuli
and environment. Equilibriumists treat behavior either by
introducing or by removing stimuli, or both. There are
two kinds of stimuli--rewards and punishments. "Rewards"
involve the administration of positive stimuli or removal
of aversive stimuli. "Punishment" involves the administration of aversive stimuli or removal of positive stimuli.

Equilibrium practitioners have used stimuli in numerous ways. The simple application of rewards is the best-
known and most widely used technique. Equilibrium theorists'
range of techniques goes far beyond this, however, and some
are quite complex and sophisticated. Albert Bandura describes six separate methods of behavioral change.[7] We will
use his list and describe each briefly with our own examples. The six are modeling, positive control, aversive
control, extinction, desensitization through counterconditioning, and aversive counterconditioning.

a. Modeling

People change merely through observing others' behavior and its consequences, and then trying the same behavior
themselves. This is how small children learn from siblings
and peers. It probably is the way adults in group therapy
make initial changes. They watch how other group members
act and then select what fits themselves best.

b. Positive Control

The most important and widely used method of behavioral change is tangible rewards that positively reinforce
desired behavior. Rewards have been most notably used to
treat stuttering. They also have been used along with
modeling to treat autism. Counselors at the David School
in Chicago teach autistic children sign language by modeling
signs. They give rewards when the children make the desig-
nated sign. Amazingly, over several years the autistic
children have learned to use signs, and even words, to make
requests and express themselves.[8]

Lawrence Kohlberg's method of moral education is also
based on the use of positive reward. Kohlberg views moral
cognition in terms of a six stage hierarchy. Students
change their views of the moral world at one stage when
they encounter moral reasoning that better accounts for
what they know. Students are not aware that their structure
of moral reasoning is changing to a higher stage. They

merely respond to the intellectual challenge of discussing
and solving Kohlberg's interesting moral cases. Each moral
stage is a Piagetian "schemata" or self-contained scheme of
moral reasoning. One's thinking scheme gradually changes
when stimulated with moral thinking at one stage higher.
Kohlberg and his colleagues have found that if students are
exposed to moral reasoning two stages above their own, their
reasoning does not change.[9] By resolving cognitive dison-
ance, an immediately higher stage of moral reasoning functions as an enticing positive reward. The higher stage
makes more sense of the individual's own experience. As
students adopt a more complex stage, they pave the way for
a new cognitive reward, the next step higher again in the
moral hierarchy. Kohlberg's concern with the complexities
of moral reasoning is unusual for an equilibrium practitioner, and his interest in symbolic and cognitive issues
typifies both conflict and fulfillment approaches. Yet
basically he utilizes an equilibrium practice of positive
rewards in his moral education.

   c. Aversive Control

   Aversive control is an equilibrium technique that involves the application of aversive stimuli or the removal of
positive reinforcers. Everyday child-rearing examples would
be scolding and spanking (aversive) or depriving a child of
dessert. Using these methods of behavioral change on adults
or on persons outside one's own family raises many people's
ethical concern. Behaviorists from B. F. Skinner to Albert
Bandura caution that aversive control is not a very effective means of behavioral change. They also acknowledge that
it can produce unwanted side effects and do not recommend
it as a sole means of behavioral change. Retarded and
autistic children have eliminated destructive and self-
destructive behavior by being physically confined to a chair
as soon as they behave violently. Institutionalized delin-
quents have also been individually isolated for their violence, but such control bascially manages the immediate
violence and does not have the long run effect that it does
with retarded and autistic children.

   d. Extinction

   Extinction is a deconditioning procedure. In deconditioning one unlearns or disassociates stimulus-response
pairings one had previously associated. With extinction
formerly learned behaviors are displaced through the removal
of the stimuli that reinforced them. For example, undesirable behavior is often a response to some prior anxiety.
The deviant or undesirable behavior functions to avoid society, and as long as it does so, the behavior will be maintained. If one talks incessantly because he is afraid of
what others will think of him, and the talking reduces his

80

anxiety, this reinforces the incessant talking. Thomas
Stampfl primarily uses extinction as a therapeutic technique.
His Implosive Therapy is designed to extinguish reinforcement like incessant talking by bombarding patients with
great amounts of anxiety-eliciting material. For example,
Stampfl would detect what causes the incessant talker's
anxiety. It might be the opinion he imagines others would
have of him if he were silent. Stampfl would tell his
patient to imagine the absolutely worst situation in which
his silence would lead others to reject him. By imagining
and reexperiencing what they fear the most, patients learn
to cope with their anxiety. They do so without resorting
to the undesirable behavior which they previously used to
cope with the anxiety. As a result the undesirable behavior is not reinforced and gradually disappears.

   e. Desensitization through Counterconditioning

      Counterconditioning, like extinction, is a decondi-
tioning procedure. In the extinction example above, the
patient disassociates feelings of anxiety from rejection
by others. In desensitization the patient replaces feelings
of anxiety with different feelings. This means that
patients gradually desensitize themselves from feared objects or situations. Joseph Wolpe uses relaxation techniques to replace phobic feelings of anxiety. If a patient
is afraid of cats, for instance, Wolpe sets up a desensitization gradient, from least to greatest fear. He might
set a cat at a point where the patient feels comfortable,
say twenty feet. He then teaches the patient relaxation
techniques such as deep breathing. Slowly he brings the
cat to a point where the patient begins to feel anxious.
He has her relax and breathe deeply. He then moves the
cat a bit closer and repeats the breathing procedure. Wolpe
also uses a gradient of imaginary situations, such as first
imagining holding a small furry toy animal, then a large
one, then a live kitten, next a live cat, then several cats,
etc. In desensitization the patient associates a response
(relaxation) with an old stimulus that the patient formerly
associated with anxiety. The new response counters the old
one, in that one cannot do both at the same time. You cannot be anxious and breathe deeply simultaneously. Desensitization thus involves a reinforcement schedule to decon-
dition fears. Desensitization is also a popular sexual
therapy technique for treating male impotence.

   f. Aversive Counterconditioning

      The most controversial of equilibrium techniques is
aversive counterconditioning. Here patients' behavior is
potentially quite harmful or goes against cultural taboos,
as in the case of addictive or deviant sexual behaviors. The
therapeutic goal is to pair painful stimuli with stimuli

the patient previously responded to with pleasure. Drugs or electrical shocks are customarily used, for example giving male homosexuals mild electric shocks when they respond erotically to pictures of nude males. As with aversive control, aversive counterconditioning needs to be used with other methods. Success is also more likely when the method is used with the patient's voluntary consent.

3. Equilibrium Loyalties

The equilibrium approach has played a paradoxical moral role in the field of psychology. Behaviorists once prided themselves on their scientific (value-free) objectivity. Subsequently, they drew moral fire from psychoanalysts and humanistic psychologists. Now we find behaviorists like B. F. Skinner writing on freedom and human dignity and challenging other behavioral scientists to be clear about their values.

Generally equilibrium therapists have shared three basic value assumptions--the importance of scientific objectivity, the goal of efficient personality functioning, and the necessity of socially appropriate behavior. Scientific objectivity is the overarching equilibrium loyalty. "Science" is an instrumental value which can mean many things. It can mean a non-moralistic approach to a patient's dilemmas. Equilibrium therapists are concerned to be objective and nonjudgmental about the problems patients bring, even if others, including the patient, find the problem despicable. "Science" can mean dealing only with empirically observable behavior rather than intangible abstractions like Oedipal complexes and conditions of worth. "Science" may mean a hard-nosed, realistic, specific approach to personality which can be replicated and evaluated, in contrast to the intuitive and less verifiable approaches of other therapies.

The use of punitive techniques by behaviorists, however, raises moral questions about acceptable scientific means for influencing personality. Equilibrium therapists tend to become very simplistic at this point. The goal of their enterprise is <u>efficient personality functioning</u>. Equilibrium therapists can be so committed to this goal that they do not question the moral validity of means toward it. They would not see scientific method as a basic loyalty, then, but only as a neutral procedure or treatment tool.

Equilibrium practitioners certainly have humanistic concerns, or they would not be interested in treating people. When pushed about their loyalties, however, many equilibrium therapists shy away from ethical reflection. They respond by distinguishing between desirable and

82

and undesirable behaviors, sometimes called <u>socially</u> <u>accep-</u>
<u>table</u> <u>and</u> <u>socially</u> <u>deviant</u> <u>behavior</u>. When questioned about
what makes a behavior acceptable or not, two well known
behaviorists have stepped forward to answer.

B. F. Skinner makes his ultimate ethical criterion
"cultural survival." This determines which behaviors are
desirable. To the concern of many, Skinner does not say who
will decide which behaviors will contribute to cultural
survival and which do not. This raises the spectre of
totalitarian control. At the other end of the spectrum,
Albert Bandura places behavioral theory in the context of
individual liberty and democratic participation. He
believes the individual should decide whether his or her
behavior will be altered. Bandura's and Skinner's concern
for ethics acknowledges the loyalty dimension and its
implications for equilibrium practice. This means that
sooner or later some notion of "right" and "wrong" behavior
emerges in this approach. This simple <u>dichotomy</u> in thinking
about moral behavior concerns ethicists who conceive human
action in more complex terms. The dichotomy fits right
in line with other moralists, however, particularly with
those holding what we call a dualist orientation toward
society.

Many equilibrium theorists approach the loyalty dimension in a tantalizing, yet incomplete way. O. Hobart
Mowrer and William Glasser have drawn a strong readership
among religious audiences with their focus on "responsibility." Yet specifying and justifying a moral norm like
responsibility in a pluralistic society like ours is a
difficult task. To whose values is a client responsible,
his own? The therapist's? An institution's? Clearly
equilibrium theorists have a moral lion by the tail and are
wrestling with the role of moral values in psychology along
with conflict and fulfillment psychologists.[10] This is the
point where the approaches to personality need to look
beyond themselves toward ethics and social theory.

D. Conclusion

We have classified three alternative visions of personality as conflict, fulfillment, and equilibrium approaches.
Our ideal-typical analysis highlights the distinctive theories, loyalties, and practices of each. Sigmund Freud, Carl
Rogers, and B. F. Skinner are classic representatives of
each approach because of their theoretical clarity and
because of their consistent attention to issues in all three
dimensions. Fewer therapists today use practices, theories,
and loyalties from only a single approach. Most mix motifs
from all three.[11]

By highlighting the distinctive characteristics of

83

each approach we have identified the unique alternatives each offers. This is especially important for people with interdisciplinary concerns. A pastoral counselor, for instance, may come with the problem of assessing a client's improvement. A fulfillment therapist might tell the counselor to ask the client to assess his own improvement. A conflict therapist might look behind any reports by the client for a reduction of bodily and psychic tension, and for more relaxed functioning in everyday activity. An equilibrium practitioner would suggest looking at observable changes in behavior to indicate that an individual is solving personal problems.

The assessment of a client's improvement is an important issue in pastoral counseling. Pastoral counselors need to decide which of several criteria of psychic progress to adopt. They may choose a combination of alternatives. In doing so, however, their choice of differing approaches should facilitate discerning rather than haphazard judgments. Counselors will carefully assess clients' reports that they are "feeling much better" when traces of tension are visible in their faces. They will balance evidence of ostensible behavioral change with intuitions about how clients inwardly regard themselves. Likewise, they will check people's jargon about their "OKness" against observations about their behavior in relation to others.

By pressing an issue in any one of the approaches, such as the matter of a client's improvement, we encounter choices. The value of charting personality as we have is in sorting out the likely alternatives to an issue. Because each approach has its particular wisdom about personality and interpersonal relationships, we need to take each seriously. The following chart of approaches to personality summarizes the breadth of knowledge and practice each approach represents.

APPROACHES TO PERSONALITY

	Conflict	Fulfillment	Equilibrium
T **H** **E** **O** **R** **Y**	Neurosis Instincts Renunciation Symptoms Defenses Cure Ego, Id, Superego	Actualization Needs Barriers to Growth Self-Actualizing Person	Stimulus-Response Reinforcement: Positive and Negative Environment Schedules of Reinforcement
P **R** **A** **C** **T** **I** **C** **E**	Interpretation Free Association Dream Analysis Resistance Transference	Mirroring of Feeling Interpretation Values-Clarification Encounter Groups Hitting and Yelling Dream Work Self-Assertion Role Playing Fantasy Trips	Rewards Punishments Modelling Positive Control Aversive Control Extinction Desensitization Aversive Counterconditioning
L **O** **Y** **A** **L** **T** **Y**	Cure Managing Tension Capacity to Love and Work Conflicted Human Nature	Self-Fulfillment Individual Autonomy "Rational" Motives Intrinsic Human Goodness	Science Efficient Functioning Acceptable vs. Deviant Behavior

CHAPTER SIX

SOCIETY

We need not travel widely in the realm of personality before realizing that individuals and interpersonal relationships do not exhaust the fullness of human affairs. People act because of laws, mores, customs, group pressure and wide-spread "forces" that go far beyond their personal contacts or psychological states. This awareness fosters the inquiry of sociology, with its allied disciplines of political science and economics. We will be using the term "sociology" in its broadest sense to indicate the disciplined study of these supra-personal dimensions of human affairs.

People acquire a societal perspective when they see war, for instance, not as the expression of aggressive individuals, but as the outcome of population pressures, arms, races, the self-interests of specific elites or institutions, as well as of decisions by specific authorities. The extent to which the motivations and psychological conditions of individuals or even small groups is considered in a societal perspective varies among theorists. But the identifying mark of all sociologists is that they direct primary attention to social structures rather than to individual wills.

The general concept of social structure is central to any sociological perspective. It indicates any set of patterned relationships. Individuals enter into them rather than create them. Thus the system of law is a social structure, for people act by taking into account what the law expects or prohibits. A business corporation is a structure, which, because of its internal organization, can act somewhat as a unit over against other corporations and institutions. What people do in a corporation results not so much from their inner dispositions or psychic condition but from their job description, offical duties, or fear of sanctions.

Societal analyses of human affairs have been made since Aristotle, though what we take for sociological analysis was often expressed in terms which we now associate with philosophy, religion, or poetry. Over the past two centuries a separate discipline of sociology has emerged parallel with specialized study of the unique dynamics of the psyche.

Quite briefly, sociology is the study of "society." It originated in response to the rise of industrial capitalism and liberal democracy around the time of the French and American Revolutions. People were faced with new ways of ordering their economies and governments apart from the seemingly "natural" relationships established by family, aristocracy and estate. To grasp these new dynamics and to control them, intellectuals developed the inquiry which came to be called sociology.[1]* The dynamics of industrialization and liberal democracy have shaped sociological inquiry at many points. Each approach set forth here has responded to these challenges in different ways.

The other set of factors affecting the character of sociology has been the rise of scientific method. Sociology strives to be a "scientific" study of society. It pays close attention to empirical, historical facts which can be observed by anyone given the scientific method. There are indeed wide disagreements about the nature of scientific method in sociology.[2] Some sociologists have thought we could establish "laws" of society, just as we talk about "laws of the universe." Others have held that we can only establish relatively stable correlations among structures and events. Some have held to a "hard quantitative" notion of what constitutes a fact. Others have been more liberal in defining the facts to which all sociological theory is accountable.

In responding to the pains and catastrophes of the industrial period sociologists have also sought to reform or reconstruct the society. The commitment to science was not construed merely as a formula for passive description. It also had some normative component, a prescription for society. Even the most descriptive sociologists among the founders, Max Weber, was clearly a defender of liberal democracy and specifically of the emerging Weimar Republic in Germany. Conversely, even the most activist and militant of the founders, Karl Marx, was firmly committed to a scientific appraisal of the social order.[3] An exploration of society involves both objective appraisal and prescriptive exhortation. The experts here can be committed to revolution as well as to reaction.

There are basically three approaches to society--the systemic, the dualist, and the pluralist. Each of these

---

*Notes for this chapter being on page 244

offers a different perspective on the basic dynamics of society.[4] Though supporters of one of these approaches may have differing loyalties they tend to put concepts together in similar ways within the theoretical dimension. Even when moving into the practical arena they tend to make similar moves. For instance, Ortega y Gasset and Marx both share a dualist approach to society, but they differ drastically in their loyalties, the former wanting the ruling elite to consolidate its position, the latter desiring to overthrow it. These differences in societal loyalties may spring from a variety of sources, including psychology and theology. We are not going to discuss the origin of these loyalties and normative visions here. Our task is to present these dominant approaches and some of their representatives.

A. The Systemic Approach

1. Systemic Theory

The systemic approach embraces the work of Emile Durkheim, Talcott Parsons, and Robert Merton, as well as cybernetic social theorists like Walter Buckley and Karl Deutsch.[5] Systemic theorists inherit the tradition of social theory in which societies are understood as (analogous to) "bodies." They therefore tend to see society as a unity oriented toward survival, growth, and development. Systemics seek to explain why societies survive. They try to show how they achieve the degree of unity that they exhibit. They search for the ways a society grows and develops from infancy to maturity, and sometimes to death. Thus, the concept of evolution is often associated with systemic approaches, though it can be used in various ways.[6] In any event this cluster of terms focuses the process of inquiry. It also can become the basis for normative social visions.[7]

Societies exist and survive only because of a basic compatibility and harmony among all the parts. Each part of the society serves some function with regard to all the other parts. This interrelationship is sometimes depicted with a mechanical model, sometimes with an organismic one, depending on the wider purposes of the theorist. Both "organicists" and "mechanists" share, however, a systemic view.

A society, then, consists of certain structures, such as the family, economic organizations, governments, and armies, which supply various needs of the whole society. Social structures are the basic "organs" of society. The cells which comprise these are roles. Institutions, the basic manifestation of social structure, are complex arrangements of roles. The family, for instance, consists of the roles of husband and wife, mother and father,

daughter, son, and various relatives. The family, as an
institution, then fulfills certain basic societal needs,
such as procreation and socialization.

Each society may have different kinds of structures,
but they all share certain universal functional needs.
Function, in its general sense, means the effect of one
part upon another in the social system.[8] More precisely
it has come to mean certain effects that are necessary if
a society is to exist. These "functional prerequisites"
comprise such societal needs as reproduction, education,
defense, securing of food and clothing, handling fear and
anxiety, and the like.[9] Sometimes an institution will
explicitly seek to serve a certain function, as in the
case of marriage and reproduction. The raising of new
members of the society is a "manifest function" of the
family. Sometimes, however, an institution will have other
functions which are not recognized, as when churches serve
as places for making business contacts rather than worship-
ping God. Robert Merton has called these "latent functions."
A keen systemic will always be concerned with identifying
both kinds of functions.

Societies tend toward a state of equilibrium in which
the various structures achieve an optimum functioning relationship with each other. This point of equilibrium is not
necessarily a static one, however. It may change as the
overall social conditions and environment change. The model
of ecological balance is used here to understand societal
processes.

Equilibrium results from adequate social integration.
The various structures have to be integrated with each other,
each fulfilling its appropriate function. Persons have to
be integrated into roles, and roles have to be integrated
with the overall requirements of institutions. Societies
strain toward integration in order to meet their functional
needs.

The search for ways that structures can fulfill the
necessary functions of a society can lead to differentiation
as well as integration. As long as the basic culture holds,
structures can become increasingly specialized, and distinct
from one another. The culture itself may become more complex so that central values, such as justice or love, can be
related to a greater variety of institutions. All these
differentiations, however, are knit together by common
culture. They are yet more sophisticated ways of meeting
the society's needs.

In the process of differentiation the means for relating persons to the wider society may also change. In a
simple society, the offical relationships of military,

90

governmental and economic institutions may be closely inter-twined with the more personal relationships of family and friendship. A complex society develops a distinction between primary groups and secondary groups.[10] Primary groups are characterized by face-to-face relationships. They are personal, affective, and multi-purpose. Secondary groups consist of relationships which are more impersonal, specialized, and official. While we tend to be born into primary groups, we join secondary groups for specific purposes.

From the point of view of many systemics, the indus-trial revolution shifted the basis of society from primary to secondary forms of association. In the famous terms used by Ferdinand Toennies, communities (Gemeinschaften) gave way to societies (Gesellschaften).[11] Some may view this shift with alarm and nostalgia. Others can see it simply as a further development in the means by which persons are integrated into the wider society. First they enter into primary groups, which then, in the process of socialization, introduce them to ever wider circles of secondary association.

Culture provides the basis for this overall complex integration.[12] Culture is the sum of basic symbols, ritual actions, beliefs, values, worldviews and customary disposi-tions of a people. Culture is fundamentally a set of values that integrates persons into their roles, their roles into institutions, and the institutions into the total society.

The society, therefore, is not integrated by force but by compliance with values that are deeply internalized in its members from birth. Thus, systemics give considerable attention to the role of religion, symbols, and communica-tion. Individuals within the society therefore do not feel they are being compelled to perform their roles, because the values they espouse already lead them to do what soci-ety needs to have them do. The society appears voluntary at the same time that it seeks its own survival.

Both the integration and differentiation of a society depend on the way the common cultural substratum is tied to specific social structures, like government or the family. The terms authority and legitimation are the pivotal hinges between society and culture. If culture represents the ground for a society, legitimation concepts represent the foundation stone and authority the walls. There is a log-ical progression from the more fundamental commitments of culture to a conception of what makes certain relationships legitimate within that culture. There is then a logical progression to the articulation of what constitutes legit-imate relationships of authority. The systemic tends to emphasize the importance of the ultimate cultural claims and the commonly held sense of legitimacy these entails within a society.[13]

Systemics trace problems in society to some kind of
dis-integration. Somehow, the existing structures are not
fulfilling the society's functional prerequisites. This
may be because the environmental conditions have so changed
that the old structures no longer suffice. This challenge
to adaptation, however, can only be met if the society is
sufficiently integrated.

Durkheim pin-pointed this kind of problem with the
concept of _anomie_.[14] Anomie can afflict the society in two
ways. The values of the culture can become disconnected,
contradictory, or incoherent. The society may try to pursue
such contradictory values as success and equality at the
same time. This value conflict then undermines the authority of basic institutions.

Anomie can also occur when persons have not effectively internalized the culture's values. Inadequate
socialization then results in deviant behavior. In either
case anomie points to a problem in the basic values of a
society, whether in their relation to each other, to institutions, or to individuals. Social problems are ultimately
value problems.

2. Systemic Loyalties

Systemics are usually committed to the _preservation_
of the system. This does not mean a commitment to a static
world, but to _growth_ and _development_ emerging from the
natural forces in the system.

Once this basic commitment has been made, integration,
socialization, and unity enter in as instrumental values for
achieving societal growth and survival.

It is important to point out here that the value of
societal survival is not conceived as being at the expense
of the individual. Systemic theories, as we shall see
later, tend to assume that individuals can gain their own
true end only if the society can exist in relative unity.
The process of socialization is closely allied with that of
personal actualization.

People may, of course, analyze a society as being
highly systemic. However, they are not loyal to that systemic integration. They may criticize such a society and
try to move it in the direction of more pluralism or even
to a sharper polarization. Generally, however, the normative vision of systemics flows directly from their descriptive model.

3. Systemic Practices

Because of their commitments to system survival and integration systemics tend to focus on practices in two areas--system adaptation and integration. At the center of practices for system adaptation stands <u>planning</u> and <u>coordination</u>. Planners inevitably seek to treat societal pro<u>blems</u> from the standpoint of the whole. The problem lies in detecting threats to the system from its environemnt. Thus, ecological reformers, land use planners, and economists tend toward systemic perspectives and practices. Problems must be solved in the context of long run societal survival. This demands research into all the possible system consequences of any particular social reform.

Effective planning and its implementation demands coordination. Therefore, systemics seek out those who stand at the centers of power in order to guide their planning. Thus systemics seek to advise elites, to create a general public consensus about the direction society should take, and plan out in detail how to move in that direction. This is indeed social engineering, but it is an engineering that does not seek to impose a pattern on society as much as to advance its central functional tendencies in the direction of survival.

The problem of coordination leads directly to practices to enhance integration. Integrative practices can be directed at the cultural dimension or at personal socialization. Systemics take the role of religion, communication, and symbol very seriously. Therefore, they emphasize various practices that will affect and change the culture so it can guide people in a non-coercive way to fulfill society's needs. They engage in <u>cultural action</u>. Ritual demonstrations, theater, the shaping of civil ceremonies receive prominent attention. Others emphasize the importance of communication patterns in the society, whether through computers, books, or mass media. Still others seek to reshape the rites by which we pass from childhood through maturity to death. Cultural action, then, includes all those practices aimed at shaping the patterns of values, symbols, and ritual which, from a systemic perspective, finally govern social survival.

At the personal and small-group level systemics pursue the goal of integration through processes of education and shaping of primary groups. <u>Education</u>, whether as a process or an institution is the <u>major means</u> by which people are socialized. Education is the process of relating persons to the wider society. The kind of education a systemic prefers is one that is consciously aimed at <u>socialization</u>--securing a job, learning social values, <u>gaining an identification</u> with the society's heritage, and

93

and learning to overcome selfish impulses for the sake of the common good.

Adequate socialization cannot rely on processes of education alone. Education is usually assigned to secondary associations in the society. However, the heart of socialization lies finally in the primary group, for it is here that generally societal values are most firmly anchored. Emile Durkheim, in searching for responses to the problem of anomie, sought ways to strengthen secondary associations based on occupation. At the primary level we inevitably turn to the family. Not only must the relationship of the family to the rest of society be strengthened, so must the relationships within the family. The family, with its clear system of functional need, is a microcosm for the whole social system. Whatever happens in this microcosm is therefore decisive for the rest of society.

The specific techniques systemics may choose to advance practices of adaptation and integration depend on their psychological assumptions as well as assessment of the facts at hand. To see the issues at stake in choosing these kinds of practices we must compare them with those taken in the other two approaches to society.

B. The Pluralist Approach

While pluralists share the systemic concern for groups, their wider assumptions and typical loyalties lead them to a distinctive position which has gained increasing prominence in recent years. Among its proponents we find not only practitioners like Saul Alinsky, but theorists like Max Weber and George Herbert Mead. James Madison's famous position in the Federalist Papers is also typically pluralistic, as are the writings of the famous nineteenth century French student of American affairs, Alexis de Tocqueville. In our own time, political thinkers Robert Dahl, Henry Kariel, and Hannah Arendt have been major proponents of pluralist views. More recently Andrew Greeley and Pierre van den Berghe have tried to articulate the meaning of ethnic and racial pluralism. [15]

1. Pluralist Theory

One reason pluralists and systemics appear to be the same is that pluralism seems to mean the same thing as the systemic concept of differentiation. But what we have here is something with greater gaps and conflicts than mere differentiation. Differentiation implies that something is still holding the parts together. That "something" for systemics is the mutual interdependence of the parts and the common cultural bases they share. The partially conflicting structures require each other in order to meet all the functional needs of individuals as well as the society as a whole. Conflicts among them can be resolved by appeal to the cultural loyalties internalized in each person in the society. Pluralism, however, means that the relations among these structures are very loose. They exist not because of functional need, but because of some kind of contractual obligation or historical accident. Their relation is more one of concordat than of interdependence. A great variety of culture, ideas, values, politics, ethnicity, and style is possible within a single population. From this standpoint, there is no "society" with a clear boundary but congeries of groups and institutions with various interrelations.

With regard to the problem of industrial capitalism, pluralists have generally defended the theses and claims of liberal democracy over against both Marxists and fascists. The kind of pluralism connected with liberal democracy is highly voluntaristic and rational. Rooted in the viewpoints of Madison, de Tocqueville, and Calhoun, it seeks to promote voluntary association among free individuals and small groups. However, pluralism may also rest on involuntary, or natural, groups. Students of apartheid and ethnic pluralism find plurality rooted in the natural relations of race, family, language, region, and nationality. The distinction between voluntary and involuntary pluralism deeply affects our vision of society and leads us back to fundamental loyalties.

Voluntaristic pluralists have emphasized the importance of political structures and political action in the face of economic and ecological forces. Pluralists search for some kind of public in which political beings can resolve, at least temporarily, their differences through persuasion, vote, and compromise. Problems are met through the competitive but limited interplay of various interest groups and associations.

Because of this political orientation, pluralists direct our attention to the prominence of power and interest in human affiars. Power has an expansive quality. It must either be exercised or it withers away. The dynamics of power are unpredictable and upset any calculations based on the supposition that human life inevitably is governed by a set of interlocking functional needs. The concept of power has received many definitions, each exhibiting the particular face arising from its position in an overall social theory.[16] We do not need to settle the question here except to point out that in all cases it differs from authority on the one hand and sheer force on the other--with systemics emphasizing the former and dualists, as we shall see, the latter.

95

People seek and exercise power primarily out of self-interest. Self-interest is neither the plain desire to meet biological need nor is it a response to the functional needs of society. "Interest" denotes something that someone has a stake in. People have a variety of self-interests--psychological, cultural, political, as well as economic. Moreover, they perceive them in a variety of ways that govern their action. Pluralists generally deal only with people's conscious interests. These are what is crucial for social action. Because of the multitude of combinations between objective self-interests and subjective perceptions of them, the pluralists maintain that people do things for all kinds of reasons. Therefore they can offer no general explanation for the way societies are organized. Society is a continual process of conflict among changing interest groups.

The picture of continual conflict and plurality almost conjures up an image of sheer anarchism. This, however, is not the pluralists' contention, for they focus attention on groups rather than isolated individuals. While the acts of geniuses and heroes can be decisive in human affairs, it is the interrelations of groups which determine most significantly the course of social life. A certain kind of individualism does arise in voluntaristic pluralism, however, because it emphasizes that groups arise "from the bottom up," from the interests, claims, drives and commitments of individuals with specific self-interests. Thus almost any kind of group is possible. Moreover, the checks and balances exerted by a plurality of groups can protect individuals from tyranny by a single ruling group. In addition, individuals can construct a unique "personality" out of a variety of commitments and associations.

Because of this unpredictable concatenation of social forces the pluralist faces greater dilemmas in discerning the way stable structures of authority can exist in a society. We have already seen how systemics identify the ties between culture and authority. However, it is a pluralist guide, Max Weber, who has given us the most influential description of legitimate authority.[17] In stressing the possible conflicts among legitimacy orientations Weber moves away from the systemic concept of an all-embracing social substrate to the existence within and among societies of ultimate orientations with radically different characteristics. Legitimation is the ground for authority and social order. But the ultimate loyalties present in this ground do not spring from the functional needs of enduring social orders, as culture seems to do for the systemics. Legitimation orientations from which social authority arises are not a matter of rational choice but of historical contingency. They need not have any necessary roots in biology, psychology, or reason. This theoretical possibility for a variety of conflicting legitimacy orientations leads us to avoid a search for any "laws" of social order. Because of the divergence between alternative ultimate loyalties, the conflicts in social life are less tractable to persuasion and peaceful adjudication.

Weber himself tried to order this welter of legitimacy orientations which the historical records present to us. He was able to develop a typology of three kinds of orientation --charismatic, traditional, and rational-legal. Since we are interested only in the overall concept of legitimation, we will provide only a cursory presentation of these orientations. The charismatic is a form of legitimation in which the authority of commands is referred back to some distinctive and overwhelming personal attribute of the commanding person who is seen to be working "under the Spirit,"--as did the Judges or King Saul in ancient Israel. Charismatic authorities have a direct relation to an ultimate power-- whether it is YHWH as with the Israelite prophets, the spirit world, or the forces of history. From the standpoint of ordinary humans, this kind of authority is very personal. It revolves around the specific utterances of the charismatic person.

The traditional pattern of legitimation refers all commands back to custom. Every present action has to be squared with the past. Present innovations have to be "rediscoveries" of forgotten traditions or further elaboration and development of traditional principles, policies, or customs. The Roman Catholic Church comes closest in most people's minds to dependence on this type of legitimation.

Rational-legal legitimation refers all commands back to a formal, usually written, agreement or description of the rights and duties of a particular office or set of offices. Within these rational and logical prescriptions policies may seem to become traditional, but in fact they are justified and can be criticized by appeal to law or to job description and formalized procedures. Bureaucracy is the best example of this approach to social order.

These orientations are usually present to some degree in any society, with one dominating the others. Plurality exists not only at the level of power and interest, but at the deepest level of legitimation. While pluralists appreciate the dynamics of legitimation and authority, they approach them in terms of conflicting tendencies. The tensions among legitimation orientations, combined with those produced by the thrusts of power and interest, makes social order a precarious matter. Because of the divergence between alternative ultimate loyalties, the conflicts in social life are less tractable to persuasion and peaceful adjudication.

Social order exists to the extent to which there is
some consensus bringing together interest with legitimate
authority. Some kinds of legitimate authority contribute to
social stability more than others. Charismatic authority
is inherently unstable and must take on either traditional
or rational-legal "routinization" in order to create internal organizational or social order. In Europe and America
routinization is dominantly a matter of "rationalization,"
in which the original goals of the charismatic innovator
are fitted with increasingly refined and logical means in
the form of bureaucratic organizations.[18]

Pluralists may differ on where they locate the plurality in society. Some follow Weber to a concern for the
variety of legitimation forms. Others focus on the plurality of formal institutions, others on ethnic groups,
communities, or interest groups. Rather than concentrating
on the sweep of evolutionary advance, as do the systemics,
they seek to tell us the history of the conflicts and ac-
commodations among these groups.

2. Pluralist Loyalties

Pluralists generally seek to achieve or maintain a
pluralistic society. However, as we mentioned before, this
coupling is not irresistible. People committed to a systemic vision of society may use pluralist theories to
describe the "fragmentation" of the society and its need
for more overarching cultural unity, integrated growth,
or survival. Similarly, persons committed to what we will
call a conservative dualist position may seek to secure a
society in which the leadership of a single elite emerges
clearly from the welter of conflicting interest groups. In
the description of pluralism here, however, we are describing those who not only describe society from pluralist
perspectives but also seek to secure or enhance this
pluralism.

Genuinely prescriptive pluralists, however, are loyal
to the dispersion of power among social groups. They seek
as much decentralization as possible so as to enhance the
self-determination of these groups. They often champion
the strengthening of intermediary associations, such as
professions, churches, voluntary associations, and private
enterprises, to buffer the impact of massive institutions
on families and individuals.[19] Voluntaristic pluralists
will emphasize the capacity of individuals to move freely
among these groupings. They will seek legal equality among
persons in order to sustain their capacity for associating
freely. Involuntarists will emphasize the need to strengthen racial, ethnic, familial, or regional groups in order
to promote plurality. Unlike the systemics, who strengthen these associations in order to enhance societal

integration, pluralist's strengthen them because of their loyalty to the groups themselves and the way they limit the totalitarian tendencies implicit in "integration."

3. Pluralist Practices

The kinds of practices appropriate to a pluralistic perspective generally involve political power processes and the mobilization of groups.[20] We have already seen one possibility in the community organizing practices described in Chapter Three. Alinsky-style organizers try to discern the interests of persons and groups in an area. They focus conflict on particular issues and mobilize groups and coalitions of groups to compete for power in the public arena. While voluntarists and naturalists may differ on the kinds of groups they seek to strengthen, they all agree on the significance of these groups.

Because pluralists generally lack any overall plan or science of history, they engage in piecemeal reform movements through voluntary associations, interest groups, lobbying, and introduction of utopian alternatives, such as communes, cooperatives, pilot projects, and independent schools, parties or unions. They try to break out of existing systems or dualistic oppositions by proposing "third ways" and maximizing choice through some market process (such as a voucher system in public education) or democratic procedure (as in movements for industrial democracy). Pluralists usually pose these as alternatives within the present society. They do not espouse revolutions or even systematic planning, because those practices tend to sacrifice too many other values, goods, and minority group interests.

While pluralists have a special affection for political processes, they do not restrict their activities to these spheres. In fact they are also found defending the integrity of the non-political sphere, whether it be "private life" or economic organization. They assume that there must be some private spheres in which to develop and nurture alternative visions and unique personalities. Moreover these have to have some independent economic base in order to stand in effective competition with other powers in the society.

Pluralists are most likely to promote the protection of the liberties of individuals through civil and constitutional law. They will mobilize minority groups to defend their interests in the face of overwhelming majorities. Systemics tend to override the distinctions among sectors and groups in order to expose or create the common interrelations and commitments within a society. Dualists, as we shall see, are impatient with such a preoccupation with

99

the rights of individuals or groups, for it only obscures the essentially dualistic struggle which constitutes society. Pluralists are inveterate associationalists. They believe that the freedom to form associations with particular as well as general interests is more important than the supposed benefits of societal growth or economic equality.

D. The Dualist Approach

The dualist approach to society shares a number of pathways with both systemics and pluralists. On the one hand they approach society as a certain kind of system. On the other hand they focus our attention on the struggle, conflict and warfare that constitute that system. What is distinctive about dualists is that the social system is a system of conflict which takes place between two opposed groups or classes.

1. Dualist Loyalties

While dualists have a common model for describing the social scene they tend to divide into two camps with regard to their loyalties. Either they are radical dualists, like the Marxists, who want to overturn and end the class struggle, or they are conservative dualists, like the proponents of apartheid, who seek only to institutionalize the dualism rather than eliminate it.

Even among the radical dualists we find two streams, namely between those who are striving for a completely egalitarian society of personal freedom and those seeking a new hierarchal order which will guarantee justice. The former is represented by the "humanist Marxists" and other followers of the "young Marx" who appeared especially prominently in Europe in the 1960's. The latter is represented by the tradition from Engels, Lenin, and Stalin.

The value conflict between equality and inequality also divides dualists. For conservative dualists inequality is simply a scale against which one measures the relative inferiority or superiority of the two opposed groups. Proponents of apartheid in South Africa or Aryan superiority in Nazi Germany have both been concerned with inequality, but see it in a positive light. Most modern dualists, especially in Marxist and American populist traditions, see inequality in a negative light and seek to implement the value of social equality. In either case the dualist examines inequality with regard to every human criterion of power, prestige, ability or virtue, whereas the pluralist is mainly concerned with political and legal equality and the systemic with equal participation and membership.

Dualistically inclined analysts of society may also

seek to institutionalize a pluralist model of society in opposition to the tendencies toward polarization. This position is found among many Americans, and reflects the position of James Madison and Robert Dahl.

We place this statement about loyalties at the beginning of our treatment of societal dualism because controversy over the normative aspect of dualistic theories is so central to the significance of the social sciences for theology. The discussion to follow pays attention to the difference between radical and conservative dualists, but we should not ignore the role that pluralistic or systemic models may play in the normative decisions of dualists.

2. Dualist Theory

Among the radicals, and possibly among all contemporary dualists, stands the towering figure of Karl Marx. Recent variations on the radical theme have been sounded by Ralf Dahrendorf, Herbert Marcuse and C. Wright Mills.[21] Some of these radicals are committed to a thoroughgoing class analysis, others to an analysis of elites who stand over against the masses. Like all dualists they direct our attention to a single line of opposition running through the entire society. This single line of cleavage can be characteristic in many ways--oppressor-oppressed, elite-mass, haves-have nots, powerful-powerless. The radical dualist seeks ways to overcome this unequal struggle.

Conservative dualists likewise see a single line of cleavage but do not seek to eliminate it, because it is either impossible or undesirable to do so. It may be seen to be impossible because the cleavage is rooted in "nature," race, or heredity. Change may also be undesirable because the dualism enables the "higher" race, class, or group to manifest the fullness of humanity. The slaves make possible the superior achievements of the chosen few. The elect are inevitably a select elite in the midst of a mass of rabble. Warfare and conflict between them there may be. But conservatives do not seek to end the battle or the dualism which constitutes it.

Dualists are inevitably preoccupied with equality and inequality as concepts for understanding society.[22] This focus on equality and inequality leads dualists to see human organization in terms of patterns of command and subordination. The classic pattern of military hierarchy becomes a model for social organization. The compliance of the subordinate to the commands of the superior is the product of fear and habituation. In either case it lacks that quality of reasonableness and culture dear to the systemic or the enlightened self-interest characteristic of pluralist views.

In describing the fundamental struggle constituting
society dualists occasionally imply the concept of an elite.
It is important to distinguish the dualistic use of this
term from pluralistic and systemic usage.[23] Pluralists
speak of the presence of elites in the society--groups who
gain ascendancy and power through special powers or skills.
Dualists, however, see only a single elite, as with C.
Wright Mills' famous term, "the power elite." The power
elite is not to be confused with the whole ruling class. It
is, however, its heart and brain. Though its members cannot
step outside the interests and needs created by their class
position, they make the decisions concerning the specific
tactics and policies of that class.

This dualistic conception of a single elite sounds
very close to the reality described by some systemics. For
systemics, an elite is a group at the nerve center of the
society. It comprises those with access to information,
communication, and expertise. Dualists agree with this
analysis to this extent. But whereas systemics see the
elite as tending to respond to the interests and needs of
everyone and every institution in the system, radical dualists see it serving only the interests of its class at the
expense of the oppressed and alienated class. The systemic
claim that such power arises from knowledge or cultural
superiorty is described by dualists as mere propaganda mask-
ing the actualities of power and exploitation.

The conservatives, by basing the dualism in some
natural quality of race, character, ability or intelligence,
inevitably tend in a systemic direction. The opposed groups
are not seen to be opposed to the good of the whole. The
ruling class knows what is best for the masses and create a
system in which everyone's interests are met appropriately.
The radical, who pursue the warfare to its end, stand at
the center of the dualist vision in modern times. Because
Karl Marx's approach to this inequality has been so important in contemporary behavioral science we will now concen-
trate on the radical vision, leaving aside the claims of the
conservative dualists.

For the radical, societal dualism is a historical
creation. It is created by people who oppress one another,
whether or not they are aware of it. Whereas systemics
would speak of deprivation, dualists speak of oppression and
exploitation. Marxists have analyzed this exploitation with
the concept of class.[24] Social thinkers of many persuasions
use this term, but with different emphases and meaning.
Pluralists will emphasize the way class is constituted out
of the many positions of status common to a group of people.
But their statuses may rest on all kinds of cultural, political, or personal bases. Systemics usually speak of class
as "social stratification," groups of individuals with like

102

incomes, who stand in a hierarchy like overlying beds of sediment. Marxists, however, emphasize that a class is a set of people with the same position in the mode of production. Their position in the productive activity then determines their position educationally, politically, culturally, religiously, and residentially. Thus managers have big salaries, live in nice residential areas, run for public office, get tax breaks, and hold the high offices in their community associations, service agencies, churches, universities and other boards. Day laborers (the working class) get paid poorly, get a poor education, live in undesirable places, and rarely hold positions in organizations.

The dualist presumes, moreover, some kind of solidarity among all the members of a class or an elite. This solidarity overrides any formal categories of law, office, or nationality. Beneath the formal superstructure of society lies an essential solidarity of the class, race, or elite. Solidarity easily becomes a prescriptive value as well as an analytic assumption. Conservative dualists appeal to the ruling elite or race to affirm its solidarity over against the inferior group. Radical dualists, on the other hand, appeal to the inferior group to affirm its solidarity and then, through violent revolution, establish a universal solidarity of genuine brotherhood, fraternity and equality.

The set of derangements represented by class conflict are usually gathered together in the concept of alienation. Alienation is what is wrong with society. Unfortunately this term has become a popular symbol rather than a precise concept. It is often confused with anomie, the typically systemic concept.[25]

For radical dualists alienation describes a person's or group's lack of control over their works, their property and their lives. It is a condition of powerlessness and lack of self-determination. The archetypal example of alienation is the factory worker who sells his labor to a factory owner and loses all control over product, machine, or weapon that he produces. Instead he is paid a wage dictated not by his needs or the worth of his work product, but by the availability of labor on the labor market. He is caught in a system of exploitation in which he is powerless. But his powerlessness is not merely an individual problem, it is a condition he shares with all other members of his class. It is caused not by a problem of values or cultural breakdown, as with anomie, but by a specific institution--industrial capitalism. It therefore can be overcome through historical struggle.

Marxists respond to the problems of the modern age by

focusing on the economic institutions of industrialism.
Only economic change will make it possible to overcome
alienation.   As we have seen, systemics focus on the
cultural institutions and pluralists on the political ones.
To the extent that our age has been characterized in
economic terms (the industrial age, the capitalist era) the
dualists come closest to striking boldly and baldly at the
heart of the problem.

Since most modern dualists trace the fundamental societal conflict to economic opposition, they tend to be sus-
picious of cultural or philosophical explanations for social
affairs. They reject the systemic emphasis on culture's
primacy as well as the pluralist's affirmation of the effi-
cacy of political action.

This suspicion about ideas and culture permeates the
Marxist version of dualism. Karl Marx's discussions of
ideology launched this preoccupation and Karl Mannheim gave
it its distinctive terminology and theoretical elaboration.
Subsequently Jürgen Habermas and others of Frankfurt's
Institut für Sozialforschung have tried to resolve the
problem of ideology back into a pluralist direction.[26]

For Marx the world of ideas and culture is a creation
of the ruling class. Only they have the power and leisure
to write history, commission art works, and protect intellectual life. Moreover, all ideas serve class interests.
Ideas are preserved and created because of the consequences
they will have for enhancing a class's material interests.

Mannheim developed Marx's observations into a theory
of the ways relatively detached ideas interact with material
interests. Detached ideas, like "free enterprise,"
"democracy," or "the sanctity of marriage" appear either as
ideologies or as utopias. Ideologies function to legitimize
the ruling class and reinforce the existing power arrangement by blinding its potential critics. They also tend to
blind their proponents, which is why ruling classes often
behave so obtusely. Utopias tend to undermine the existing
order but without providing any positive strategy for changing things. They offer a better vision of society without
indicating in a practical way how to achieve it. What is
significant from the Marxist position is that neither set of
ideas transforms the power relations which generate ideas
in the first place. This transformation, if it is possible
at all, demands a revolutionary reversal.

Revolution is the outcome of the increasingly intense
contradictions which constitute society. To understand
revolution we must first understand the fundamental importance of contradiction in the dualist vision.[27] The idea of
contradiction once again helps identify dualists in relation

104

to the other approaches. Dualists see life in terms of this ultimate struggle between oppressor and oppressed. But they do not go so far as to say that this struggle can really be equated with warfare between two societies. There is genuinely one social order. But this order has internal contradictions which are essential to its existence. History is the production and resolution of these societal contradictions. However, Marxists disagree intensely over the extent to which contradiction disappears within human history. In contemporary history this debate revolves around the question of whether Soviet or Chinese society has created new contradictions with their accompanying alienation and new class struggles.[28] Those that entertain some possibility of new contradictions come closer to a conservative dualist position or a pluralist one. Either the contradiction becomes a continuous one through history, or it is replaced by a plurality of conflicts.

Because society generates contradictions rather than systemic "strains" or pluralistic conflict, it necessarily must be transformed totally in order to remove alienation. That is, its fundamental base must be changed in order to eliminate the possibility that the contradiction might reappear. That is why radical dualists support total revolution rather than mere reforms. Real changes occur only through revolution. Marxists differ from conservative dualists in holding out the hope and conviction that fundamental social change is possible. C. Wright Mills and American populists in general, when they have not joined the ranks of the pluralists, have held to a similarly optimistic view.

3. Dualist Practices

Both conservative elitists and radical Marxists set about training an elite (in Marxist terms, a vanguard) to guide the historical or natural forces. Conservatives, leaning on an appeal to the nature of human beings, educate the elite in order to maintain the proper power relation and to take care of the serving class. Radicals, appealing to history, prepare a vanguard who will raise the consciousness ("conscienticize" in present discourse) of the proletariat so that they can engage in revolutionary activity.[29] While each approach emphasizes the role of an elite, the particular tasks of those elites sharply distinguish them. The conservative elite manages a social system composed of two types of human beings. The radical vanguard arouses the oppressed class and prepares to lead it through the coming revolution.

Because this duality is so pervasive nothing short of total environmental control can guarantee the success of the effort to train and retrain the elite. The opposition is so great and so bent on domination that only a new environment

105

can insulate the new elite from its force. In this light
we also see the less pronounced dualism between the perfect
community, such as B. F. Skinner's Walden Two, and its
hostile environment. While such total environments usually
move in a pluralist direction they can also exhibit pronounced dualistic theories, loyalties, and even practices.

Marxists, however, engage in organizing the working
class for revolution. Because the societal contradiction is
rooted so deeply in the forces of economics, race, or biology (to include some neo-Marxist views), it can only b
resolved through some kind of revolution. For some radi-
radicals, however, this is a slow and long revolution.[30]
For others it is an imminent and violent warfare which is
further hastened by polarizing the latent contradictions.
This polarization can include such practices as coercion
and terrorism. The military practices that revolution finally entails are more a matter of military history than of
any particular dualist theory justifying their use. Need-
less to say the use of military force by conservative
dualists has dominated the fields of warfare to this day.

D. Societal Loyalties

In presenting each approach we have tried to show that
a similar analysis of the dynamics of societies can lead to
quite different efforts to change or preserve them. A person loyal to a pluralistic vision of society might analyze
society as a system. Systemics seeking to bring about a
more integrated society might use a pluralistic model to
analyze the present "fragmentation" in society. People with
a basically dualistic perception of the dynamics of society
might seek either to replace them with an egalitarian
solidarity or to maintain the present dualism. Moreover,
with the radical dualists we have to distinguish between
those with pluralistic commitments and those who seek a more
radical equality among individuals.

In all these cases it is therefore very important to
ascertain whether a model is being used to describe what is
actually going on or whether it is being presented as an
ideal yet to be attained. Moreover, we must be aware of the
way that descriptive theories can begin to function as prescriptive norms, or the way that societal ideals can mask
over the realities of the present situation.

Loyalties can permeate the sociological effort in
other ways as well. People may be loyal to certain practices for describing the society as well as for changing
or preserving it. Some people are committed to survey
methods while other gravitate toward analysis of formal
organization. Some prefer opinion polls, other pursue class
analysis. Some are loyal to an approach focusing on

economic factors, others to those emphasizing cultural or
political factors. In this case they have certain methodological loyalties leading them to a certain range of
descriptive outcomes. Choices of loyalties also decisively
affect the practices pursued to bring about social change,
as we saw in the fundamental disagreement between radical
and conservative dualists.

E. Conclusion

As in the previous chapters on Christianity and
personality we have presented an ideal typology of basic
approaches to a realm of concern. Pure exponents of any one
approach are rare indeed. Most of use have a bias or emphasis which places other perspectives in a subordinate role.
However, these three approaches do represent, on the whole,
quite divergent orientations in the present world. These
are the alternatives which engage theologians and psychologists most acutely when they seek out sociological partners for developing their own concerns.

There exist, both in classical and contemporary forms,
some typical connections among the various approaches in
these three realms. We are now ready to describe them and
then turn to the critical questions they raise. Before
turning to that endeavor we summarize the important theories
and practices emphasized by each approach to society in the
following chart.

APPROACHES TO SOCIETY

	Systemic	Pluralist	Dualist
T	Anomie	Conflict	Alienation
H	Authority	Consensus	Basic Forces (Natural,
E	Culture	Countervailing Groups	Economic, Military, etc.)
O	Differentiation	Groups (Voluntary,	Class, Race Sex
R	Function/Structure	Involuntary)	Command/Subordination
Y	Integration	Interest	Contradictions and
	Legitimation	Pluralism	Polarizations
	Equilibrium	Polity	Elite/Mass
	Evolution	Power	Equality/Inequality
	Primary/Secondary Groups	Public	Exploitation/Oppression
			Ideology and Utopia
			Solidarity
P	Communication	Experiments, Alternatives	Forming an Elite or
R	Cultural Action	Intermediary Associations	Vanguard
A	Differentiate Structures	Mobilization of Interest	Revolution
C	Education	Groups	Warfare and Terrorism
T	Formation of Primary	Political and Legal	Total Environmental
I	Groups	Reform	Control
C	Planning	Voluntary Association	Coercion
E			
L	Development	Decentralization	New Hierarchical Order
O	Coordination	Dispersion of Power	Preservation of Present
Y	Growth	Group Self-Determination	Domination (Conservative)
A	Planning	Legal Equality	Social Equality (Radical)
L	Socialization	Personal	Solidarity of Oppressed
T	System Survival	Self-Determination	or Elite
Y	Unity	Plurality	

PART III

DRAWING RELATIONS

The second step in critical thinking is drawing relations. In Part III we draw together the disciplinary components we distinguished in Part II. In Chapter Seven we
relate approaches from the three disciplines according to
their typical "triadic" affinities. In Chapter Eight we
align the separate dimensions according to the principle
of congruence.

In Chapter Seven we show how one approach from each
discipline implies an approach in each of the other two
disciplines. We believe that, for instance, as soon as
one had chosen an approach in Christianity, he or she has
implicitly chosen an approach to personality and to society
as well. We believe there are three primary triads and
three secondary triads throughout the history of Christianity, each triad consisting of compatible notions of
Christianity, self, and society. We explore these in detail through the writings of classical and contemporary
Christian authors.

In Chapter Eight we look at the affinities among the
dimensions of theory, practice and loyalty. The term
"congruence" refers to the relative degree of fit among
dimensions across disciplines, for instance between a
Christian value, a societal theory, and a psychological
practice. Interdisciplinary conversation is filled with
implications about such affinities. In Chapter Eight
we bring these to awareness and some systematic
clarification.

CHAPTER SEVEN

INTERDISCIPLINARY TRIADS

We have devoted the last three chapters to ordering
a vast amount of data into a coherent typology. Each
discipline offers three dominant approaches to its subject.
Each approach in turn involves dimensions of loyalty, theory, and practice. We now draw together these disciplinary
components according to their perennial affinities.

We have assumed that considerations about Christianity,
personality, and society have many points in common. From
the Christian side in particular, there exists a drive for
linkage with personality and social concerns. We see this
each time a theologian or minister uses behavioral science
considerations. At the same time we believe that personality
and society matters both relate to one another and have
definite associations with religion as well. We see this
most obviously in the psychology and sociology of religion.
Of equal importance are behavioral scientists' concerns
about values and ultimate commitments.

In Part I we noted the wide scope of the theology-
behavioral science conversation. We also showed the implications of Carl Rogers' and Saul Alinsky's work for theological and religious concerns. In these early chapters we
noted that the search for affinities and connections in the
behavioral science-theology conversation was intuitive and
precritical. Professionals with interdisciplinary concerns
simply followed what seemed to be intrinsic connections
among approaches in the three disciplines. They gave
little attention to comparing alternatives among approaches,
or to exploring the wider ramifications of the connections
they were making.

However, we believe that interdisciplinary intuitions
have a long and fairly consistent history. Indeed, we have
discovered certain perennial structures of these intuitions.
In this chapter we will be mapping the forms these intuitions have taken.

The affinities we have discovered among contemporary
participants in the theology-behavioral science conversation
have their predecessors in more classical forms. St. Paul,

Augustine, Luther, Calvin and Wesley had their respective
approaches to personality and society. While the associations they made existed in the cultural frameworks of their
times, they still bear similarities to associations being
made today. We can understand what these classical figures
did in our own formulations and gain new ways of understanding our traditional religious inheritances. At the same
time we can see how the rise of the disciplines of psychology and sociology has stimulated more sophisticated connections among concerns for Christianity, self, and society.

Therefore, in each of the presentations in this chapter we will attend both to contemporary representatives who
use triadic patterns, as well as to the way interdisciplinary intuitions have appeared in classical theological
figures. By "triad" we simply mean a set of conjoined
approaches made up of one approach from each discipline.
A cultic (Christian), systemic (societal), and conflict
(personality) set is thus a triad. We propose that certain
triads have appeared with such great frequency and perennial
vigor that they deserve to be called "primary triads."
Others which have less viability but still possess considerable attraction and importance are called "secondary triads."
They are secondary in that they have greater internal
tension and historically have been less durable.

These triads are not inevitable or necessary connections. They are the result of decisions people make in
light of the complex interplay among loyalties, theories,
and practices. Our claim that certain triads are more
stable than others rests on an examination of the logic that
holds them together and of their actual history.

There are three primary triads--cultic, prophetic,
and ecstatic. We have named them after their Christian
partners because they are our own points of entry into
the interchange. Cultic, systemic and conflict approaches
constitute the cultic triad. A prophetic triad combines
prophetic, dualist, and equilibrium approaches. Ecstatics
construct a triad with pluralist and fulfillment partners.
The secondary triads are movements away from each of these
primary groupings, especially in their personality choices.
We will take up these secondary triads in conjunction with
their primary forms.

A.   The Cultic Triad

1.   The Primary Form

On historical as well as logical grounds cultic theologians tend to choose systemic approaches to society and
conflict approaches to the self. We can understand these
affinities first by recalling some central characteristics

of a cultic emphasis in Christianity. Our own notion of cultic Christianity stands close to what Ernst Troeltsch called "church type" Christianity.[1*] The church type is grounded in the act of redemption by which God's grace has been made available to all people. It therefore seeks to support a stable order in which this redemptive power can permeate people's lives. The concept of cult, like that of "church," underlines the existence of some definite actions performed by officials in the church. This independence of these actions from the spontaneous acts of persons helps guarantee the objective availability and effectivenes of the grace made manifest in the cult.

On the one hand this means that a definite institutional structure exists to conduct these rites and sacraments. This institutional church, with its stability and comprehensiveness, enables members to be related to these sacraments and cultic actions as individuals Thus, within a cultic type of Christianity people tend to think in terms of a set institution grounded sacramentally on the one hand, and individuals who receive grace through its cultic acts on the other.

We can already begin to see why cultics would adopt a systemic view of society. This relation of self to whole institution is typical of a systemic approach, in which the main problem is one of relating individuals to the social system. This is why systemics are so concerned with processes of education and acculturation. These processes work within the self to make persons full members of the pre-existing society. The institution, the source of grace, precedes the individual, but it works within the individual from infancy to develop a social self.

Crucial to this development is the cultivation of the self's loyalties and fundamental orientations. These loyalty orientations, at a pre-cognitive level, are the real centers of our personality. We are, in this sense, our loyalties. Therefore whoever can finally command our loyalty and ultimate orientations exercises the decisive control over our lives.

We have already pointed out that this concern for education, socialization, and acculturation reflects an overarching emphasis on culture. It is culture which makes a society what it is, enables it to survive and to achieve higher integration. Culture is, etymologically and sociologically, simply the extension of cult. At the center of culture stands cult--some ongoing set of symbolic actions

---

*Notes for this chapter begin on page 250.

that make human life possible. The cult-culture connection is a very strong and durable one. In many ways it summarizes the primary affinity that exists between cultic Christianity and systemic sociology.

Historically within Christianity, whether in St. Paul or in Thomas Aquinas, a cultic emphasis has taken on "Body of Christ" as its dominant symbol of the Church. Participation in the Church's cult is really a participation in the life of that one high priest--Jesus Christ. People have access to the power that enlivens and guides them through a symbolic union with Christ, lived through sacraments of baptism, eucharist, marriage and ordination. Christian cult tends to center on these dominant motifs in Christ's life, especially his self-sacrifice. Sacrifice figures prominently all through the cult of ancient Israel. It is condensed in the person of Christ. Christians participate in this self-sacrifice when they exist in Christ. Having sacrificed their self they can gain a glorious self in resurrection.

Having understood the Christian life in terms of participation in a body, cultic Christians tend to think of society in the same way--as a kind of body for the natural life. This kind of "body thinking" has a deep affinity with systemic models of society. Body ecclesiology leads to body sociology. The internal harmony existing in Christ's own self is extended to the structure of the Church as well as to believers individually. The harmonious actions of the well executed ritual are a miniature condensation of the whole cosmic harmony. Sociologically, along the connection of cult-culture, this implies a harmony within the larger society gathered around its cultural center.

This kind of thinking leads to an emphasis on social order, both as a precondition for regular participation in the cult and as a result of the internally harmonious models articulated in cultic action. These actions are oriented to individuals whose eternal destiny is at stake, rather than to the welfare of the social structures, which are secondary in importance to the care of souls. However, this does not mean a simply anarchic disregard for society, since cultic Christianity cares about the preservation of the Church and its priesthood on the one hand, and for meeting the minimal needs of people on the other. Since the Church has charge of a very particular and specified spiritual need of individuals, it can delegate the responsibility for mundane tasks to other orders, structures, or aspects of the society. Thus a cultic church is more ready to divide up various functional needs of individuals (food, clothing, defense, law, spiritual nurture) among various institutional organs of the society, all of which work or can work harmoniously with the Church.

Within cultic Christianity we see a distinctive individualism as well as a collectivism. Just as the collective side has a distinct geography so does the individual side. Cultic theologians choose a conflict theory of self on a number of related grounds. The most important theological consideration here seems to be the emphasis on the grace of God. God's grace is all-sufficient to bring about and certify salvation. God alone, working through His chosen priestly representatives in the world, effects grace within people. We cannot manufacture this power and quality on our own. It is produced beyond our individual power. We cannot satisfy our need for grace alone. We need the Church, its Sacraments, its worship.

This immediately implies that there exists a fundamental disorder within individuals which can only be filled from without. Sometimes this lack is interpreted as actual rebellion within the self--a battle within the self between flesh and spirit. On these grounds cultic theologians choose psychologists like Freud and Erikson, who view the self in terms of conflict.

The second reason cultics adopt conflict theories of the self arises from their emphasis on the institutional "body of Christ" which in its cultic action makes Christ's power available to people. The church community does not arise from the individual wills of the believers but is in some fundamental way the wordly and historical extension of Christ himself. As such it has an independent existence over against individuals, who must be conformed to its pattern of life. The will of Christ, as set forth in the Church and its saints, seeks to transform and perfect the natural drives of the self. For the sake of the soul's eternal well-being, the Church rechannels these natural drives to produce a new being, a higher humanity. Within this context the self is therefore perceived as a creature of two forces--that of natural instinct (libido, as the Freudians would say) and that of conscience (the super-ego, in Freudian terms).

These demands from the church community are not merely external ideals placed on the self. These demands, from the earliest awakening of the person, are to be internalized to become an intrinsic part of the self. Conformity to the Church and its law is never a purely external conformity. It is produced as the "law is written on the heart." It is a result of conscious formation, education, and self-mastery. Only in this way can believers really be members of a body of love, rather than one of fear and coercion. The ideal society, i.e., the Church, is one in which all action results from an internalized sense of the community's needs rather adherence to a set of general rules. The kind of institutional structure that this orientation

115

supports ultimately presses beyond law, contract, and explicit promise to one of brotherhood, love, and paternity. The ultimate conception of the Church is one of a family directed by a loving Father.

The cultic triad also rests on affinities between personality and societal approaches. The systemic and conflict orientations tend to reinforce each other. This connection is beautifully exemplified in the work of Emile Durkheim and Talcott Parsons. For Durkheim the society is an independent power apart from the wills and minds of its individual members. Moreover, this power is a moral power. It exists for the good of its members. Without its constraints, guidance, and formation individuals would follow their own natural instincts to their ultimately destructive end--an end symbolized by suicide. Thus we find that Durkheim's theory of education is really one of discipline to authority.[2] The self is truly led out of its bondage by being placed under social authority. Only in this way can persons gain the upper hand against the chaos of forces which threaten to undo them from within.

While Parsons is not as openly authoritarian as Durkheim, he takes a similar path in selecting Freud as his psychological guide.[3] Though Freud's own formulations give Parsons' psychology an added sophistication, Parsons' thinking differs little from Durkheim's. Societies survive only to the extent that they can socialize the new members born into them. Social values and orientations must be inculcated into them so that most actions flow voluntarily from the individual members. Since the society is more or less disposed to meet the real needs of socialized individuals, most conflicts and problems are seen as a result of the psychological conflict between individuals' internalized social self and their natural or egoistic drives (which hardly constitute a "self" at all). It is important to notice that this focus on internal conflict is the logical accompaniment of the systemic concern for social harmony and educational development without external coercion. The one implies the other.

Thus the cultic triad is knit together by a variety of ties. Cultic action predisposes us to cultural action in the social system. Societal harmonization and integration require an elaborate handling of the intrapersonal conflicts. Before presenting two illustrative cases it might be helpful to point to one common idea running all through this triad, i.e., its attitude to the "natural." In each approach in this triad we see a deep appreciation and validation of the natural. The cultic must assume that the natural things and events of life--bread, wine, marriage, and the like--can be the bearers of divine grace. Nature is to be permeated with grace. The systemic likewise deeply

116

appreciates the natural way that societies seek their survival by developing structures to meet their functional needs. This is especially true for the more organic thinkers on the systemic trail. Conflict explorers of the personality, Freud pre-eminently, maintained forcefully that the natural drives must be given their due. Personality abnormalities result from an inadequate attention to these drives. However, in each case these drives of nature are not left to their own direction and given free reign. They are transformed, taken up, sublimated, and perfected so that they go beyond their purely natural course. In the Thomistic formulation, "grace perfects nature."

Within this orientation, regardless of discipline, there is an ambivalence toward nature and the natural drives. There is always a tension in this triad--whether to give greater weight to the natural component or to bear down on it even harder in order to assure the achievement of the higher goal. The secret of the cultic triad lies in preserving the delicate balance between the two.

a. A Contemporary Case: B. R. Brinkman

The English theologian B. R. Brinkman is not well known, known, yet his work represents a sophisticated effort to draw together the themes we have associated with a typical cultic triad. The substance of his effort, presented in five issues of the Heythrop Journal, attends to most of the concerns we associate with this set of approaches.[4] Though Brinkman's thought is not a pure case of the triadic logic at work, it is one of the best examples we know that systematically relates all three approaches in a cultic vision.

In brief, Brinkman seeks to articulate a contemporary theory of Christian life within the thought frames provided by the behavioral sciences. Yet he does not want to reduce Christian doctrine to the claims of psychology or sociology. He does not begin with pre-existing Christian theology, but with an examination of language and symbol. His analysis is heavily informed by Jungian (and in the background Freudian) psychology. He sees persons in the light of their cultural capacity, their use of symbols, and the rootage of these symbols in fundamental natural activities such as eating, drinking, and sexuality.

One of the central problems Brinkman wants to overcome is external or "extrinsic" Christianity. To him, true religion rests in the interior. Cultic action is not an external performance but is a kind of paradigmatic life constituting the very core of the self. At many points Brinkman walks a very narrow edge between preserving the objectivity of the life of grace offered by God (and hence the relative integrity of Christian discourse) and his belief that such life is already at the heart of things.

The gradual transformation of the self in true sacramental action presupposes and creates a community. The symbolic life and "the way in intimacy" demand at the same time a "socially operation way." This is the sketchiest part of his work. It is still clear, however, that Brinkman greatly appreciates the kind of work done by Anthropologists Victor Turner and Mary Douglas (herself more of a mixture of societal perspectives) and sociologists such as Hugh Duncan and Talcott Parsons.

Brinkman is careful and judicious in the way he draws on the behavioral sciences. He does not collapse them into each other. He recognizes tensions but sees clear affinities among the disciplines. His work is a significant example of recent efforts to link cultic theologies with the behavioral sciences.

b. A Classical Case: St. Paul

The cultic triad arises from a mutually reinforcing arrangement among cultic, systemic and conflict orientations. Because of the many grounds on which this mutuality rests it forms a fairly stable and perennial triad. We find its classical expression in St. Paul. While Paul is a rich and complicated thinker indeed, we find his approach to be fundamentally a cultic one in which prophetic and ecstatic emphases are strong but subordinate. For Paul the essence of the Christian life is to be "in Christ." We become new beings in Christ through participation in his body and blood in Eucharist. This is Christ's continuing presence in history. By being a communal event, Eucharst is safeguarded from private mysteries, gnostic cults and wild imaginings of lone mystics or religious demagogues. In entering into Christ's body we leave behind a human slavery to our own passions and to the life of the flesh and enter a new slavery to Christ. In taking on a new authority we are freed from bondage to an old allegiance which would lead us to our destruction.

Even within this new structure of Christ's authority, we still struggle against our fleshly urgings, the desires of the old self. The warfare within us enters a plain of victory but never ceases. The vivid portrayal of the divided self that we find in his Letter to the Romans is typical of conflict theories of the self. The conflict is resolved only by being taken up into the body of Christ which is the Church.

Paul makes extensive use of the body metaphor in order to legitimate a church in which people's special gifts are used to benefit the whole. While these gifts of the Spirit "naturally" are oriented toward the welfare of the whole body they also must be schooled and disciplined, like the athlete's skills, in order to attain their end. For Paul, the body of Christ is both a eucharistic symbol (which we internalize) and an organizational symbol (to which we give allegiance).

When Paul comes to articulate the wider societal dimensions of Christian existence he also relies on a systemic approach, in which rulers exercise their power as a function of the whole society. They have their appropriate functions in the same way that Christians perform various functions in the Church. While there are still some heavily dualist strains even in Paul's mature thought, his emphasis is strongly systemic.

In Paul we see a sophisticated intertwining of themes which, in the present conversation, we call cultic, systemic and conflict. Pauline thought, with its attendant practices, has exercised a powerful influence on Christianity, one which finds renewed force in the present conversation between theology and the behavioral sciences.

2. The Cultic Triad: The Secondary Form

We mentioned earlier that the cultic triad, through its validation of "nature," can give great emphasis to the compatibility of the life of grace with the unfolding of properties already inherent in the self. When this emphasis is pushed far enough we find ourselves on a different path altogether in the personality realm. This is a new triad consisting of cultic, systemic, and fulfillment approaches. This is the secondary form of the cultic triad.

This triad pushes the internal conflict of the old self into the background and highlights the natural potentialities of the self. Rather than being in tension with societal demands, they are basically compatible. The drive to sociality is prominent among the natural instincts. The social order merely provides form and structure for them.

This has been a very popular move, not only in contemporary cultic expressions of Christianity but also in more classical versions. It seeks to combine the high degree of social order and "objectivity" with the free expression of the natural self and the cultic celebrations of the Church. In the contemporary conversation it is well represented by Urban Holmes. Thomas Aquinas presents us with a classical formulation.

a. A Contemporary Case: Urban T. Holmes

Like many other Anglican theologians Urban Holmes

119

places concepts of cult and sacrament at the center of his concerns.[5] While giving attention to "sacramental person" and "sacramental word" Holmes relates them all back to the central emphasis on "sacramental rite." It is this which stands at the center of life and Church. It is this which must be purified by the attention to person and word, lest it degenerate into mere form or fancy.

How does Holmes gain a critical lever for reinvigorating sacramental rite? He turns to anthropology and specifically to the concept of liminality offered by Victor Turner--a largely systemic thinker. "Liminality" is the social or personal condition in which we are between the stable roles or institutions that give us an objective status in the world. It is the time when we are no longer a child but not yet an adult. It is the time when the old order binds us but the new order has not yet made its claims. It is this liminal condition which offers the presence of the truly sacred.

On this basis and with this equation of sacrality and liminality Holmes reconstructs genuine sacramentality. Because liminality is basically a condition for persons, however, true sacrality enters the world through these liminally situated individuals. In their deep intuition of the pre- and post-social realities they help put us in contact with the transcendent. The Spirit wells up and through them and appears in a communal form united around the sacramental, liminal person.

It is here that Holmes' preference for a fulfillment psychology becomes evident. The kind of personality Holmes depicts is not so much one struggling with the conflict within, but one which releases out of its deepest roots a true humanity prior to and beyond socialization. The kind of community in which this occurs is equally pre-institutional, but none the less genuine for that.

This kind of move in Holmes' work creates tension with the more conventional claims of a conflict personality theory. Holmes is attentive to this (between the lines) and spends considerable time seeking ways in practice as well as in theory to balance the claims of the large institution and the embracing society with those of the liminal community and the sacramental persons. Finally, he relies on patterns of differentiation, both structurally and functionally, to accommodate the charismatic and the institutional elements, the subjective, personal epxerience and the objective, societal structures. The outcome is a provocative set of theoretical and practical proposals set out along the lines of the secondary cultic triad.

b. A Classical Case: Thomas Aquinas

With Aquinas we have a fundamentally cultic approach, thought it is tempered with the more monastic orientation toward contemplation. The contemplative element inevitably draws in a more pronounced ecstatic element. The experience of the person is given a high priority. The second factor leading to his selection of a fulfillment emphasis is his Aristotelianism. Thomas places much greater emphasis on the natural development of the self toward its good. The life in grace is more a completion of the drives of the self than it is their control or replacement.

With both of these factors we find an emphasis on the continuity between reason and faith, between cognition and intuition. Reason appears less as the way to self mastery than as the wondrous apprehension of the self's ultimate destiny. This has much greater affinity with a fulfillment approach than with the conflict theories of personality.

Moreover, on a number of grounds, Aquinas continues and reiterates the social nature of the self. The fulfillment of the self, in this world at least, is in community. Here we might recognize Aristotelian roots as well as Christian and typically medieval claims. This, along with his conceptions of subsidiarity and social differentiation, place him clearly within the systemic perspective.

The Thomist triad was very important in legitimating a new configuration of person and society in the 13th century. It has again become very important in legitimating a new alignment of cultic theology with the 20th century America scene, where fulfillment views of the self find widespread acceptance.

B. The Prophetic Triad

1. The Primary Form

Prophetic theologians have a predilection for dualistic approaches to society and equilibrium approaches to personality. These three constitute the primary triad for Christians with a prophetic orientation. We will first sketch in the basic logic which ties this triad together and then introduce some representative contemporary and classical figures pursuing it.

The biblical prophets, who are our most important source for this type of Christianity, portrayed history as a struggle between God and man, the elect and reprobate, Israel and the world. Other themes are present, but they have a subordinate place. Various Christian groups and churches have developed and preserved this view. The cosmic

struggle between the powers of good and evil is seen to sum
up all the lesser struggles of life. In it are posed the
crucial questions of reconciliation, wholeness, and
reunification. This way of thinking in prophetic polarities
attunes believers to dualities in society. The loftier
conflict between the City of God and the City of Man,
between the innocent and the wicked, between good and evil,
is referred to specific groups, classes, nations or races.
It is placed within history. This is the first connection
between a prophetic and a dualist approach.

Inasmuch as the prophetic point of view is biblical,
it tends to focus on the Exodus from Egypt and the coming
reception of God's promise. In our own time numerous theologians have used this fundamental symbol as a springboard
for moving into a radical or Marxist vision of the liberation of the oppressed. Black as well as Latin American
theologians of liberation have used this path extensively.[6]
Many observers have noted other ways in which the specific
symbols associated with the prophetic tradition have deep
affinities with a Marxist perspective.[7]

Both radical and conservative dualists share another
point of connection with prophetic Christianity. Both
tend to view things from outside the situation. The prophet juxtaposes human affairs against the plumb-line of
God's justice. It is from the standpoint of this external
rule that we can see the true state of affairs. Regardless
of how happy and comfortable everyone may think they are,
the present state of affairs is far from the from true life
to which they are called and commanded. Similarly, dualists
use a transcendent concept to discern their division of
society--whether it be race, class, or sex. Many things
may be going on to the eye of the involved observer, but
from the standpoint of the fundamental criterion everything
is actually a manifestation of the single line of division.
The adoption of this transcendent point of view offers a
strong line of connection between prophetic and dualist
persuasions.

Finally, both tend to think of things in terms of an
opposition between structures, what St. Paul called the
"principalities and powers." These enormous networks of
power, dominion, and might are pitted against each other in
a way that overwhelms the imagination and strength of individuals or particular institutions. Whereas the cultic
triad emphasizes the relation of individuals to the whole,
the prophetic triad emphasizes the importance of vast
structures pitted against each other.

What then is the connection between this theology-
sociology dyad and the equilibrium approach to personality?
We have just noted that the prophetic temperament,

122

especially in its apocalyptic strains, tends to push conflicts onto a plane of cosmic opposition. The outcome of
this cosmic conflict determines the fate of all finite
beings. From this standpoint we can see that the destiny of
individuals devolves from this external combat between God
and the demonic power. Gustav Aulen has called this notion
of a cosmic struggle for man's soul the classical theory of
the atonement. We can easily recognize the affinities
between this view and an equilibrium theory of the self.
The condition of the self results primarily from the balance
of forces impinging upon it. The way to save individuals
is to save their cosmic environment. The "Law" or Torah
is not a repressive force as much as it is a kind of environment in which we can best grow to perfection. The prophetic perspective, especially when joined with a dualist
sociology, emphasizes this kind of equilibirum psychology
within the context of cosmic struggle.

The commitment to an external objective standard,
common to prophetic and dualist exponents, also figures
importantly in the choice of an equilibrium partner. As
we noted in Chapter Five, the equilibriumist emphasizes
the importance of right thinking and right action. What
is right is ascertained from the standpoint of the external
observer. Equilibriumists are often called behaviorists,
because what is generally observable is only external
behavior. It is, as the prophets reiterate, right deeds
that count before God. It is the observing public who
provide the touchstone of reality for ascertaining the
"true" state of psychological affairs.

This common commitment leads us to yet another point
of affinity. All three approaches look to external intervention to resolve the problems they face. The prophet,
while exhorting the people to change their sinful ways,
ultimately looks to God's act of intervention to set things
right. Sometimes this emerges in a strong notion of pro-
vidence, as it does with Calvin. Sometimes it emerges in
a vision of redemptive apocalypse as with the Revelation of
St. John. Dualists also tend to look to some elite, vanguard, or conquerer to set society aright, or, with conservative dualists, to maintain the duality. Finally, equilibriumists, when they turn to therapeutic practice, look to
the directives of the therapists for the solution to mental
illness. Direction lies in the therapist's hands. The
therapist, like God, like the elite, know what is right and
good for the patient and then set about applying the correct
procedures. The focus of outside intervention and direction from one who is "in charge" links the prophetic triad
together at yet another point.

In contemporary times we find further evidence of a
direct affinity between Marxist social theory and

equilibrium psychologies. Some of this is due to theoretical connections, some to practical ones. By fixing our attention on the conflict between oppressor and oppressed, radical dualists imply that the resolution of societal alienation will terminate all psychological alienation. Only the harmonization of societal forces will produce psychological harmonization. This is why most Marxists have looked upon conflict psychologies such as Freudianism as merely a symptom of bourgeois culture with no lasting contribution to make to human welfare. While Freudians take culture and society as a given within which we must achieve the capacity for love and work, Marxists seek to change the social conditions themselves by direct action.

From the practical side, in the Soviet Union and other states operating under Marxist theories, equilibrium psychologies have been adopted because they tend to raise fewer questions about the adequacy of social engineering. Social planners need not worry about what might spring from the inner resources of the self or the subterranean flow of libido. The self can be re-educated in order to conform to the image of "the new socialist man" in a rational way. Thus, Soviet psychology has been dominated by behavioristic approaches to self-transformation.

We have here a great deal of corroboration for holding that the prophetic-dualist-equilibrium triad is a primary one by virtue of its inner logic and its historical experience. Once again, since we are dealing in thought and action, we cannot make any claim to the deterministic tightness of these connections. They exist as a perennial tendency among those who engage in serious interdisciplinary exchange. In a moment we will cite the secondary prophetic triad. First, however, we will note briefly three figures representative of this primary triad--two contemporaries and one classical author.

   a. Two Contemporary Cases: Gustavo Gutierrez
       and Jose Miguez Bonino

Latin American Liberation Theology is the literary expression of many different movements for social change in Latin America. Their theological exponents have been articulate and learned as well as committed to social justice. Since we will analyze a work by Gutierrez later we will only mention his effort here. Bonino, with his statement, <u>Christians and Marxists</u>, takes an even more deliberate stance along the lines of the primary triad.[8]

Bonino first of all is "a person who confesses Jesus Christ as his Lord and Savior." He simultaneously is one who believes "that revolutionary action aimed at changing the basic economic, political, social and cultural structures and conditions of life is imperative today in the world." Through reflection on efforts to achieve these changes he seeks to establish correlations between these two spheres of loyalty, both theoretically and practically.

Bonino pursues this "correlation" more consistently than do some others. We wish to point out here those places where, rather than departing from the primary connections, he works along them. First of all, he attempts to dissuade Christians from the embrace of "third ways" that might mediate between the polarized powers. These always have proven to be fruitless. In any event, polarization will finally force them to one side or the other. Thus, he eschews the usually attractive pluralist option.

Secondly, he takes a more consistent psychological stand. While indeed he consults Freud, he places him in the context of the social forces of his time. Internal conflict is seen primarily as a manifestation of the social oppression around persons rather than as a perennial dilemma. Thus, considerable more weight is given to environmental change as the key to personality change. This environmentalism, however, must then be tempered by theologically based efforts (implicitly ecstatic ones) to realize the freedom and subjectivity intrinsic to individuals. Bonino takes two chapters to show how, within this primary triad, such claims can be compatibly advanced.

Finally, he takes the prophetic commitment to an external standard to its logical conclusion. God's demands stand over against the Church and all human societies. Moreover, so do those originally envisoned by Marx himself. Marx's "humanist vision" stands in judgment over all Marxist regimes, even though these have, he claims, generally advanced human welfare more than liberal democratic or capitalist ones. Thus, the common commitment to transcendence, so crucial for the prophetic mind, maintains a continuing openness to change.

b. A Classical Case: John Calvin

While there are other classical figures, such as Thomas Münzer, who fit the primary prophetic triad even more purely, Calvin's greater reknown makes him more accessible as an illustration of these motifs.[9] Once again, in highlighting the basic orientation in his thought and practice we do not mean to ignore ways in which he incorporates or touches upon other approaches.

The Word of God, both in Scripture and in preaching, stands at the center of Calvin's theology. This Word stands objectively over against the believer. While this external objectivity places believers in judgment and anxiety, it also is able to save them. The only possibility of salvation lies in God's power alone to save--and this through the perfect obedience of the Son.

God's will, then, as made known in his Word and in the life of Christ, lies behind any act of salvation. His will dominates the world in creation, providential intervention, and in redemption. His will also lies behind the evident damnation of some lives. The system of God's righteousness and the glory that it manifests demand that some should fall to destruction while others rise to eternal life.

This double predestination in the light of God's eternal decrees gives to all of Calvin's theology its prophetic duality. This is not the dualism of the Manicheans, in which flesh and spirit are pitted against each other. It is not the dualism of the Marcionites, in which creation and salvation are attributed to different divine sources. It is the ethical dualism typical of the prophetic temperament.

We are therefore not surprised by the ways in which this duality is translated into societal terms. The tension between Church and world is intensified. Calvin fought bitterly with his fellow Genevans to maintain the Church's independence from the secular powers while at the same time he wanted to give the Church dominion over the ethical, moral and cultural life of the city. Secondly, in his political theory he is sharply attuned to the difference between the people of virtue (the elite, the aristocratic) and the untutored masses. While some democratic process was conducive to proper government, the central power should be in the hands of a body of distinguished people.

Calvin's societal dualism was in essence a conservative one, not the radical kind found either in his radical contemporaries or in revolutionaries of the present day. Moreover, the sharpness of this social dualism was attenuated by his reluctance to bring the cosmic dualism between elect and reprobate down to earth. Only God knows, in truth, who these are. Neither the Church nor the governing elite can claim to be the elect. God's sovereignty always tempers the drive toward a closed dualism in the society.

Both of these thrusts in Calvin's theology and church practice are taken to their logical end in his psychology. While conflict within the self is seen as an intractable warfare, and while the self has a hidden nature struggling to become free, it is an equilibrium approach that dominates the horizon. With regard to salvation, the self is a receptor of the divine Word. Within individuals there is nothing that can create the peace and righteousness of salvation. We are saved by God's intervention, just as we are seduced into damnation by the cunning strength of the Devil.

126

Moreover, the Church, for Calvin, is conceived as a school in which we are trained within the proper environment for sanctity. We are continually led astray from our path because of the weakness of our will. The Church, with patience and prodding, keeps us on the right path of thought and action.

And finally, the Church so tries to dominate the society ethically that it guarantess a total environment which will stimulate us to do the good, even when our intentions are wrong. Through divine intervention, the schooling of the Church, and the discipline provided by the whole society, we are transferred from bondage to evil into a life of true righteousness and peace.

In these three respects--theological, sociological, and psychological--Calvin purses a prophetic triad with rigorous logic and profound attention. Subsequent Calvinists have been able to take his societal dualism in racist and conservative directions, as in South Africa, or in revolutionary and even libertarian ways, as in England and America. In these later cases as well as in Calvin's own thought, an awareness of his basic choices can illuminate the ways in which he deviates from some typical conclusions in order to take on other ideas, loyalties and practices.

2. The Secondary Prophetic Triad

The secondary prophetic triad is formed when prophetic dualists select a conflict rather than an equilibrium psychology. The basic logic of this move is quite simple. The duality already evident in prophetic ethics and intensified by a dualistic social theory is then pushed into the depths of the self. The ethical claims of the prophet cannot be actualized completely in society and personality because the conflict within the self has independent roots unamenable to the behavioral modification pursued by equilibriumists.

Here again we see the importance of the distinction between a conflict and equilibrium view of the self. The equilibrium may grant the presence of conflicting motives or behaviors within the self, but attributes this to environmental conditioning. The true conflict theorist, however, sees in this conflict the expression of biological, mental, or even metaphysical processes that cannot be explained or resolved by environmental approaches.

If we recall that the conflict alternative is part of the cultic triad we can see that the choice of this psychology by prophetic dualists leads them to concern for culture, symbol, sacrament and cult. Their revolutionary

127

thought and practice (if they are radicals) takes on a
concern for cultural change and symbolic manipulation. If
they are conservatives they give greater heed to the role
of cult, culture, and symbol in maintaining societal dualism.
This frequently leads them to a more systemic approach to
society.

This secondary triad has always been quite popular.
It is a move that complexifies interdisciplinary exchange
and leads to its own kind of tensions and instabilities.
We have chosen Martin Luther to illustrate the classical
form of this triad and Reinhold Niebuhr the contemporary one.

   a. A Contemporary Case: Reinhold Niebuhr

In some sense our use of Niebuhr to illustrate this
triad is an argument about the development of his thought.
If we look at three of his important works written over a
span of more than 20 years, we see the working out of the
implications of his dominant triadic emphases.[10]

The first work, Moral Man and Immoral Society, reflects a dualistic analysis shaped by Niebuhr's encounter
with Marxism. While persons may be "moral" in their private
lives, they may participate in and benefit from an immoral
configuration of vast social forces in the economic and
political realms. These overarching forces are pitted
against each other in a way that usually results in an
opposition between rich and poor, powerful and powerless.
The actual fact of this dualism calls into question all the
ideology of democratic pluralism and social process through
which privately "moral" people hope to end injustices.

Even here, however, we see the beginnings of a critique against the utopians, who believe that a new society
can be constructed by regenerate humans, and against the
Communists, who believe that even immoral people can bring
about a more perfect social order. Niebuhr can of course
appeal to historical evidence, which shows that, regardless
of personal sanctity, no perfect order has ever existed.
But the logical and theological grounds for his claim that
social perfection must lie beyond history seems to result
from his encounter with conflict psychology, especially
Freud's.

The outcome of this appropriation of Freud can be
traced in The Nature and Destiny of Man. Freud's own
research corroborates and deepens a theme that goes back
to Augustine. Pride, selfishness, arrogance, anxiety and
power-seeking will always corrupt the use of power. These
qualities can never be eliminated, because they spring from
the awareness of death, of biological drive, and finitude.
It is this reality which forces us beyond history, social

transformation and personal improvement to a salvation of
a different order entirely.

In the Self and the Dramas of History Niebuhr rounds
out these convictions and explores even more extensively
the problem of participating responsibly in historical
change without illusion and without despair and resignation.
His commitment to conflict psychology never draws him away
from a simultaneous commitment to a prophetic type of Christianity and a basically dualistic analysis of social
dynamics.

b. A Classical Case: Martin Luther

Luther's basic theological position is quite similar
to Calvin's. Calvin himself expressed his deep indebtedness
to the reformer of Wittenberg.[11] Similarly Luther's social
thought bears out a number of dualistic themes. With Luther
we find the notion of "two kingdoms" to be much more pronounced. The polarities of Gospel and Law, Church and World,
the Cross and the Sword, cluster around this key Lutheran
thesis about the double way God governs the world and leads
people to salvation. Moreover, the cosmic struggle between
God and Satan receives more passionate and vivid attention.
The two-kingdoms duality subsequently leads, in ways found
also in Calvin, to a dualistic social theory, usually a
conservative one. Today, however, some Lutheran theologians
have found ways this can be taken in a radical direction as
well.[12]

While Luther pursues a primary prophetic course with
regard to social theory, his psychology is much more pro-
noundedly conflictual than Calvin's. Historically, we might
trace this to his own Augustinian heritage. Luther probes
the depth of the intractable conflict within the self to a
greater extent. He is much more aware of the way that God
and Satan conduct their warfare within the self. It is here
that the work of salvation resides in a special way. Little
wonder, then, that contemporary Freudians like Erik Erikson
have found special reward from examining Luther's thought,
life, and work.[13]

And finally, it is this greater attention to psychological conflict which lends to Lutheran thought a more
systemic cast, a greater attention to sacrament and cult,
a more conservative thrust. The prophetic and dualistic
commitments remain dominant, however, and create perennial
tensions within Lutheranism to this day.

3. Cult and Prophecy, Church and Sect

The prophetic triads have many ramifications. The
secondary pattern places the primary form in frequent

juxtaposition to the cultic triad. Students of Ernst
Troeltsch will probably recognize in these two triads a
corroboration or refinement of Troeltsch's two great forms
of Christianity--the church type and the sect type. In
our formulation we have clarified, under the impact of the
behavioral sciences, the dynamics of these two types and
how they can feed into one another. The prophetic triad
embraces many sectarian motifs as well as the "church"
motifs of traditional Lutheranism and Calvinism.

It was also Troeltsch who pointed out the increasing
importance of yet a third, though historically subordinate,
type of Christianity--the mystical or spiritual type. While
ecstatic Christianity does not parallel Troeltsch's conception exactly, it bears rough resemblance ot it. Though it
may not have been as prominent historically, it has received
increasing support and attention today. It has its own
integrity and its own typical triadic moves.

C.   The Ecstatic Triad

1.   The Primary Form

The primary ecstatic triad brings together ecstatic,
fulfillment, and pluralist approaches. This combination
arises from the implications of ecstatic religion as well
as from affinities that lie between pluralist sociology
and fulfillment psychology.

Ecstatics recognize personal experience as the fundamental vehicle of the sacred. Personal transformation or
conversion assumes the place of primary value. Ecstatics
often symbolize transformation of energy and change of
state in the self by fire, as with images of Pentecost or
John Wesley's famous "warming of the heart." Faith for the
ecstatic means a deep inner conviction and experience of a
justifying love which leads to an outpouring of the self
toward others. Under the impact of the Spirit's amazing
gifts, ecstatics are optimistic about the human spirit and
its capacity for perfection. The inner experience of grace
naturally permeates the self and leads to service of others.

Consequently, ecstatics frequently practice common
prayer, confession of sins to each other, and mutual care
and support in small groups and communities. These practices, especially among evangelical Protestants, are often
complemented by large scale revivals in which preaching and
enthusiastic singing play prominent roles. Among the more
quiet minded, especially Anglicans and Catholics, mysticism
and meditation have had a favored place. In either case,
ecstatics aim to nourish and rekindle the Spirit within
Christian believers.

Because the impact of the Spirit is so personal, the process of ecstatic thought and reflection often leads to autobiographies rather than institutional histories. Though each autobiography is unique, it can be instructive and inspiring for others. The history of Christianity tends to be conceived as a succession of spiritual autobiographies.

All of these themes clearly give to ecstatic Christianity a bias against large institutions. While cultics tend to see spirit working through structure, and prophetics see structure working against structure, ecstatics tend to see spirit working against structure. Structures of themselves never can give life. They can only kill it with letter, law, and legality. Only the free-moving spirit can give life. It must spring up anew constantly to give life to dead structures.

When ecstatics do develop an ecclesiology it is one that gives primary authority to the inspired opinions of individual believers. It is therefore radically democratic. As we will point out shortly, this gives ecstatics a strong preference for voluntary associations and the pluralism they imply.[14]

All of these ecstatic concerns find their most congenial partners in fulfillment approaches to the self. Fulfillment therapists conceive of the individual as a pilgrim on a journey from an old self to a new self, and the journey is marked by steps that can be defined and celebrated. Fulfillment guides evince optimism about the journey, as in Rogers' value of self-actualization and Maslow's theory of growth. They are cognizant of human imperfection, as are ecstatics, but tend to be criticized for being naive or romantic about human nature. This is because they focus their attention more on the destination of the pilgrim than on the hazards along the way. Rogers' notion of the fully functioning person attracts ecstatics desiring to identify concretely the qualities that accompany the inner spiritual realities of faith. Ecstatics are further drawn to Rogers to understand more precisely how the self can be strengthened in a life of selfless love. As we cited earlier they are especially attracted by the analogy between what Christians call "agape" and what Rogers calls the capacity for unconditional positive regard.

In addition to these parallels in theory and loyalty, there are many similarities in practice as well. Fulfillment therapies offer techniques like Rogers' mirroring of feeling, which elicit closeness and intimacy. Thomas C. Oden cites the numerous parallels between the small group practices of pietism and modern encounter groups.[15] Both movements cherish flexible formats, free expression of self, and a mutual care leading to intense feelings of intimacy and group solidarity. It is intimacy in particular that ecstatics find attractive in fulfillment practice. This follows the ecstatic emphasis on the nurturing of persons.

Modern ecstatics are typically first intrigued by the personality realm rather than the societal. Nevertheless, with varying degrees of awareness they tend also to employ a pluralistic social theory. Their very establishment of spirit-led small groups immediately introduces practices fundamental to pluralism. These groups are the seedbed of voluntary associations established to serve the interests of their members and to transform the social order. They do not seek to transform the whole society from a common cultural base, as in systemic approaches. Nor do they pit a saving class against its enemies, as in radical dualist theories. They attempt to transform society by transforming individuals in the context of small groups. This occurs in the Church through the action of the Spirit. It occurs in society through the banding together of like-minded persons. In the Church, decisions are reached through seeking the minds of the inspired individuals. In social groups, the reasonable or enlightneed interests of the participants, that is their wills, is the touchstone for policy.

Once voluntary association is legitimated as a leading of the Spirit, any division of the society into two camps becomes very difficult. Ecstatics will thus practice their faith in society alongside other voluntary groupings that may directly contradict their efforts. This makes sense to ecstatics, however, because they see transformation to be an intensely personal affair that cannot be programmed for all. Ecstatics are thus content to ply their trade in the market place where a plurality of competing groups co-exist. Moreover, they do so under a wide diversity of social and political structures, as long as these permit them to further their own particular interests.

The ecstatic triad can also be developed from the behavioral science side. Frank Goble interprets Abraham Maslow's psychology as assuming that each mature person following his own interests will also serve the interests of society. [16] This social theory has historical roots in Adam Smith's concept of the "invisible hand" and John Locke's notion of the sympathetic self. Smith and Locke were political economists, while Maslow is a psychologist. Both approaches assume that the essential instincts of the self are socially beneficial if only given a chance to blossom. Each theory rests on pluralistic assumptions about the nature of society. [17] Because of its evaluation of human tendencies to self-actualization, fulfillment psychology typically implies a pluralistic social theory.

Fulfillment exponents, when seeking a religious partner, normally choose an ecstatic one. Their emphasis on
personal experience and inner fulfillment attunes them to
the ecstatic's reverence for personal religious experience.
Maslow, for one, is quite interested in religious experience,
and many humanistic therapists are attracted to mysticism
and Eastern spirituality. Were a fulfillment theorist to
choose a cultic or prophetic partner, he would have to
attenuate the value of individual autonomy and self-
direction. In those approaches the self is always subser-
vient to greater ends, whether conceived in terms of the
will of God (prophetic) or of the perpetuation of the Body
of Christ (cultic). Thus the ecstatic-fulfillment-
pluralistic option logically has interlocking affinities,
regardless of one's starting point.

a. A Contemporary Case: Thomas C. Oden

The ecstatic triad is a popular one in contemporary
pastoral theology. Especially within the pastoral counseling movement, many theoreticians infuse their ecstatic
Christianity with some school of fulfillment psychology.
The subsequent connection to a pluralist social theory is
more often implied than developed to any extent, though
the openings usually are there. Thomas C. Oden's work
involves a move in the direction of an explicit social
theory.

In his <u>Kerygma and Counseling</u> Oden brings together
evangelical proclamation and client-centered therapy.[18]
Firmly believing in the importance of the believer's
experience of the kerygma, Oden looks to Rogers' work to
see how individuals open themselves to the depths of reality.
Oden even treats Rogers as a theologian. Rogers speaks of
the movement from unconditional worth into incongruence and
defensiveness and then, through therapy, to full functioning.
Oden parallels this with the Christian's journey from original righteousness into sin and bondage of the will and
then into new life through God's grace.

In the tradition of Seward Hiltner's method of correlation, Oden juxtaposes theological and psychological theory.
Oden goes on to make a confessional move that is his own,
however, claiming that effective therapy is ultimately
rooted in the kerygmatic claim that God is for us.

The uniqueness of Oden's alignment of ecstatic Christianity and fulfillment psychology is that he follows
through on its implications for eccesiology and social theory.
Oden's choices here are complex, and we will treat his overall triadic pattern in detail later. Part of his societal
choice, however, is a concern with small groups and Christian community, or with what pluralists call voluntary

associations. Oden believes that human authenticity is the prime vehicle of the sacred. Psychotherapy and group therapy thus function as a locus of Christian revelation. Through small groups, Oden claims, the divine-human encounter continues to flourish. Groups also provide a means of rejuvenating Christian community and liturgy in an age of religious boredom and stagnation.

b. A Classical Case: John Wesley

Our classical representative of the ecstatic triad is John Wesley. Wesley was the founder of the 18th century movement known as Methodism. While best known for his pastoral leadership in that movement, in recent years he has gained recognition as a theologian as well.[19] Wesley's theology is essentially ecstatic. His societal approach is pluralistic, and his personality vision is primarily a fulfillment one.

Though raised in the dominantly cultic patterns of Anglicanism, he came to view the great truths of his Anglican tradition through the lens of individual experience. His experience of God's love and forgiveness one evening at a society meeting on Aldersgate street marked a turning point in his own life. There he realized that God had truly forgiven him. Wesley's famous phrase, "I felt my heart strangely warmed," is a glimmer of the transformation by fire that many ecstatics report. Wesley's Aldersgate experience was sparked by someone reading Luther's Preface to the Epistle to the Romans. It is not unusual, therefore, that the notion of justification through faith became the core of Wesleys' own theology. Wesley differed widely from Luther in that he believed that by grace man achieved a present dominion over sin, not merely a hope for ultimate victory over it. Wesley's optimistic conviction about salvation in spite of sin is expressed in his conviction that "holiness is happiness."

As the founder of the Methodist movement and as one of the leaders of 18th century Protestant pietism, Wesley's practices included both open field preaching to large audiences and the supervision of souls in small bands called "societies." The societies were groups of five to six Christians who wanted to perfect their moral and spiritual lives. Wesley himself supervised many of the societies. Their activities included prayer, reading of scripture, self-examination and confession of sins, and bearing "one another's burdens." Members of the societies often generated intense enthusiasm over God's salvation. In retrospect we can see how these practices intertwined with Wesley's concept of justification and his commitment to transformation and holiness.

134

As is typical for an ecstatic, there are fulfillment leanings in Wesley's scheme. His emphasis on personal experience is clear. Wesley's concept of self-examination is taken up in that of introspection. This parallels Carl Rogers' conviction that only the individual truly knows himself. Wesley took the total depravity of man as seriously as Rogers takes human sufferings. Yet both are also optimistic about the destiny of the individual. Each grounds his convictions differently, to be sure--Wesley in God's grace, Rogers in man's self-actualizing tendency. Rogers would see the fully functioning person in Wesley's vision of the soul who has achieved Christian perfection. Though Wesley was ambivalent about the possibility of achieving Christian perfection in this life, his orientation to that ideal shaped his thought and practice, just as orientation to the fully functioning person shapes Rogers'.

Wesley's concept of justification has important affinities with fulfillment psychology. Wesley always denied that justification came through works. Early in his own career, he was active in visiting people who were sick and imprisoned. If anyone's, Wesley's deeds manifested holiness. Yet for him salvation was much more a matter of the inner spirit than of outward action. Similarly, for Rogers the characteristics of the fully functioning person are always inner traits or attitudes (empathy, acceptance, congruence, tolerance, and prizing of others). Rogers does not refer to specific acts or behavior patterns that would typify the ideal personality. For both Rogers and Wesley inner experience is a central value. This focus on inwardness is what draws classical pietism and the fulfillment perspective so closely together.

Wesley's practices are also similar to those pursued by fulfillment therapists. His use of small groups for confession and support among group members is also found in contemporary encounter groups. Even the motifs of confession of sin and forgiveness have their parallels in the patient's self-revelation and the therapist's acceptance. However, Wesley's practices of prayer and fasting and his appeal to a divine ground for all human transformation set him noticeably apart from Rogers. Moreover, Wesley used the more violent symbols of fire and energy to describe the soul, while Rogers uses the more peaceful metaphors of growth. The basis for these differences lies in Wesley's concentration on a divine-human synergism as opposed to Rogers' appeal to the organismic roots of the self. That is to say, they operate in quite different spheres, each possessing their own integrity. Yet the many parallels between the integrity of the inner self and Wesley's own notion of the soul reinforce our claim that this ecstatic theologian presumes a basically fulfillment approach.

135

Ecstatics also utilize pluralistic social motifs in
their work. John Wesley is no exception. Wesley's societies were voluntary associations serving the interest of
personal holiness. In establishing the societies, Wesley's
aim was not to replace or overthrow existing structures.
He faithfully kept Anglican doctrine and sought only to
renew its observance. He preached regularly in Anglican
pulpits until forbidden to do so, and he remained an Anglican priest until his death. His only break with the Church
of England came over the ordination of priests for areas
deprived of them--impoverished Britain mining towns and the
American colonies. In spite of that, Wesley never intended
to start a new church, but rather to reform the old by
invigorating Christian lives.

Similarly Wesley never sought a radical change in the
political or social structures of England. Though he
ministered to the miners at Bristol, he sought to promote
only their individual salvation and holiness, not to challenge national economic or social policies that oppressed
them.[20] Out of the Methodist movement, however, sprang
a whole host of societies to oppose slavery, worker exploitation, and political disenfranchisement. In Wesley we find
a union of spiritual reformation and liberal democracy
typical of English and American traditions. Had Wesley been
dismissed by the Church of England, he possibly would have
tended in more dualistic social directions. Yet this did
not happen, and his Methodist societies formed part of the
plurality of groups and institutions of 18th century England.

2. Secondary Ecstatic Triads

Ecstatic Christianity tends to take on a much greater
variety of behavioral science partners than do its Christian
companions. Therefore, it is less easy to single out one
secondary form. However, three patterns are worthy of some
attention.

The most frequent secondary form involves the selection
of a conflict psychology. This tends to arise when ecstatic
Christians become more aware of the conflict within the self
between the new identity under the Spirit and the old
identity. The higher life in Christ struggles against the
natural inclinations of everyday life. Moreover, that which
appears to be the Holy Spirit may in fact be a false "imagination of the heart," a lure of the devil. In short, the
self needs some discipline or continual formation under the
guidance of reason or righteousness. This kind of shift
runs through much of the literature of the early church in
the New Testament as it turns from the ecstatic moments of
Pentecost, healing, miracles, and enthusiasm to the longer
range cultivation of the fruits of the Spirit in personal
life.

Another frequent secondary move involves a variation on the secondary cultic triad. Earlier we showed how a connection could be made between a fulfillment psychology and a systemic sociology. System integration and personal fulfillment flow into each other. In this secondary ecstatic triad, the usual pluralist choice is replaced by a systemic one. Sometimes this arises because the ecstatic and fulfillment perspectives simply assume that society exhibits characteristics similar to those of the self. The systemic view is closest to that kind of assumption. Other times, ecstatics begin to take on the more typically cultic attitude that society has a functional need for religion. The ecstatic finds it possible to fulfill that function--in this case not one of cultural integration and legitimation but one of personal regeneration and motivation. A good deal of this secondary choice flows through Oden's work as we shall see in the next chapter.

Finally, it is worth noting a most unusual constellation filled with tension, in which ecstatic, dualist, and conflict approaches are aligned with each other. The conflict and dualist motifs are associated in the way we described with the prophetic-dualist-conflict triad. However, here the life in the Spirit still stands at the center of the Christian choice. The people of the Spirit occupy one side of the societal dualism and await their liberation both societally and personally with Christ's second coming.

D. Critical Implications of Triadic Patterns

We have now described the interlocking affinities that link various approaches in the three disciplines. The triads that result have a logic and a history. Some are quite stable. They tend to endure and recur in the course of history. They are perennial patterns. Others are less stable. These secondary and tertiary connections tend inevitably to move toward a more primary connection.

The primary triads can be set forth in schematic fashion.

PRIMARY TRIADS

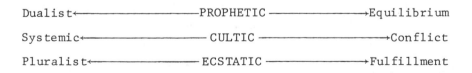

Dualist ←————————— PROPHETIC ————————→ Equilibrium

Systemic ←————————— CULTIC ————————→ Conflict

Pluralist ←————————— ECSTATIC ————————→ Fulfillment

We can then indicate the secondary patterns with dotted lines.

SECONDARY TRIADS

Dualist ← ————————— PROPHETIC ———— ⟍   Equilibrium

Systemic ← ——— 3 ————— CULTIC ———— ⟍   3 ⟍→ Conflict
          ⟍   2 ⟍

Pluralist ← ——— 1 ————— ECSTATIC ← = 1 == 2 ———→ Fulfillment

While we have claimed that these patterns dominate the trilateral interchange, there is no reason to exclude any of the 27 permutations possible in this scheme. Most assuredly they have all played a role in Christian history under other forms and in the contemporary exchange as well.

E. Critical Questions Raised by Triadic Patterns

This triadic scheme constitutes a set of hypotheses concerning the relative persistence and viability of various relations between Christianity and the behavioral sciences. On the basis of these hypotheses we can then begin to analyze any particular effort to relate the disciplines.

We can inquire about the reasons by which an author or actor includes certain elements in a trilateral construction. The more the inclusion of an element draws the construction away from a primary triad the more intense our inquiry becomes. The list of usual affinities supplies us with these questions and constitutes a check list for analysis.

For example, when examining a construct that moves dominantly in a cultic triad, such as Urban Holmes', we are acutely alert to the problems raised by his inclusion of obviously ecstatic elements. How will they be subordinated to his dominant framework? How will he handle the typical tensions between the ecstatic and cultic triads?

The triadic scheme also helps us ask why certain elements are excluded from a construct. Have certain elements usually present in a triad been excluded because of a Christian loyalty? Or have they been excluded on the basis of some choice in the personality or societal realm? For instance, why does a prophetic theologian not take up fully the equilibrium implications usually found in a primary prophetic triad? Have Christian eschatological loyalties

138

caused him or her to adopt a conflict psychology that drives
the tensions of the salvation struggle into the center of
the psyche? Or has a quite independent loyalty to, for
instance, a pluralistic social order, tempered the thoroughgoing Kingdom ideal usually found in prophetic theologies?

The schema can also help us <u>fill out</u> an otherwise
undeveloped construct. If an author takes up a psychoana-
lytical interpretation of the Eucharist we can then infer
that a systemic approach to society stands not far off in
the wings. We can then inquire further about the compatibility of such an extrapolation, including the possible
ways that such an expansion, taken along the primary triadic route, would threaten some initial loyalties, theories,
or practices.

We realize that the kinds of claims advanced through
these hypotheses may call into question some popular presuppositions. Perhaps most striking is our claim that conflict psychologies are usually tied to systemic societal
positions, while equilibrium approaches have a basic affinity to dualistic ones. However, many people who pursue the
secondary prophetic triad hold that a conflict psychology
such as Freud's is most closely related to Marxian sociology.
Our own claims call this marriage into question and illuminate the tensions found in a person like Herbert Marcuse,
who ties Marx and Freud together. Theologians who take up
Marcuse have handled the implied tension between cultic
and prophetic strains within Christianity, as well as the
ambiguity within Marcuse's own social theory and practices.

These remarks only begin the discussion about the
critical implications of the triadic hypotheses advanced
in this chapter. Awareness of these triadic options and
tendencies can become a checklist for accounting for various alternatives that claim our attention in a comprehensive engagement between theology and the behavioral sciences.
They are a means for analyzing the work of others as well
as for guiding our own constructive thought in a systematic
fashion. In subsequent chapters we will explore further
ramifications of the critical thinking made possible by
this triadic framework.

PRIMARY TRIADS

SOCIETY	CHRISTIANITY	PERSONALITY
DUALIST →	**PROPHETIC** →	**EQUILIBRIUM** →
Overcome (radical) or maintain (conservative) the fundamental conflict	Understanding, accepting and doing God's will	Right thinking and acting in proper environment
Society the product of conflict between two groups, sexes, classes, races, etc.	God's will known in Bible, Word, preaching	Self results from learned responses to stimuli; self a system of habits
Society rests on force or nature	Jesus as prophet, rabbi, teacher	Self changed by unlearning and re-learning; rewards and punishments
Alienation, exploitation, contradiction, revolution (Marx)	God transcendent judge, governor	Behavior modification, implosive therapy, cognitive development studies
Command/Subordination structures	Sin as rebellion, disobedience, wrong-doing	B. F. Skinner A. Bandura
Warfare, hierarchy, discipline	Minister teaches, exhorts	A. Ellis L. Kohlberg
K. Marx C. Wright Mills	Church distinguished from world by word and deed	
I. Illich	Amos T. Münzer	
	M. Luther J. Calvin	
	G. Guttierrez	
SYSTEMIC →	**CULTIC** →	**CONFLICT** →
Society an organic whole to be preserved, integrated, kept in equilibrium	Communion with God through symbolic action, cult, rite, sacrament	Rational management of natural drives for sake of love and work
Selves to be socialized into society	Christ as priest and sacrifice	Fundamental conflict between conscience and instinct--produces symptoms (neuroses, defenses, psychoses)
Social structures arise to meet system needs	Church as Body of Christ	Self-understanding and insight key to therapy
	Creation capable of incarnate presence of God	

Directed, interpretive therapy

Psychoanalysis; dream analysis

S. Freud   E. Erikson

C. J. Jung

FULFILLMENT

Self to achieve creative, personal autonomy, congruent with inner needs, feelings

Self continually seeks to grow and actualize itself.

Actualization results from meeting inner needs

Problems arise from imposed conditions of worth, non-acceptance, esp. of feelings

Acceptance produces growth

Client-centered therapy, meditation, much of Transactional Analysis and Gestalt Therapy

C. Rogers   A. Maslow
W. Schutz   A. Adler

Sin as impurity

Cult under care of Church and priesthood

St. Paul   K. Rahner
E. L. Mascall   U. Holmes
B. R. Brinkman

ECSTATIC

Personal experience of the Holy Spirit; personal union with God

God known in personal emotional experience

Christ is personal savior, mystical fount

Church is fellowship of believers, of regenerate persons in the Spirit

Free worship; democratic ecclesiology, "movement" and individualistic forms

J. Wesley   P. Tillich
T. Oden   J. Eckhart
G. Fox

Societies evolve; society tends toward equilibrium

Anomie produces social problems

Culture is key to integration and societal survival

Planning, development, education, communication, cultural

T. Parsons   E. Durkheim
R. Merton   W. Buckley

PLURALIST

Mobilization of interested persons in variety of competing ethnic or interest groups

Society a plurality of groups in competition and coalition

Variety of power bases and outcomes to conflict

Minimum consensus of law necessary to constrain conflict

Politics best model for society

Voluntary association, law and constitutionalism, organizing

G. H. Mead   M. Weber
S. Alinsky   R. Dahl
J. Madison

PRIMARY TRIADIC AFFINITIES

(SOCIETY)	AFFINITIES (CHRISTIANITY)	AFFINITIES (PERSONALITY)	AFFINITIES (SOCIETY)
D **U** **A** **L** **I** **S** **T**	**P** God at war with Satan **R** God transcendent and absolute **O** God provides external, objec- **P** tive standards of judgment **H** God's Word demands either/or **E** response **T** Obedience as path to true **I** freedom and salvation **C** Behaviors, not intentions, count as commitment The oppressed deserve God's justice The elite are God's chosen ones Grace available to the few who choose God's side	**E** Cosmic struggle determines **Q** personal destiny **U** Salvation through external **I** intervention **L** Self a member of Kingdom of **I** God or Kingdom of Satan **B** Self known through deeds, **R** behavior; self judged **I** according to God's law and **U** order **M** God's order as salvation environment Ministry as teaching elite	**D** Societal position is key to **U** character of self **A** Self determined by social **L** conditioning **I** Self faces decision between **S** two environments; opposed **T** options are clearly defined Society and self evaluated by external, objective criteria Right thinking and action arise from environmental change Self is its cognition and behavior
S **Y** **S** **T** **E** **M** **I** **C**	**C** Body of Christ an organic **U** unity **L** Institution in harmony with **T** natural functions **I** Spirit works through body **C**	**C** Internal struggle managed **O** through participation in **N** Church's symbolic action **F** Grace and healing present **L** in community of symbols **I** **C** **T**	**S** Self formed through long pro- **Y** cess of socialization **S** Self and society rooted in **T** natural drives, functions **E** Self finds integrity through **M** adaptation to culture **I** **C**

142

SYSTEMIC	**CULTIC** Grace available to all within the church system Centrality of symbol Cult and culture Sin and anomie Individual sacrifice maintains the system, integrates selves Governance by professionals	**CONFLICT** Self as body taken up and perfected in Body of Christ Natural as bearer of grace Self-sacrifice necessary to social existence Church symbolism rehearses family and natural drama Ministry preserves and presents symbols	**SYSTEMIC** Cultural symbols, myths key to personal dynamics and consciousness Self sacrifices instincts for sake of social functioning and higher values
PLURALIST	**ECSTATIC** Church is invisible, known only by personal witness Impossible to structure or institutionalize the Spirit Church is spontaneous and voluntary, springs from inspired wills of members Democratic; Spirit harmonizes gifts of members Many gifts, talents, interests, and small groups	**FULFILLMENT** Personal experience the vehicle of the sacred Life in the Spirit realized in conversion, personal transformation Spirit works in heart, yields fruits in dispositions, actions Theology as autobiography Life of church in small egalitarian groups Members witness, confess to each other Church as voluntary association for nurture and expression	**PLURALIST** Personal experience is basis of reality Self must find and express its needs Individual diversity valued Self-acceptance leads to acceptance of others Self is basically social, self-assertion in harmony with sociality Self should seek power, autonomy, self-expression, authenticity

CHAPTER EIGHT

CONGRUENCE

In the previous chapter we drew together specific
approaches from sociology, psychology, and theology and
called them triads. Now we turn to relate the dimensions
of these same disciplines under the notion of congruence.

In its simplest form, congruence indicates appropriate
relations, a mutual "fit." In our context it means a fit
among theories, practices, and loyalties, Its opposite,
incongruence, is a disjunction or inappropriate relation
among these same dimensions. Incongruence generally means
that one dimension does not fit with the other two--a
practice not fitting in with a loyalty and theory, for
instance. We assume, from the standpoint of systematic
and ideal-type thinking, that theory, practice and loyalty
naturally must be taken together. They have logical implications for one another. Congruence is an issue within a
single discipline, as well as in relations among the three
disciplines. Congruence also has two different forms,
simple congruence and functional congruence. We will
treat simple congruence first.

A. Simple Congruence

1. Congruence within a Discipline

The relation among theory, practice, and loyalty within
any discipline is never perfectly congruent. Rather, the
dimensions exhibit only a relative degree of congruence.
Relations which are too loose or disjunct, however, raise
certain questions about priorities among disjunct dimensions. If a loyalty does not match a practice, for instance,
which dimension should be changed? Which sould be maintained? These choices, which the notion of congruence
raises, reveal our underlying commitments and priorities.
We will illustrate this with examples from each discipline
and then with interdisciplinary examples.

Carl Rogers' client-centered therapy provides a fine
example of a tight fit between the value of autonomy, the
practice of reflection of feeling, and the theoretical
concept of unconditional positive regard. Rogers' prime

loyalty is the autonomy of the client. Too many therapies, he claims, direct clients and rob them of their own internal directions. By being non-directive and by reflecting clients' feelings back to them, Rogers helps clients get in touch with their own inner thoughts and feelings. Rogers presents no interpretation or diagnosis to the patient. These might get in the client's way. This is designed to facilitate the value of client autonomy. At the same time the reflection of feeling communicates unconditional positive regard to clients. Unconditional positive regard clearly relates the value of autonomy to a particular practice as well as to the rest of Rogers' theory. It penetrates the therapist's style as well as leads to particular techniques. It is also tied to the theory that clients have not had sufficient unconditional positive regard as youngsters, but received stultifying conditional worth instead. According to Rogerian theory, unconditional positive regard will help clients become self-actualizing and whole.

The interlocking logic among loyalty, theory, and practice is clear in Rogers' case. One dimension has direct implications for another, regardless of where one starts. In his later work Rogers became more confrontive with clients and increasingly expressed his own thoughts and feelings in therapy. This was accompanied with a change in practice to include group therapy. However, Rogers never followed these changes with basic alterations in his theory, as we might expect. To clarify this deficiency we must turn again to the notion of barriers to growth. As he envisions the therapist becoming more active (and thus more directive), Rogers needs to account for the client's maintaining an investment in not growing and thus requiring direction and confrontation. This is where his later practice and earlier theory lack congruence. Awareness of this congruence leads us first of all to clearer insight into the therapeutic process as well as into the dynamics of interdimensional congruence. At this point we do not judge Rogers' effort as right or wrong. Rather, we see tension in his work and begin to look for solutions to such tensions. Identifying such tensions usually leads to some decision about the theory-practice-loyalty relation in his work that will reduce the apparent incongruence.

Saul Alinsky's community organizing provides another example of congruence and incongruence, this case in the realm of society. Alinsky was committed to the goal of gaining participation in decision-making power through organizing. This naturally fits in with the pluralist practice of action and conflict to gain access to media and power interests. The value of participation and the practice of demonstration both fit in with Alinsky's theory that society is a plurality of groups competing for power to

146

further their own self-interest. Thus in his case pluralist theory, practice, and loyalty are congruent with one another.

However, in Chapter Three we noted that much of Alinsky's rhetoric seems to be quite dualistic. Organizers speak speak in terms of "us" and "them" and go to great length to polarize opinions in favor of a community's self-interest. At second glance, Alinsky's theory seems to be dualist, not pluralist, and thus incongruent with his practices and loyalties. We need to make some judgment about Alinsky at this point. Would he move in the direction of revolutionary practices to align practice with theory? Or is the talk of the community organizer a rhetorical technique designed to achieve pluralist goals and values? In Alinsky's case, the latter seems to carry the day. Alinsky's practices and values take precedence over this theories. A disjunction of the three dimensions in his case leads us to a closer look at Alinsky's overall work and an assessment of his priorities among theory, practice, and loyalty.

Sacramental celebration provides us with an example of the problem of congruence in Christianity. From the cultic perspective, for instance, sacramental action is the prime vehicle of the sacred. Through regular participation in such sacramental action as the Eucharist believers pursue their primary loyalty of living in communion with God. A theology congruent with this loyalty and practice then seeks to describe the meaning of communion with God through sacrament.[1]*

Cultic theory has generally seen the priest as a special mediator of the divine in sacramental celebration. Then when the practice of "passing of the peace" among parishioners during worship was introduced, some balked, having no theory to support this practice. The implicitly egalitarian values of this practice conflicted with those of elevating the priest to a higher position. Conceptions of the priesthood emphasizing the priest's brotherly (and not just fatherly) role have arisen now that are congruent with this transformation in liturgical practice. This in turn has put priestly values and self-understanding in tension with old spiritualities and roles.[2] Thus the relation among theory, practice, and loyalty is not a static one. There continues to be some necessary relation of congruence such that a change in one dimension leads to tension with the others until a viable congruence is restored.

2. Interdisciplinary Congruence

Congruence is also important in relations among the

---

*Notes for this chapter begin on page 253.

disciplines. Theories, loyalties, and practices can be related among disciplines as well. Homiletics, church administration, spirituality, liturgy, social justice, and pastoral counselling are all areas of Christian life that have been affected by the disciplines of psychology and sociology. Today Christian theology, values, and liturgical and spiritual practices are attended to by psychologists as well as sociologists.

We believe that in the theology-behavioral science conversation congruence is a helpful notion for the second stage of critical thinking--drawing interdisciplinary relations. As is the case within a single discipline, when we happen upon an instance of incongruence, we have located a decision point. The disjunction in dimensions signifies that some interdisciplinary shift is occurring, some commitment is being made, or some novel association is in the works. This implies that interdisciplinary dialogue opens one up to exploration, dialogue and change. Indeed, incongruence is often a lever for disciplinary change in interdisciplinary conversation. In Chapter Nine we will investigate what changes might occur in the exchange. At this point we will cite several examples of the tension among theories, practices, and loyalties when we begin to juxtapose dimensions among the three disciplines.

Our first example concerns the priest who is a community organizer. The priest himself may be attracted by the many parallels between Alinsky and St. Paul's organizing of early Christian communities outside of Jerusalem. They see that both Paul and Alinsky lived in an era of social upheaval. Both travelled widely to provide embattled communities with an awareness of their unique interests and requisite discipline. Both urged their communities to conflict with prevailing powers and both faced conflict as a necessary part of building up community.

A decisive question for contemporary priests doing organizing is, which loyalties shall they appeal to in order to motivate their communities? Should they appeal to self-interest as many Alinskyites do? Or should they appeal to a "higher" Christian good, such as the love of neighbor? What do the Christian themes of self-sacrifice or obedience to God mean in this context? How can the concepts of power and self-interest central to community organizing be reconciled with these demands for altruism from the Christian side? More pointedly, how can the cultic themes of communion with the self-sacrificing Christ be reconciled with the advance of political self-interest?

To resolve this incongruence priestly organizers may decide to reinterpret the notion of Christian self-sacrifice (their cultic loyalty) to conform to their appeal to

self-interest (their pluralistic practice). They might
emphasize the importance of seizing the power and freedom
which Christ's sacrifice has made possible. Or they might
take on more strongly the prophetic loyalty of struggling
against the powers of evil in this world. In doing so
they would make their societal practice and values deter-
minative for their Christian loyalties or theology. Their
Christianity would be reshaped in the light of their
societal commitments. Incongruence would lead to a change
in disciplinary commitments.

Priest organizers often find themselves amidst another
interdisciplinary tension. Cultic theologies usually adopt
organic concepts of society, i.e., a systemic social theory.
This involves transferring organic imagery of the Church as
Body of Christ onto the whole society. This also entails a
conception of the Church's mission as a spiritual function
which basically harmonizes with other functions in society
played by family, corporation, and the state. The Church's
main role is to provide the cultural base for legitimating
the authority by which social conflicts can be adjudicated
in peaceful manner.

Alinsky's organizing social theory is quite different.
His is pluralistic and even dualistic. He sees society not
as a system, but as numerous groups motivated by their own
self-interest and competing for power. For the pluralist,
conflict is a natural and desirable state of affairs. It
mobilizes people, preserves their vitality, and prevents
the rise of tyranny produced by concentration of power.
Indeed, without it the cultural base defended by the systemic might never be revitalized through reinterpretation
in the light of current history.

Thus priests who do community organizing have a
theological heritage in which conflict and active pursuit
of self-interest are subordinate to broader cultural aims,
yet they engage in practical activities in which conflict
and self-interest are essential. They experience incongruence between their cultic loyalties (with their systemic
implications) and their pluralistic practices.

This does not mean that cultically committed community
organizers need give up either their social practices or
their faith assumptions. They can be aware of how their
own theories, practices, and loyalties are incongruent at
different points. Merely identifying the source of interdisciplinary incongruence can be extremely helpful. Such
analysis may also point out ways they may achieve greater
congruence.

There is no single way of dealing with incongruence.
Its solution depends on the individual's or institution's

commitments and priorities. One priest may expand his
organizing practices to take in the need for integrative
cultural action. Another may drop his organic social theory.
Still a third may lessen his incongruence by a shift in
loyalties within Christianity. A fourth may make no change
at all, but live within incongruence as an everyday state
of affairs. This choice, however, would then demand specific attention to personality practices in order to handle
the consequent psychological and professional tensions.
The notion of congruence functions to locate tensions and
decision points and to identify available options.

The issue of congruence in interdisciplinary relations also arises in the use of client-centered therapy by
a pastoral counselor. Ministers have been trained in Rogers'
nondirective method for years. The reasons for this are
many. His method does not require training in diagnosis
or psychopathology. Rogers does not use esoteric psychological jargon in describing his method. Reflection of
feeling is a simple method, and it builds on the capacity
of every human being to care for another. We also noted
in Chapter Two how Rogerian values are similar to those in
Christian tradition.

Pastors schooled in client-centered practice will
probably experience some disjunction with the concept of
sin in their religious traditions. Traditionally, the
Christian attitude toward sin is to forgive it, not "accept"
or merely "own" it. Practically, the non-directive pastor
will deal with sin by empathic listening. But what account
will he or she give of Christian judgment, of the call to
repentance, and of divine forgiveness? Clearly there is a
tension between Christian theory and Rogerian psychotherapeutic practice.

Again, there are numerous alternatives for resolving
such dimensional and interdisciplinary incongruence. Thomas
Oden takes the route of redefining the theological notion of
sin in terms of not attaining authentic humanity.[3] Lowell
Colston interprets the notion of "judgment" in terms of a
mutual discernment between pastor and client.[4] Eduard
Turneysen, however, roots pastoral counseling in the Word
of God and believes that the pastor sooner or later must
stop listening and bring the judgment of God to bear on
the parishioner and his problem.[5]

Each decision reflects the respective commitments of
the pastor. Oden chooses a fulfillment psychological notion
of sin over the dominant Christian idea of moral transgression. Colston chooses not to follow the biblical notion
of prophetic judgment, but moves to the mutual engagement
compatible with an ecstatic position. Turneysen, on the
other hand, puts psychological practice totally in the light

of the prophetic emphasis of Calvinistic theology. In these crucial decisions incongruence reveals one's interdisciplinary commitments.

From these examples in pastoral counseling and community organizing we can see the diversity of choices that are possible in response to the need for congruence. We see what substantive commitments authors and practitioners really hold. They may ground their commitments in practical considerations and let theory and loyalty follow. Their proficiency with certain familiar techniques and the success they feel they have attained through them overrides the claims of incongruent theories and loyalties. Or, they may follow the deep symbolic and emotional pull of certain symbols and values and take steps to learn new practices and theories. As another alternative, they may find their theoretical framework so embracing and logically satisfying that it becomes the dominant point around which loyalties and practices are accommodated. They may even resolve incongruence by committing themselves to another discipline altogether.

These kinds of judgments are the basis for constructive transformation in the interdisciplinary interchange. We inquire into other disciplines because of our commitments, obvious or undisclosed as they may be. In the process of making connections to other disciplines, we find the implications and consequences of our choices. We discover the tensions between triads, as we saw in Chapter Seven, and we encounter the tensions of incongruence. In dealing with these tensions and contradictions we are forced to new and often novel constructions in the three dimensions.

In the light of congruence we can see more clearly how the triads function. They are not watertight compartments or boxes that label or restrict our efforts. By forecasting the implications of our positions they can guide us in our interdisciplinary choices. The triads do not determine our commitments, but shed light on where our commitments may lead us. Patterns of triadic affinities and dimensional congruence form an interdisciplinary map, but we must choose the direction and goal.

B. Functional Congruence

We now turn from simple congruence to a more complex form we call functional congruence. Simple congruence deals with how tightly or loosely dimensions fit together, either within a discipline or among dimensions of several disciplines. It deals with the ways elements in the three dimensions imply each other, especially on a logical basis.

Functional congruence examines this relationship from

151

a different angle. From a functional standpoint, disjunction of dimensions indicates much more than illogic, lack
of awareness, or naivete. Functional incongruence indicates
that a position is incongruent from the standpoint of actual
human thinking, feeling, and acting. Functional congruence
deals with the relation of theories, loyalties, and practices to actual human activity.

Functional congruence raises questions like: How does
an idea, value, theory, technique, or institution arise in
or affect human life? What kind of activity does it produce? What kind does it hinder? What does it legitimate
or delegitimate? These questions go far beyond a simple
matching of theory, loyalty, and practice.

The functional notion of congruence is a specific
outcome of the interchange with the behavioral sciences.
It emphasizes the key position that real human activity
plays. This emphasis is also a concomitant of our concern
to see all three disciplines not as detached intellectual
activities, but as professional endeavors in which thought
and commitment are always, even if sometimes latently, tied
to practices.

Within the trilateral interchange, however, this matter leads to some very complicated considerations. We are
led back to our assumptions about which human activities are
the fundamental ones. Each discipline assumes that some
basic practical reality exists to which all else must be
attuned in order to achieve congruence. Psychologists
attend to psychological reality, sociologists to societal
reality, and theologians to the interaction of divine and
human reality. Each discipline has a different orientation
to what is fundamentally "real." Because of the importance
of these differences, we want to clarify functional congruence within the trilateral framework.

The question seems to involve three types of considerations. The first inquires about the prescriptive versus
the descriptive function of a theory. The second deals with
the three approaches within any discipline. The third
involves an interdisciplinary perspective. These three
types of considerations represent increasing states of complexity in the examination of functional congruence. At
each stage some commitment is being made to a particular
pattern of human reality which provides the standpoint for
examining the function of some theory, loyalty, or particular practice. We will take up each of these considerations in turn.

1. Prescriptive vs. Descriptive Uses of Theory

In the three disciplines functional incongruence can be

caused by confusing the descriptive and the prescriptive
aspects of theory. This is commonly called the "is/ought"
problem. The seemingly descriptive concept may in fact
have a high significance as a loyalty and be functioning
in a prescriptive way to bring about certain kinds of
activity. In psychology, for instance, Erik Erikson dis-
avows any attempt to make his eight-stage description of
the life-cycle into an achievement scale whereby personal
worth might be measured. Erikson believes that no psycho-
social task, once attained, is secured once and for all.[6]
He is aware that parents can use his theories to pressure
children into achieving parental ideals rather than per-
mitting them to grow in their own unique ways. Such a use
of his scheme undermines the value that he believes people
should embody, that of mutuality. The subtle prescriptive use of descriptive theory can function to thwart
achievement of the loyalties he seeks to pursue. The shift
from descriptive to prescriptive use results in functional
incongruence. Not the theory itself, but how it is functioning in a situation is the key to what is really going
on.

We face similar issues in analyzing functional congruence in the realm of society. Sociologists frequently
employ the concept of ideology to describe functional incongruence. Karl Mannheim, drawing on Marx and others,
set forth the dominant framework for the ideology question.[7]
Ideology first of all involved the slippage from descriptive to prescriptive functions of a set of ideas. Ideology
is a set of ideas that seems to describe social reality, but
is so detached from empirical confirmation that it actually
disguises (and thereby reinforces) existing power relations.
For instance, "The American economy is a free enterprise
system" seems to be a description of American economic
practices. However, upon searching for specific social
facts fitting the criterion for "free enterprise," we find
that the term applies either to very small areas of the
American economy or to none at all. It is not really a
description but seems to have taken on the status of symbol
and loyalty. It plays some practical function in social
affairs. It manifests some kind of functional incongruence.

Finally, we can develop analogous themes in an exploration of the meaning of functional congruence within Christianity. The idolatry we mentioned earlier can arise simply
in the shift from descriptive to prescriptive uses of
terminology. We may hear the claim that "The Church is the
Body of Christ," or that "It is a fellowship of believers."
However, upon empirical investigation we find that this "is"
statement is really an "ought" dressed up in idealistic
clothing. This seemingly descriptive claim can lead Christians, and especially church officals, to believe that their
ideas really are true belief, or that the existing

153

institutional church really is the form commanded by Christ for the Church. In short, this kind of functional incongruence can be seen as pride, self-righteousness, and idolatry.

Each discipline, then, seems to have its own way of approaching the problem of functional incongruence. In the realm of personality science we see the terms "rationalization," "integration," or "full functioning" pointing to the relations among the dimensions of personality. Neurosis and psychosis can be seen as psychoanalytic terms for describing disintegration in personality. Sociologists often speak of incongruence in terms of ideology. The opposite of this disjunction between theory and practice is then called "praxis," the mutual interaction of thought and action in the effort to change social reality. For theologians the concept of idolatry assumes an analogous place. Functional congruence, theologically speaking, can then be seen as righteousness and knowledge. True knowledge of God always involves the whole self in action, disposition, loyalty, and thought. It designates a harmony of belief and action.

These are indeed analogous conceptualizations in the various disciplines, expressed in terms of the fundamental reality they presuppose--whether it be the self, society, or the divine-human interchange. But we cannot rest with the simple analogies, for here too, the varying perspectives within the disciplines make their effect known. To the degree that the differing approaches see the fundamental ground of reality differently they will see the problem of functional congruence differently.

2. Intradisciplinary Functional Congruence

The problem of functional congruence becomes more complicated when we realize that there are varying approaches to reality within the disciplines. At this point we do not work merely within one perspective, as in our examples above, but have to see how these approaches reflect particular biases, thus casting the problem of congruence in other terms.

To illustrate this divergence we will return to the problems of therapy, "free enterprise," and idolatry.

a. Personality

A therapist, for instance, may encounter a client who describes her own condition in an intellectual or analytical way that hides her feelings about that condition. The self-description that one is "schizophrenic" may hide a patient's feeling of hopelessness. Her resignation is the true therapeutic reality, not the diagnostic concept of being schizophrenic. The therapist can pick up the patient's non-verbal communication and give the patient the support or confrontation she needs to deal with her despair. Therapeutic jargon is not the prime reality, but how it functions in the patient's activity overall is the key to what is really going on.

Eric Berne, the originator of the new psychological language known as Transactional Analysis, was pre-eminently aware of this form of therapeutic incongruence. He describes the game of "psychiatry" in which the therapist and patient exchange psychiatric analyses but avoid getting down to the business of cure.[8] In such instances, therapeutic language (ideas alone) frustrates the therapeutic process.

But Berne was a key bridge for those moving from a conflict to a fulfillment approach in psychology. The fulfillment approach would tend to see fundamental human reality in terms of these issues of feeling, disposition and the autonomous activity of the self in playing such games.

Conflict theorists would claim that with regard to the fundamental human reality they assume, contact with feelings will produce only transitory effects or only immerse the client more deeply in various transference effects that mask over the deeper conflicts which need to be brought to light through painstaking analysis of dreams and memories.

Equilibriumists can also get into this quarrel by claiming that the owning of feelings will lead nowhere unless reinforced by observable environmental controls. From their standpoint the therapeutic effort of people like Berne, along with the theories and values accompanying it, also represent a form of functional incongruence with regard to the real ground of practical life--observable human behavior grounded in systems of psychological equilibration.

b. Society

Analysis of the functional congruence of the concept of "free enterprise" can also benefit from seeing it in terms of the three approaches. According to a Marxist analysis, for which the concept of ideology has been very important, the free enterprise theory masks the existence of the capitalist class which controls the marketplace as well as the means of production through interlocking directorates, banks, and monopoly practices. At the most it may function in a "utopian" way to legitimate the struggle of small businessmen against the vast conglomerates. In

155

either case it does not really reveal or further the underlying class struggle, which is the fundamental social
reality.

At this point proponents of other approaches to social
reality enter the scene to interpret the nature of the functional incongruence. Pluralists attend to the way this
concept of free enterprise legitimates intervention by
government, through anti-trust regulations, to open the market further. Moreover, the continual thrusts by the small
business groups are not to be discounted in this rather long
interim before the predicted outcome of class polarization.

Systemics would perceive the issue of congruence here
from an even different angle and indicate that the real
function of this cultural symbol is to enunciate and further
undergird an overarching American culture grounded in the
belief in personal and small group participation in decision-
making. The problem of economic disparities has to be
understood within the total American context of law, religion, culture, family, and education, as well as that of
economics. Moreover, a systemic might argue, we have to
see that the wider ecological system is putting increasing
constraints on capitalist accumulation and may be forcing
us to respect once again the natural scale of things. This
scale is pointed to by the notion of free enterprise, which
implies a number of small entities in association with one
another.

c. Christianity

We have already indicated that theological concepts
such as idolatry, righteousness, and knowledge probe the
problem of incongruence in Christianity. In taking up the
concept of idolatry we are first of all led to the perspective of the prophets, who testified constantly to the
transcendent Word and judgment of God. All human claims in
which persons begin to take on pretensions to judgment or
goodness are immediately suspect in the light of God's
transcendence and ethical demand. The real function of
these claims, in light of this ultimate interaction with
God, is to mask over the actual sin of the world and distort the real nature of the situation of the world before
God and His pure reign.

The only release from this situation is true conformity to God's will through repentance in word and deed.
Ultimately, the only way out is to be received into God's
new creation by His own gracious action. But righteousness,
as ecstatics would hasten to point out, is not merely an
external behavior. It is an internalized knowledge of God,
a quality of one's action. This is why faith is the essence
of righteousness (Galatians 3, 4; Hebrews 11). Righteousness

is already present in us as we believe. From this perspective the functional incongruence of these claims about the Church may be that they mask over and hide the actual life of faith that lives, often "invisibly," within the Church as an institution. It diverts our attention from the true life of faith that speaks quietly and humbly within believers through the Spirit.

From a cultic approach, however, it would not be enough to draw attention to this actual life in the Spirit behind the organizational pretensions. All Spirited life in the Church is nourished by, formed by, and sustained by the actions of worship, sacramental celebration, and the total ritual life of the Church. The Spirit is only the manifestation of the fact that these symbolic actions have really "taken" within the life of a person or community. Therefore, the real functional incongruence that appears in the claim that the Church is the Body of Christ, for instance, lies in its diversion of attention from that "body" which is present in the Eucharistic elements onto the institutional structure or sheer physical presence of the members of the Church.

In each of these cases attention is drawn to the real character of the divine-human engagement in order to ascertain the nature of the functional incongruence detected initially in the purported description of the Church. All of these represent approaches to the problem of idolatry and yet each bears its characteristic stamp and emphasis.

In these first two steps into the problem of functional congruence we encounter complexities caused by the existence, not only of the three dimensions of loyalty, theory, and practice, but also of different approaches to practical reality within each discipline. Functional incongruence is not merely a problem of confusion between prescription and description, it is also one of assessing quite different approaches to practical reality within each discipline.

With this comparative awareness within the disciplines we should now be ready to move to the third consideration in assessing functional congruence--diverging approaches to practical reality among the three disciplines.

3. Interdisciplinary Functional Congruence

We have just been stressing the divergence of approaches to personal, societal, and Christian reality in the search to grasp the nature of functional congruence. However, these divergences are still variations within some wider common assumptions. We face even greater divergence in interdisciplinary analysis. Each discipline views the

deeper human reality underlying functional incongruence
differently. Psychotherapists point to psychic processes.
Social theorists point to the trans-personal interplay of
institutions. Theologians point to the divine-human engagement with the Triune God present in Jesus Christ.

Each discipline will therefore tend to interpret the
real function of some theory, loyalty or disciplinary practice in terms of its own perception of this ultimately
real practical ground. Since the thrust of such a comparative approach to the problem of functional congruence should
be somewhat evident by now we will give only some short
illustration of the issues involved.

Sociologists, for instance, regardless of their persuasion, when coming upon a claim such as Berne's concerning
the problem of feeling, intellectualization, and therapy,
do not inquire into the effectiveness of Berne's therapy
in bringing about personality transformation. They will
instead ask, what function does this therapeutic practice
play in social reality? Is it an attack on the existing
psychiatric associations, with their monopoly of access
to medical facilities, support, and approval? Is it an
adaptation of therapy to the middle class, especially as it
suffers under the increasing squeeze between big capital and
the demands of the working class? Or perhaps it is a symptom
of the decline of culture and willingness to deal with its
demands. All of these questions concerning function produce, in short, some kind of sociology of psychology, or
similarly, of religion.

Psychologists, upon hearing a religious claim, such as
that advanced concerning the Church as the Body of Christ,
will pursue their own analysis in terms of a psychology of
religion. What psychological function is this statement
really playing? Perhaps it is a displacement and projection
of repressed feelings about our own bodies, a kind of
institutional narcissism. Perhaps it is an attempt to adopt
a relation to the Church as the body of the mother, from who
whom one expects warmth and affection. In any case, the
functional congruence or incongruence is examined with regard to the ground provided by the discipline of psychology.

Finally, of course, we have, from the Christian standpoint, a "theology of..." which examines the religious or
Christian function of incongruencies arising from the other
domains. The real function of the quest for personal wholeness or social justice may be a perverted form of the search
for reconciliation with God. However, these societal forms
and personal forms are only partial realizations and therefore can always lead not only to disappointment but also to
manipulation by unscrupulous therapists or political
demagogues.

We can now see that the problem of congruence is a many-faceted one. It involves not only the simple congruence concerning the logical mutual implications of the dimensions. It also involves the functional issues of prescriptive and descriptive uses of theory, of differing assessments of practical reality within disciplines and of differences among disciplines about the ultimate grounds of human activity. The first issue, prescription and description, raises arguments over the relation of loyalty to theory and the tendency to confuse one with the other. The second raises such questions as whether the "unconscious" or observable behavior is the real psychological ground for therapy. The third drives us to assess the relative commitments to person, society and religion as the key to human reality.

In the course of this exploration we have touched upon two issues which bear brief consideration in order to fill out the significance of the problem of congruence in the trilateral interchange. They are the issues of meaning and of ontology.

C. Congruence and Meaning

The awareness of how language functions pervades the theology-behavioral science dialogue. Even though each discipline has in some sense its own distinct "language," they all struggle with certain common problems of meaning. The problem of ideology, intellectualization, and idolatry involve a discussion of the meaning of ideas, concepts, symbols, and words. In the interchange of Christian and behavioral disciplines a certain conception of meaning emerges around the issue of congruence, especially functional congruence. We call this functional meaning. Because the idea of meaning has figured prominently in theological discourse, it may be helpful to point out the impact of the idea of functional congruence on the concept of meaning. To understand this impact we must see functional meaning in terms of two other kinds of meaning--referential meaning and contextual meaning.

The most common notion of meaning is as a relation between a term and a referent. The meaning of the term is found when we find the referent to which it points. We know the meaning of the term "table" when we see, touch, use or direct our action toward a certain kind of object. This simple referential notion of meaning sets the ground rules for scientists' struggle to describe exactly the relations between terms, many of them mathematical, and discrete observable objects. Many of the debates over method in the behavioral sciences are disputes over the use of this conception of meaning when employing concepts to describe human action.

However, numerous opponents of this conception of

159

meaning, at least as an exclusive definition, have contested this course and countered with a conception of meaning which we call <u>contextual</u>. The meaning of terms must be understood in view of their place in a network of relationships with other terms, symbols, and words. It is their position in the structure of a grammar, worldview, web, of psychological associations, or a whole language which gives them their meaning. Meaning arises out of the whole configuration of terms in a system.

With this conception of meaning we have an easier entree into the world of metaphor, allusion, and symbolism. A contextual approach helps us grasp more immediately the phrase, "He tables the motion," or "She chaired the meeting." It grasps the difference in meaning between the Swastika as it appeared in Egyptian and early Christian culture and as it appeared in the complex of Nazi symbolism. From the contextual perspective the search for meaning does not begin with the search for an object of reference but with the search for the symbolic context in which a term or symbol exists.

Both of these conceptions of meaning are important, even in behavioral or theological inquiry. Certainly a great deal of theology has assumed that its symbols and terms had an exclusively referential meaning. The objects for such terms were only indirectly present in this world, however. "God" simply referred to a being in another sphere. Theology was understood to be pointing to some other world. The contextual meaning gives us a richer approach to the meaning of these terms and helps us to see the theological system itself as a web of relations which can serve as guide or mirror for human relations.

In the interchange with the behavioral sciences, however, we encounter yet a third conception of meaning which incorporates many elements of the first two. A <u>functional</u> conception of meaning assumes that the referent for a term is the action which the term produces. From this perspective the language of theology is a set of symbols evoking a community and way of life in a particular cultural setting. The functional meaning of words and symbols can also be latent. For instance, the functional meaning of baptism in the late medieval Church can not be understood apart from seeing its connection to the right to participate in public life, not just in the Church.

The functional conception of meaning understands terms in the context of a system of action. The critique of ideology searches for the actual function of terms rather than their ostensible referents (as if human affairs were an object to be referred to) or even their linguistic or symbolic contexts. The behavioral sciences bring to a focus

160

those particular conceptions of reference and context to inquire persistently after the functional meaning of terms. This analysis is fundamental to the process of critique among the disciplines.

D. Functional Congruence and Ontology

The difference among the disciplines are not only a matter of differences among language games. Our discussion of congruence has brought out even more sharply that they have differing perceptions of "ultimate human reality." They do not necessarily exclude one another, but they are qualitatively different and their relation to each other is quite problematical.

This divergence, with its ensuing arguments, raises quite sharply the philosophical question of ontology. What can we say about "being" in this context? We are not here going to go through this very attractive door into another discipline. We simply point out this important connection to philosophy. We do not, however, want to give the impression that the discussion we have been pursuing here can simply be translated into the language of ontological philosophy and carried on at a "higher level." Something crucial would be lost in that move, namely the intractable attention to particular historical practices that lies at the heart of the trilateral interchange.

This empirical reference is as important to Christianity as it is to the behavioral disciplines, although each Christian approach would give slightly differing reasons for its concern. Not only is this an empirical concern for persons and institutions. Christian theologians have also taken on the empirical concerns of the natural sciences as well.[9] We must also point out that the empirical concern of the behavioral sciences is not at all necessarily that of a positivistic natural science. Indeed, there are at least some psychological schools, such as the Jungian, that verge on the metaphysical.

E. Congruence and Critique

The problem of congruence is not a simple one. We have attempted here to lay out its parameters within the perspective of trilateral analysis. We have not tried to resolve the arguments over ideology and its companions, nor find a sure way that theology or theory can avoid the pitfalls of incongruence.

Our main task in Part III has been to lay out a map of interdisciplinary conversation. We have drawn together both the approaches and the dimension of the three disciplines We have claimed that certain patterns of triadic

161

relations can predict participants' direction and choices. We can thereby see the implications of taking certain pathways. This itself is helpful in locating our own choices and in forging new paths. It opens up for us the possibility of criticizing the triadic connections that we or others try to hold together.

In delineating the patterns of congruence and incongruence we also began to open up the possibility for critique among approaches, dimensions, and disciplines. We are therefore now ready to move to the final step in trilateral analysis. The conceptual framework we have laid out in these two chapters provides a basis for the process of trilateral critique and transformation to which we are committed.

PART IV

INTRODUCING CHANGES

Introducing changes is the third and final step in
trilateral analysis. As participants in the theology-
behavioral science conversation begin to draw elements of
the disciplines together, they need to decide which elements
to include, and how to fit them together. These choices
confront us with our basic loyalties. The dialogue inevitably leads to decision and change.

This third step demands trilateral criticism. By
trilateral criticism we mean analysis and evaluation based
on our trilateral map of Christianity, personality, and
society. It includes the three approaches, ·the three dimensions, and the web of primary and secondary triadic affinities. All of these then form a framework for handling the
problem of congruence.

In Part IV we show our method of trilateral analysis
in operation. In Chapter Nine we fill out our notion of
interdisciplinary criticism. We explain two modes of criticism leading to change. Then we trace six separate outcomes of interdisciplinary change. After identifying our
own notion of criticism and its relation to the critical
theology movement, we expose the formal values behind trilateral analysis.

In Chapters Ten and Eleven we explore in depth two
authors who have taken on the challenge of introducing
changes into their own disciplines. Thomas C. Oden has
developed a systematic pastoral theology, and Gustavo
Gutierrez a theology of liberation. Each is a significant
advance from the intuitive and precritical work we introduced in Chapters Two and Three. Using our method of trilateral analysis we analyze and evaluate the tension and
points of decision in Oden's and Gutierrez's careful
arguments.

CHAPTER NINE

TRILATERAL CRITIQUE AND TRANSFORMATION

Interdisciplinary conversation is by nature a critical process. Participants make criticisms of their partners as well as of themselves. The critical process is a dialogue with points of exchange, deliberation, and decision.

The process of criticism will eventually lead to some decision on the part of the participants. These inter-disciplinary decisions lead to six possible outcomes--rejection, reduction, addition, corroboration, translation, and transformation. Each of these outcomes results from particular commitments and the decisions they imply.

These decisive commitments arise and are clarified in the process of critique. Within the critical process, par-ticipants will engage in two modes of criticism--substantive and formal. Both are essential to genuine interdisciplinary inquiry. Use of one without the other either hinders or terminates the discussion.

In this chapter we want to lay out the nature of tri-lateral critique. First we will explain these two modes as they relate to the six kinds of interdisciplinary outcomes. Then we will highlight the process of reciprocal transfor-mation and its place in the development of a critical theology.

A.   Two Modes of Criticism

1.   Substantive Criticism

Substantive criticism flows from the selection of a particular loyalty, theory, or practice as normative or primary. First of all it means establishing a "homeland" among the disciplines, and refining values and priorities along with their appropriate theories and practices. While frequently this demands that we declare loyalty to a par-ticular approach as well, it usually means putting together our own blend of the basic elements of a discipline.

In making genuine substantive commitments, we must become specific enough to launch criticisms of discernible alternatives to our choices. For example we cannot simply say, "I am a Marxist" or "I am a sacramentalist." We need to say, for example, "I think there will be a cataclysmic war between the forces of God and evil within my lifetime" before we critique the gradualism and progressivism implied by systemic views of society. We need to have reasons for believing individuals have inner resources to achieve personal fulfillment before we critique the more pessimistic claims of orthodox Freudians or Calvinists.

In making our choices and refining our loyalties we build up a "substance" from which we launch specific critiques. This substance is not only a matter of choosing a particular theory of the human prospect or even of having certain ultimate loyalties. Critique on these grounds is easy enough to see. It arises from the way in which ideas and symbols of loyalty exclude each other and demand decision.

But we also build a substance of practice. We form certain institutional loyalties, customary ways of approaching problems, a reliable network of communication with others, a set of expectations about how things might work out in the future. That is, we gain interests. In one sense they shape our perception of the world. They cause us to see the world from a relative point of view. They produce "interested knowledge." On the other hand it is only by having these interests that we can see, understand, and criticize to the extent that we do. That is, there is no disinterested knowledge. Any claim to possess it becomes ultimately ideological in the worst sense.

2. Formal Criticism

Formal criticism is systematic, trilateral thinking. It lends a dimension to interdisciplinary dialogue that substantive criticism does not have. Substantive criticism is based on commitments that are dearly held but which may be parochial or unsystematic. Formal criticism opens substantive commitments to broad implications and a wider range of alternatives.

Substantive criticism is the entry point of interdisciplinary dialogue. Without interest there would be no dialogue. Yet once in the dialogue, formal criticism can verify, correct, expand, limit or change substantive commitments. What delivers substantive interests from isolated visions is not flight from interested knowledge, but the testing of our knowledge through a critical interchange with a plurality of interested parties. Thus the presence of a genuinely trilateral approach to interdisciplinary relations provides avenues to expanded knowledge, and, as we shall see, to transformation. Formal and substantive criticism work

166

together to articulate the meaning of specific commitments
amidst the competing claims of human plurality.

We need to emphasize that formal criticism, like substantive, is not an end in itself. Drawing a map of formal
interdisciplinary relations without reference to our own substantive commitments becomes merely an intellectual exercise.
Trilateral analysis is then a taxonomic, or labeling, enterprise, with no commitment on the part of the participants.
To paraphrase Kant, substantive criticism without formal is
blind, formal criticism without substantive is empty.

So substantive and formal criticism are not opposed,
but complementary modes of criticism. Substantive criticism
is rooted in the integrity of one's disciplinary homeland--
including choice of basic data, assumptive world, and method
of inquiry. It drives us to seek internal congruence among
theory, value, and practice in our discipline. Formal criticism is rooted in the comprehensiveness and interconnec-
tedness of human knowledge as well as the plurality of human
perceptions of truth. In the interdisciplinary exchange we
see four particular formal values that arise out of the very
structure of the interchange. In order to illuminate these
more thoroughly let us first describe the six possible outcomes of interdisciplinary decisions. These can show us in
a general way how subtantive and formal considerations
figure in these decisions.

B. Six Interdisciplinary Outcomes

Within the critical process participants will come to
a decision about their home discipline in relation to others.
These decisions involve some potential for change. The six
decisions are the rejection of other disciplines, the
addition of parts of a discipline to one's own, the reduction
of another discipline to one's own, the corroboration of
one's own discipline by others, the translation of one
discipline into the terms of another, and the transformation
of the disciplines involved in the conversation. First we
will describe each outcome. Then we will explore the dynamics of our preferred outcome--reciprocal transformation.

1. Rejection

One outcome of interdisciplinary conversation is to
reject the offerings and overtures made by one's partners.
Christian theologians may simply reject the Marxist or
Freudian in whole or in part. Some may, as Karl Barth
claimed to do, reject the entire behavioral sciences as
offering anything of fundamental importance for theological
formulation or church practice. Others may simply reject
certain schools. Some degree of rejection is part of any
critical interchange. When it arises as the only outcome,

167

it leads to the breakup of the encounter. In that case
substantive commitments have far outweighed formal considerations.

2. Addition

    Theology-behavioral science exchanges frequently end
with participants adding a practice or theory from another
realm to their own repertoire. Pastors utilize Rogerian
therapeutic practices. Theologians import the notion of
alienation into their vocabulary. Sociologists begin to
call all kinds of movements and institutions "religious."
Too often this addition is the result of an eclectic pursuit. It is like the tourists who wrest artifacts and sou-
venirs from their natural environment and add them to the
decor of their own homes without knowing their meaning.
Other times addition represents the outcome of a much more
sophisticated and critical process. Here the interdisciplinary traveller understands the "natural function" of an
idea or practice and deals with the implications of import-
ing it. But this usually leads to transformation on a
wider scale, a process we will take up separately.

3. Reduction

    Reduction carries with it such negative overtones that
people usually speak of reductionism when referring to this
kind of outcome. In reduction one idea, loyalty, or practice, or even approach is reduced to another. One thing is
"nothing but" another thing. This exclusiveness defines
the central character of reductionism. For example, "What
Christians have always meant by sin is really nothing but
neurosis," or conversely, "What psychologists call therapeutic growth is nothing but sanctifying grace." One participant really swallows up another. The integrity or relative autonomy of the various disciplines is ignored.

    Reductionism can also take a practical form, in which
a professional reduces his practices to those of some other
discipline, still believing, however, that he is pursuing
his original loyalties. He lives as a practical expatriate
while still seeking to retain former loyalties intact.
Priests take on the practice of community organizing as the
authentic expression of their ministry. Pastors adopt
counseling techniques as the basic manifestation of their
pastorate. This then is a selective, and very important,
form of reductionism.

    Regardless of these apparent deficiencies we do acknow-
ledge that reductionism fuels interdisciplinary dialogue.
It challenges others to affirm and articulate the integrity
of their discipline, the congruence of their dimensions,
and the distinctiveness of their loyalties.

4. Corroboration

In the fourth type of change, participants use other disciplines to corroborate values, practices, concepts or theories in their own discipline. Thus Bernard Lonergan, in his Method in Theology cites numerous psychologists from various schools to verify his speculative statements.[1]* The differences among them, their implied opposition to his own method or suppositions, and their differing contexts and purposes are not an issue in his use of behavioral science. In fact the very differences among behavioral witnesses are taken to be additional proof of the truth of their convergence. Longergan is asking "nature" (the behavioral sciences) to corroborate "supernature" (his theological speculations). The blanket category of "nature" relieves him of the task of discerning the differences among his behavioral approaches.

5. Translation

Depending on the use of analogy, corroboration is similar to the distinctly different purpose of translation. Once some parallel is established between two concepts, practices, or symbols, it is possible to hold that one is a translation of the other. They both would be saying that same thing from different contexts. The differences between translation and corroboration is that the former grants equal weight to the two partners (and sometimes even more weight to the former partner). Corroboration maintains priority for one's own side of the exchange. Thus, with Lonergan, it is clear that the theological term takes priority over its behavioral partner. However, an apologist like Paul Tillich sees equal weight between the two, or even emphasizes the behavioral partners. Thus, Tillich speaks more about alienation than sin, more of acceptance than of grace.[2]

The impact of translation is least visible in the dimension of theory, but it is extremely significant in those of loyalty and practice. To translate our loyalties from one institution to another or from one way of acting to another is a step of exclusion and can mean a radical difference. In the world of action, one thing is simply not another. It is different. Translation can become that practical reductionism we called expatriation. In the process institutional loyalty and personal role identification get blurred or confused. The relation between theory and practice begins to unravel. This kind of translation leads to a more complex form of interdisciplinary change--transformation.

---

*Notes for this chapter begin on page 253.

6. Transformation

The most complicated form of interdisciplinary change is transformation. Transformation has three patterns. We may inquire into other disciplines in order to transform matters in our own. For instance, a theologian might consult the psychologist Carl Jung for his theory of the self's dynamics. In doing so he would soon be apprized of Jung's contention that the Christian Trinity is an inadequate concept because it excludes a classic fourth figure--the Devil.[3] For Jung dynamic personality demands conjunction of opposites. Taken to its highest order this demands some kind of opposition even within the godhead. Unless the Devil is given his due at the heart of things, we fail to concretize God in human affairs. The Christian doctrine of Trinity is not incarnational enough to account for the actual creative center of human life.

Transformation does not mean that the theologian in this case would necessarily replace the doctrine of Trinity with a quaternity. It does mean that she would reassess the adequacy of Trinity as a doctrine of God in relation to the world rather than apart from it. The distinct doctrines of the Creator and of Spirit could be developed in a more incarnational way. Thus while the symbol of Trinity would be retained as a key symbol, its theory could be transformed under the impact of a Jungian criticism. This would be a domestic form of transformation for theologians.

Within this process of transformation the theologian may begin to entertain some suspicions about the adequacy of Jung's understanding of human creativity. Moreover, she may find that the demonic side of creativity is not all that Christians have meant by "Devil." Sensing that Christians have also meant the ruler of a "kingdom," she might explore some societal interpretations of Devil that emphasize his place as a ground of legitimation for a whole "government." Equipped with both Christian as well as societal tools she might return to Jung and begin to sharpen, reconstruct, and transform Jung's own interpretation of the demonic element in human life. Even without introducing the distinctions between society and personality, between thinking and legitimation, she could open up distinctions between the Devil as an eschatological loyalty and the Devil as some kind of creative ground, distinctions between worldly loyalties and the subjective freedom of the self. This would be from the theologian's standpoint foreign transformation--changes in the discipline of psychology.

When both domestic and foreign transformation occur, we have a third process, reciprocal transformation. Both partners, or all three, are transformed under the impact of their exchange. They each preserve their own integrity,

170

but also take into account in a serious manner the alternatives or implications offered by the other.

Each of these six interdisciplinary options involves both substantive and formal criticism. Weight on the substantive side tends to preserve disciplinary commitments. More weight on formal considerations tends to change those commitments.

Each of the six kinds of outcomes rests on a strength. Each has its limits as well. Reduction stresses the integrity of one's own enterprise, but tends to deny the integrity of the other's. Rejection likewise stresses this domestic integrity but ends up excluding dialogue with outsiders to one's own discipline. Addition recognizes the integrity, at least of certain components, of another discipline. However, it tends to fail to searchout the implications knitting dimensions together in either discipline. It usually produces some form of incongruence. Corroboration affirms the mutual concerns of the disciplines, but often fails to recognize the functional meaning involved or the integrity which requires mutual criticism. Translation, finally, stresses the character of dialogue within one world of concerns, but overlooks the importance of integrity and congruence.

Tendencies toward each of these outcomes has a part to play in trilateral interchange. However, each tendency has to be corrected also by certain formal considerations. Within this framework of formal and substantive values the struggle for an outcome leads us to the complex process of reciprocal transformation.

C. Critique and Reciprocal Transformation

1. The Role of Formal Critical Values

A critical interchange among the disciplines can, and we believe should, lead to transformation in each of the participants--their loyalties, concepts, practices, methods, and theories. We call this outcome reciprocal transformation. All participants are changed in the encounter. Yet this is not a haphazard change, nor is it just any kind of change. Transformation is the kind of change that occurs within the bounds of formal and substantive values.

Our substantive values arise from our particular commitments. These are not necessarily disciplinary in nature, though for purposes of this discussion we are assuming that they find specific disciplinary realizations. Our formal values are determined by the very structure of the interdisciplinary exchange as we have described it. These formal values are integrity, affinity, congruence, and

171

comprehensiveness. We will describe each formal value and then show how reciprocal transformation arises in the attempt to honor the claim they pose.

Integrity requires a mutual respect for the wholeness of each discipline. In giving weight to their own discipline participants might try to reduce things to their own framework, as when theologians look on movements in psychotherapy or social change as "religions." They may also seek to introduce some practices or theories from those movements into their own religious realm. They would be ways of being Christian or religious. They might also use the existence of these parallel "secular religions" as a way of corroborating that all people are essentially religious, or that these particular patterns of thought and action are verifications of the essential correctness of earlier religious efforts.

By giving excessive weight to the other disciplines, however, they might end up transferring to that other discipline altogether. They might join that therapeutic movement as the new way of fulfilling their old religious loyalties. They might even go beyond this "expatriation" and claim that these new movements are the essence of all true religion--a kind of "foreign reductionism." They might, however, stop short of that and declare only that these new movements are in some sense translations, but not reductions or rejections, of their existing religious approach.

The second basic value to be honored in the process of reciprocal transformation is that of triadic affinities. We have pointed out the primary and secondary patterns of affinities among the approaches to the three disciplines. Their internal logic and their historical persistence give them some special claim to our attention. First we have to pursue, across the three disciplines, the implications of our choices in any one. We need to justify why we do or do not move along these usual paths of connections. If that new therapeutic movement is essentially an equilibrium approach, we first have to show how it relates back to our own religious commitments. We would expect these commitments to lie along the prophetic path. If not, we need to show how this new therapeutic movement fits in with our religious choices. Perhaps, if we hold to a more cultic approach, identification of these factors may lead us to some criticisms of the therapeutic movement which seemed so congenial to us initially.

The third value shaping this process is that of dimensional congruence. No matter what initial moves we make, whether to reduce or add or translate the contribution of others, we have to trace the implications of that move across the three dimensions of loyalty, practice, and theory.

If indeed the millenial dream of a radically dualistic movement is the same as traditional religious visions, do its attendant practices and theories also fit traditional religious patterns? Do the overall patterns arising out of such an interchange appear to be congruent in the ways we presented in Chapter Eight? Have we taken account not only of simple congruence but also of the functional congruence that asks specifically about the relation of theory and loyalty to practice? The value of congruence offers another point of critical correction in the process of transformation.

Just as transformation has to honor the integrity of the disciplines, so it also must honor their wholeness. It must be able to grasp the fuller range of alternative approaches within that discipline. It must honor yet another value in the interchange--that of <u>comprehensiveness</u>. Comprehensiveness demands that we be open to the alternatives within and among the disciplines. Honoring this claim places us in tension, for all of us operate with some substantive commitments to particular positions within the geography of our own discipline. Ouf firm commitment to a prophetic interpretation of the Torah, for instance, makes it difficult for us to give equal weight to liturgical traditions or contemporary religious experience. And yet the legitimate presence of these alternatives within Christianity demands that we take them into account in a sympathetic way. We have to articulate their relation to our principal commitments. So it is also with the other disciplines. If, to use the example already introduced, we forge a firm alliance of some kind with a therapeutic movement emphasizing fulfillment themes, we must also attend to the critiques and claims of the prophetic or cultic exponents in Christianity, as well as other approaches in the arena of personality.

The demand for comprehensiveness of this sort reveals most sharply that all participants do have some particular commitments. The interchange would hardly be sustainable if they did not. It is a process of argument, a process honoring often conflicting values. A book like this one cannot solve the riddle of faith commitment or other specific theoretical and practical judgments that all participants must make. We can only point out here that these loyalties are essential to the vigor and critical substance of the interchange.

2. Reciprocal Transformation

All of these moves to honor certain formal values--the integral claims of the disciplines, the salience of triadic affinities, the congruence of dimensions, or the fullness of each discipline--give shape to the process of <u>reciprocal</u>

transformation. It is a process of mutual correction and
accommodation within the parameters set by these formal
values. They shape and refine the directions we take in
response to our substantive loyalties. To use John Rawls'
phrase, it is a process of seeking "reflective equilibrium."[4]
Even more, it is an attempt to find points of practical
and reflective equilibrium. It is an activity requiring
intuition and art as well as logical precision. It consists
of delicate, almost aesthetic steps in arriving at changes
in a critical manner. It is an act not merely of balancing
claims but of living and working in the field of tension
created by them.

      Reciprocal transformation is in this way a value it-
self which sums up the thrust of the interdisciplinary
encounter. Like so many important values it is never fully
achieved and secured, but offers a source of illumination
and guidance amid the complexities of the interdisciplinary
interchange. Without the correctives supplied by these
critical values the changes and outcomes we attain will lack
depth and durability. Our theological positions will lack
insight or relevance for human as well as church affairs.
Our theological symbols may become highly individualistic
and lose their import for societal responsibilities, or
primarily institutional and lose their pertinence for individual faith. Pastoral counselors may lose sight of whole
dimensions and sensitivities of clients that other realms
highlight--such as class oppression or subtleties of self-
aggression. Spiritual direction can become dry and impov-
erished without the stimulus of therapeutic and ethical
input. Ministers who go into community organizing and use
churches as a base for their activity may misjudge the practical limits of churches' involvement in community action.
Or they may reject the pietism of parishioners, thereby
overlooking important facets of human motivation that relate
to their own goals for fuller and truer community.

      The kind of critical, interdisciplinary approach we
have been developing here is indebted to the rise of critical theory in Europe and radical criticism in America.
These two movements have each had distinct impacts on theology and ministry, especially in the development of a
critical theology. Because of their importance for our
inquiry we turn to them here to spell out the meaning of
our own efforts.

D. Two Sources of Critical Theology

      Criticism is a popular virtue in contemporary theology.
It is so popular that sometimes merely a critical pose is
mistaken for theology itself. Since the term itself has
been raised to the status of symbol, we have difficulty
defining it precisely. Sometimes it means analysis. A

critical theologian examines claims or positions carefully, locating their assumptions, crucial moves, and overall logic. Criticism means an analytical stance. This concept of criticism is certainly contained in the approach of this book.

Other times, especially in the spirit of Paul Tillich's "Protestant Principle" or H. Richard Niebuhr's "radical monotheism," criticism means the devaluation of all claims in the presence of the transcendent Other.[5] Criticism is the tool of the iconoclast and spiritual reformer. It is the first task of one who would oppose all idolatry. The argument for recognition of plurality in our map of the interchange can be understood in this vein.

In many cases criticism is the first sally in the battle against the established social order. It begins a social revolution by undermining the ideological claims of the established powers. Having called the consciousness of an era into question, forces of revolt can mobilize those set free from inner constraints against resistance and revolution. While revolutionaries might clarify their own vision with our critical effort, this is not the major concept of criticism we are employing here.

Over the past two centuries this kind of criticism has first been delivered against Christian institutions--the clergy, hierarchies, parishes, holidays and the family. Marx himself summarized this strategy with his contention that "the beginning of all criticism is the criticism of religion." Since Marx and then Freud theologians and ministers have been reacting to the reductionist claims of critics. We cannot here lay out the various strategies by which they defended the faith, whether by grounding it in a "real nature of man" undetected by the reductionists or by lifting it further into a heaven of intuition and speculation. That whole era of criticism and anti-reductionist apology occurred within a societal context in which the churches still held cultural hegemony if not monopoly. The exchange was all part of the larger battle on behalf of church leaders to maintain a Christian culture or society. With the disappearance of that kind of culture under the impact of nationalisms, civil religions, and technological or mercantile ways of life, the churches have become less and less defensive about their claims and prerogatives, although this various from place to place. At one time they eagerly baptized the advent of this secular culture (as with Harvey Cox's The Secular City), but in the last decade have entered into the practice of critique themselves. They have begun to ally themselves increasingly with their former critics--both psychological and sociological. Critique has become part of the apologia of the Church, a way proponents of the faith confront the world of sin.

Some critical theologians have constructed their platforms through an unvarnished appropriation of classical Marxism or Freudianism. Others have drawn upon various revised versions of these movements, as in Herbert Marcuse or Erich Fromm. Still others have returned to the work of Hegel.[6] American theologians have been particularly affected bythe "Frankfurter Schule" of critical theory and the radical movements in sociology and psychology in the 1960's.

1. Critical Theory

The critical theory movement has been primarily a German phenomenon nourished by the Institut für Sozialforschung (Institute for Social Research). Among its most influential members have been Max Horkheimer, Karl Adorno, Erich Fromm, and more recently, Jürgen Habermas.[7] With their colleagues they explored the social and psychological vistas opened up by the Marxist tradition in sociology and the Freudian in psychology. With this combination (and its accompanying tensions) they could open up the problem of culture anew for Marxists and explore the possible psychological grounds for the failure of Marxism in societal transformation. In both cases, they laid down penetrating analyses of the interplay between ideational and "material" reality. They pushed the questions of ideology, utopia, authority, and personal and social transformation rigorously. What we have called the problem of functional congruence lay at the heart of their inquiries. Most recently, people like Jürgen Habermas have tried to break through to new understandings about the positive interaction of interest and rational knowledge. His work has influenced in turn many social theorists and theologians in Europe and the United States.

It is impossible here to present the complex relationships between critical theorists around Habermas and their theological partners in dialogue, such as Wolfhart Pannenberg, Gerhard Sauter, and Johannes Metz in Germany, or Peter Berger, Gregory Baum and numerous younger theologians in the United States and Canada, not to mention the contributions from Latin America. In Metz's work we find the essential thrust of this interchange.

Metz develops a whole theory of the church based on the task of social criticism.[8] The Church presents its message of repentance and salvation in terms of its societal critique. This critical task confronts a dilemma in the face of genuine critical theory. It must be genuinely Christian and therefore be tied both to a theological framework as well as to the Church as an institution. However, it must also be a form of objective knowledge about the society. Marxism in its classical form tended to hold that

institutional and class interests always becloud any "knowledge" that might be proposed in such criticism. Habermas
and others setting forth the tenets of critical theory maintain that the colors introduced by interests can be filtered
out through criticisms based on the general structure and
requirements of knowledge itself--canons of logic, empirical
reference, verifiability, falsifiability and the like. This
process is reinforced by the cross-criticism of public discourse. Moreover, these "cognitive interests" need the hor-
ses of material and institutional interest in order to accom-
plish their task. The Church's institutional interests may
provide motivation for its critical task without distorting
its critical claims. Its relative autonomy from other
sectors releases powers of critique never available to it in
a more established context, whether it was a political establishment, as in Europe, or a cultural one, as in the
United States.

Metz, along with other authors like Pannenberg and
Sauter, have also striven to show how theology, rather than
being necessarily an ideological consciousness requiring
external criticism, emerges as a fundamental means of critique. Theology is a rational enterprise which can call
into question the logic of ideological claims. It has a
grounding in history and a concern therefore for the empirical workings of salvation. Its rational commitments are
equal to those of Enlightenment philosophers who have given
rise to the empirical critique of ideology. Secondly, it
deals with a perfection of human life which is not in some
detached utopian paradise but is already present in history.
Therefore, while it calls men away from awestruck diviniza-
tion of human claims and institutions, it also takes these
seriously as protagonists in the drama of salvation. The
position of theology, as conceived by these critical theologians, provides it with a critical distance from events
without falling into sheer otherworldliness. From a theoretical perspective theologians can combat the error of
materialistic reductionism found in Engels and the Stalin-
ists on the one hand, as well as the error of utopianism
found in most Christian socialists and reformers.

The appropriation of the specific intellectual achievements of critical theory has been affected in numerous ways
by the radical movements within the behavioral disciplines
themselves in the 1960's. To some extent these were nourished by the solid theoretical accomplishments of the
critical theory movement. To a great extent they were the
almost intuitive reaction to the attack on established
institutions provoked by the Vietnam War.

2. Radical Criticism

At its heart radical criticism has contended that the

dominant approaches in psychology and sociology have not
changed things for the better.[9] The systemic sociology
exemplified by Talcott Parsons has been an ideology for
elitist planners, while Freudian psychologies have used
ineffectual practices which served only to line the poc-
kets of the therapeutic guild. Furthermore, each discipline or profession was criticized by radicals for not
taking the other into account. Therapists simply passed on
the attitudes and habits of the oppressing classes who were
able to pay therapist's fees. Or they did not take into
account how societal conditions produced the behavior which
therapists called "mental illness." Conversely, sociologists were critiqued for squeezing out the dynamics of
unique personalities or for not taking into account the
personal impact of actual or proposed societal arrangements,
regardless of their self-evident justice or equity.

These kinds of claims manifested themselves in various
schools, movements, and authors. For Alvin Gouldner it
meant a revision of Marxism in order to criticize Talcott
Parsons. Herbert Marcuse blended Freud and Marx to deliver
his critique of modern society in general. With considerably less play to the popular grandstand, Perry London exposed the disjunction between therapeutic claims and theories on the one hand and their actual practices on the other.
Psychologists like Thomas Szasz and Seymour Halleck have
criticized the unspoken ethical implications of their own
profession--Szasz attacking the dubious diagnostic term,
"mental illness," and Halleck the socially conforming role
of psychotherapy itself. Others, like Robert Coles, have
brought their therapeutic concerns into the broader arena
of community and social reform.

Most critical theory has presupposed a dualistic approach to society. In going beyond Marxism modern radical
critics found new cleavages in which to work their wedge
of criticism and revolution. At least three such fundamental oppositions gained the floor in this area--those of
race, sex, and knowledge.

Numerous radicals at all levels of theoretical and
practical sophistication engaged personality as well as
society in terms of racial opposition. Even a brief synop-
sis of the work of Franz Fanon, Eldridge Cleaver, Albert
Cleage, James Cone, Joseph Washington, and others would
comprise a separate book.[10] At all points, they have been
concerned to relate cultural, sociological, literary, religious, and psychological matters to the fundamental oppositions of race.

The women's movement in similar vein has heralded the
fundamental social, political and cultural importance of the
sexual dichotomy. Some, like Shulamith Firestone or Juliet

Mitchell, have self-consciously revised the Marxist heritage to critique sexism. Others in a wide variety of ways have sought to develop a whole new approach that emerges from the sexual dualism itself as it has appeared in history, culture, and personality. In the work of people like Mary Daly we find theological ramifications of this basic stance.[11]

Finally, numerous radicals have examined the fundamental societal cleavage posed by the opposition between the knowledgeable and the ignorant. Ivan Illich's work was the most popular spearhead of this critique, but others such as Christopher Jencks have carried it to considerable empirical detail. The knowledge critique has also been a very influential aspect of the general attack on technology lofted by Marcuse and others.[12]

Each of these movements of radical criticism has not only influenced developments in behavioral realms but also in Christian circles. In each case religious institutions have been deeply involved in reinforcing but also occasionally in exposing the fundamental oppositions of racism, sexism or educational elitism. Any critique of the accepted forms of these dualisms, whether they be white superiority, male supremacy, or technocratic rule, has been simultaneously an attack on the Church. However, with the increasing dissociation of the Church from other centers of power, these criticisms have also entered the armory of ministers and theologians alike.

E. Toward a Critical Trilateral Theology

Critical theory and radical criticism have been important in shaping the critical method we have been developing here. They have played a crucial role in sharpening the key question of functional congruence. However, their substantive commitments are so obvious and so strong that we have to inquire about the problems of affinity, integrity, and comprehensiveness in their approaches, especially when they take on theological allies. Using the trilateral map we can identify the shape of their constructive effort and its relation to the four formal critical values. We can then point out the specific differences between it and our own notion of critical theology. This difference lies essentially in our argument for a trilateral theology that involves both formal and substantive criticism.

1. Critical Theology in Trilateral Perspective

Seen from the standpoint of the trilateral scheme, the interchange over critical theory and the radical behavioral critiques exhibits a clear pattern of relationships. Within the societal realm, dualists have made substantive critiques of systemics and to some extent pluralists. Dualists have

179

also critiqued substantively the whole psychological realm
without exception of dimension or approach for its inattention to the oppression wrought by social structures.
Psychologists have generally depended on conflict approaches
to launch substantive critiques of sociologists. Freud's
critique of culture has been carried on with heavy fulfillment emphases by Marcuse and N. O. Brown. Within psychology
substantive critiques have usually been advanced by fulfillment proponents against both of the other approaches for
their pessimism about human freedom and self-transformation.

Perhaps in large part because of the decline of established religion, the behavioral sciences have launched
few recent substantive critiques of Christian values,
concepts or practices. However, Christian theologians have
been adding behavioral critiques or translating Christian
traditions into them. For the most part they have drawn on
dualist and fulfillment approaches for this task.

These critical movements and interchanges have
employed formal criticism to a lesser extent. The least
interesting critique has been the traditional criticisms
of the simple incongruence between Christian loyalties and
practices. In most instances this somewhat formal criticism
overlooks any careful examination of the way theology mediates between practice and loyalty. Moreover, it does not
examine its behavioral assumptions for this critique.
While Christians possess no special immunity against incongruence and its ideological symptoms, they do possess
resources that can be called upon to stimulate and guide the
struggle for greater righteousness and truer knowledge of
God. These symbols themselves can be unpacked as we have
already noted to sharpen attention to this problem. Morever,
each approach has typical means for confronting it. Prophetics must constantly measure themselves against the commandment prohibiting idolatry. Cultics must constantly test
their theology and their practices against the model of the
Eucharistic community gathered around the presence of Christ.
Ecstatics are constantly drawn to inquire about the degree
to which theories are rooted in actual experience and
produce the fruits of the Spirit.

Considerably more prominent has been the critique,
from theologians and behavioral scientists alike, of the
behavioral ideology of "value-free science." Critics have
illuminated the loyalties and theories actually at work in
the behavioral sciences. They have unveiled the actual
values and practices hidden behind the appearance of mere
theory or technique. Certainly this formal criticism has
been decisive for the approach we have taken in this book.
Discovery of the three-dimensional reality of the behavioral
sciences has upset earlier Christian hopes of using them as
value-free instruments. At the same time it has revived at

a more sophisticated level earlier controversies over the clash between "science" and "religion." Community organizing, encounter groups, and radical communities have come to be seen as surrogate churches, rather than merely behavioral practices. As behavioral scientists have made their theories and loyalties more explicit, they have forced the churches to rethink theologically their own grounds for trying to use these in a neutral fashion.

From the Christian side, the interchange with critical theory and radicalism has been carried on differently by each approach. Prophetic Christians, whether they are liberal, neo-orthodox, or evangelical, have tended to appropriate dualistic perspectives and reject systemic ones. This has been especially clear in the "radical evangelicals" movement in the United States.[13] Simultaneously, prophetics have shared the whole dualistic critique of the personality approaches. Ecstatics have supported substantive critiques launched by fulfillment critics. Primarily this has been manifested in a critique of bureaucratic or hierarchical churches that oppress individual freedom and ignore spontaneous expressions of the Spirit. Cultically inclined Christians have tended not to share in the critical debate, though there have been exceptions such as the Slant group in England. Recently, however, prophetic Christians such as Gutierrez and other Latin American theologians, working within a largely cultic environment, have entered the interchange, often transforming their indigenous cultic approaches altogether.

2. Critical Trilateralism: Some First Steps

Our own effort is an attempt to expand this movement of critical interchange from a trilateral point of view. From a formal standpoint the theology-behavioral science interchange has suffered from inadequate attention to the principles of comprehensiveness and reciprocal transformation. In the exchange with sociological dualists, theologians have often not taken into adequate account pluralistic theories and loyalties, although their practices have often turned out to be more congenial with that orientation. In their friendly relationship with fulfillment theories they have often discarded, rather than refined, their earlier appropriation of conflict theories. In addition, until very recently, they have found almost no way to engage the claims and practices of the equilibriumists, other than to reject them out of hand.

While critical theories have accomplished a great deal from their dualistic, conflict, or fulfillment strongholds, they now may suffer from inadequate attention to the claims of formal critique. This is especially true for theologians who may miss altogether the issues posed by choices among

behavioral approaches. Marx revived may simply replace
Parsons, and Freud unearthed may give way to Maslow.

Greater attention to formal critical values would
imply a reinterpretation of the ideology problem within
the context of institutional pluralism as well as a more
complex set of power relationships involving knowledge,
symbol control communication, law and voluntary association.[14] Greater appreciation of conflict approaches to the
self would instigate more penetration into traditional theories of God's grace, human frailty, and the anticipation
of ultimate victory through the cultural role of liturgy
and sacrament. A more comprehensive interchange with
equilibrium proponents could lead to a process of mutual
transformation in which Christian values of personal autonomy were balanced by a reinterpretation of the meaning of
environment in the light of the doctrine of Creation. This
doctrine in turn could correct the equilibrium over-
emphasis on simple mechanical causality in its understanding
of the self, not to mention its traditionally narrow view of
value questions.

Comprehensive expansion of the trilateral interchange
leads us inevitably to the value of reciprocal transformation. As we noted earlier, theologians have often been
satisfied merely to add or translate critical approaches to
their own realm. The rise of the critical theology movement
has often been characterized by this kind of relationship.
To some extent this has been a compensation for previous
attitudes of theological rejection of Marxism or various
behavioristic therapies. But with the present process of
addition and translation has come a willy-nilly activity of
reduction and even consequent loss of contact with the
Christian realm altogether.

Critical theology has indeed sharpened our sensitivity
to the value of functional meaning through its attention to
the problem of ideology. It has also, when coupled with
radical movements in the behavioral sciences, held theologians and ministers accountable for the lack of congruence
between their theory and practice. With our own insistence
on comprehensiveness and reciprocal transformation, we are
asking for a more thoroughgoing exposure of the reality of
loyalties, theories, and practices in each disciplinary
sphere, none of which can be hidden away by claims to
"scientific objectivity" on the behavioral side, or sheer
"allegiance to God" on the other. Simultaneously, comprehensiveness exhorts us away from simply bilateral interchanges
between Christianity and the behavioral disciplines. Not
only does such bilateralism impoverish the behavioral realm,
it also distorts the implications of fundamental Christian
symbols and theories which properly extend to both spheres
of human action. In appealing for greater efforts at

reciprocal transformation, we contest the reductionism, whether theological or behavioral, that overlooks the integrity of disciplines or that encourages a simple reductionism and escapes the critical tension among them. In the next two chapters we will examine these problems in two current attempts to move toward a more inter- disciplinary theology.

CHAPTER TEN

CHRISTIANITY AND PERSONALITY IN TRANSFORMATION:

THOMAS C. ODEN

In Chapter Seven we cited a number of classical and contemporary theologians whose work exemplifes standard alignments among the disciplines of theology, psychology and sociology. We now turn to two contemporary figures who have attempted to construct their theological positions within an explicit interchange with the behavioral sciences. One, Thomas C. Oden, has primarily engaged psychology, particularly Carl Rogers' client-centered therapy. The other, Gustavo Gutierrez, has greatly utilized the thought of Karl Marx. Each is primarily a bilateral thinker, yet each has possibilities for trilateral reflection as well. We have chosen them not only for the important behavioralists they have engaged--Rogers and Marx--but also for the creative and detailed manner in which they have treated behavioral contributions.

We will examine these efforts through perspectives provided by the trilateral scheme. The schema will be used to order our inquiry, identify the crucial critical questions and clarify the logic which holds their work together. We are not trying here to present the fullness of their thought but rather a critical introduction to some of their central ideas. We will first treat Oden and then move on to Gutierrez.

A. Thomas C. Oden's Systematic Theology of Pastoral Care

Thomas C. Oden is a contemporary Protestant pastoral theologian who has developed a systematic perspective for the theological dialogue with psychology. Although Oden does not limit his work to pastoral care, he is an important figure in the current pastoral care movement, for he brings a clear confessional stance to the dialogue with psychotherapy. With his sytematic theological perspective Oden challenges pastors to look to the theological traditions implied by their work in counseling and pastoral relations. At the same time he challenges secular counselors to look beyond their practices to see the theological grounds implied by their conceptions of psychotherapy.

Oden's theology is thoroughly dialogical. He knows
and converses with the major options and current trends in
psychotherapy. At the same time his own work involves
various strains of theology, including phenomenology and
ethics. He has been influenced by a number of sources--by
Karl Barth and Rudolf Bultmann in theology, by Martin
Heidegger in philosophy and by Carl Rogers in psychotherapy.

Oden is an important bilateral figure. His work has
important implications for pastoral care as well as for
theological reconstruction. Our basic assessment is that
he operates from the primary ecstatic triad, but picks up
important motifs from other perspectives. We shall deal
first with his commitment to fulfillment psychology, then
with his ecstatic theological commitments, and finally with
tensions in his thought between systemic and pluralistic
social theories.

1.   The Commitment to Fulfillment Psychology

Oden clearly prefers the client-centered orientation
in psychotherapy. In Kerygma and Counseling[1]* he translates
Rogers' conception of self-actualization into a drama of
individual salvation. For instance, he identifies Rogers'
notion of the self-actualizing tendency with the doctrine of
man as created in the image of God and in a state of original righteousness. He identifies the introjection of
conditions of worth with the Christian notion of the fall
into sin, and the notion of incongruence with that of the
bondage of the will. And finally, he translated therapists'
communication of unconditional positive regard toward
clients into God's communication of love to man through the
event of Jesus Christ.

In the Structure of Awareness[2] he develops an entire
phenomenology of human existence based on Rogers' thought.
This is the movement from a state of trust, security, and
responsiveness to one of guilt, anxiety, and boredom, and
then onward to a state of authenticity. Oden believes that
a psychological or phenomenological perspective, however, is
not sufficient to interpret the full meaning of human existence, and that Christian theology is necessary for that
task. So he supplements his phenomenology of individual
existence with a "covenant ontology" rooted in the work of
Karl Barth and Rudolf Bultmann.

One of Oden's unique contributions is the way he used
client-centered therapy to construct a notion of guilt.

---

*Notes for this chapter begin on page 256.

186

Guilt is a central notion for pastoral care. Its theological definition has ramifications for a theory of sin and for a doctrine of Christ's atonement and ultimately for a doctrine of God. The idea of guilt also has important ramifications for pastoral practices such as confession and penance, as well as pastoral counseling. Oden's notion of human guilt is particularly contemporary. To understand its uniqueness we must first explain the more traditional idea of guilt as moral transgression. Then we will deal with his idea of guilt as moral imperfection.

a. Guilt as Moral Transgression

One way of understanding guilt is in terms of moral transgression. A person is guilty when he breaks a moral law or disobeys certain moral restrictions held by a moral community. Transgression implies a crossing or cutting of social limits. Transgression also implies that communal, not just individual, bonds are affected, and that the moral community is endangered or influenced by the transgression. Furthermore, the moral community has certain agents or representatives authorized to handle moral transgression. In secular society, criminals are the moral deviants, and police, judges and wardens are the social authorities who handle deviation. In religious communities sinners are moral deviants and ministers and priests are authorized to deal with the deviation from community standards. This understanding of guilt as moral transgression assumes a systemic social theory in which the corporate body (social or religious) is endangered, and the deviant must be reintegrated into the social body.

Psychodynamically, a conflict psychology describes moral transgression and reintegration into the religious or occular community in the following way. The self (ego) has been unwilling or unable to control certain instincts. The resulting deviant behavior offends the conscience of the moral community. The superego, or conscience, requires some payment by the ego for its lack of discipline. Subjectively, the "payment" is the feeling of remorse and guilt. In the conflict view, since the ego is weak (it lacks knowledge or willpower), restitution involves steps to remedy the ego's lack. Thus the process of confession, absolution and penance can be seen as an attempt to strengthen the ego. Confession is acknowledging and gaining insight into one's sins, implying that this will provide some new understanding that the ego previously lacked. Absolution makes possible the release of the conscience's judgment upon the ego, and penance, when satisfied, indicates the reintegration of the self back into the moral community.

An equilibrium notion of guilt differs from a conflict notion in that the former stresses environmental controls,

rewards, and sanctions on the deviant's behavior. A conflict perspective focuses more on the stimulation of the
ego (through analysis) to prevent deviation from recurring.
Both equilibrium and conflict psychologies require a moral
community to handle personal guilt. The conflict approach
uses moral authority to provide moral insight and value
readjustment in order to reintegrate the deviant back into
society. The equilibrium approach stresses conformity in
moral thought and/or action, but is not as concerned with
it voluntariness, which is essential to the conflict view.

b. Sin as an Offense Against God

Numerous theologians understand sin as moral transgression. In their view, sin is behavior that is an offense
against God. Classically, this is Anselm's theological
position. Anselm saw people as personally responsible and
blameworthy for sin. As descendants from Adam and Eve, all
people sin, and death is their penalty. Anselm saw sin
essentially as an insult to God's honor. Sin so dishonors
God, however, that no man can possibly make due compensation.
Since no sinful man can satisfy God's honor, only a sinless
creature can possibly make the proper restitution. Thus
only God himself, Anselm reasons, can satisfy the insult of
sin. In his famous treatise Cur Deus Homo, Anselm argues
that Christ, perfect man (sinless) and perfect God, is the
proper sacrifice for God's honor. Christ willingly gave
himself for crucifixion, and thereby repaid the debt to God
that human sinfulness incurred. This is the penal-
substitutionary theory of the atonement.

In Christian theology and practice, Anselm's atonement
theory generally presupposes a conflict understanding of
guilt. Freud's pessimistic view of human instincts parallels Anselm's view that all people inherit Adam's sin. The
satisfaction of God's honor parallels the notion of the
superego's extraction of guilt as the price for moral transgression. Anselm's view of the self as a morally rational
being implies that certain superego standards bind everyone.
In Roman Catholic practice, these standards became embodied
in the moral teaching of the magisterium. The "body" these
regulations protect is Christ's body, the Church. Preservation of the social (in this case, ecclesial) organism is
an important systemic motif, and the notion of moral maintenance becomes the connection between a conflict psychology and a systemic social theory. Thus, forgiveness,
absolution and penance are steps by which the sinner satis-
fies God's honor, is reinstituted into Christ's body, and
regains access to the sacraments. This is the final tie in
forming what we have called the cultic triad--a cultic theology, a systemic social theory, and a conflict psychology.

It is significant today that the Catholic practice of

private confession and personal penance is declining. The rise of cultural pluralism and especially broadened contemporary attitudes toward sexual behavior have eroded the consensus concerning moral norms. Since a moral transgression theory of sin and guilt presupposes that people can clearly identify what is sinful and what is virtuous, penitential practices are in a state of confusion. Cultural and economic pluralism in America has put a strain on the cultic understanding of sin, penance, and Christ's atonement.

c. Oden's Concept of Guilt

Oden's approach to guilt is quite different from the cultic-systemic-conflict version we have just described. He does not describe guilt in terms of moral transgression. Instead he defines guilt as an awareness of the failure to be one's authentic self. Guilt is not determined primarily by commonly held moral standards as in the moral transgression view, but by subjectively experienced moral values. Guilt essentially is not being true to one's self. Guilt is moral imperfection.

Guilt as imperfection flows from a Rogerian model of the self. The real self (I) is the overlap of one's organismic valuing experience (III) and one's self-concept (II), as depicted in this figure.[3]

ROGERS' MODEL OF PERSONALITY

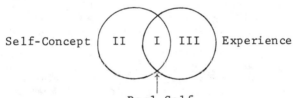

Real Self

The incongruent person has a rigid self-concept. For instance, he might believe that he is worthy only if he performs his work extremely well. Rogers calls this an introjected condition of worth. This person would believe he and others are worthwhile only when they are perfect. Whenever such a person experiences failure or imperfection, he associates personal unworthiness with it. He becomes highly anxious and tense. In terms of subjective experience this individual is often aware of a lack of perfection. Thus the self--the degree of overlap between experience and self-concept--of the perfectionist is precariously small. The degree of happiness and worthiness he would experience is minimal. This is what Rogers calls the state of incongruence. Oden calls the experiential awareness of this state "guilt."

Oden's model of guilt implies that the authentic self
grows as the overlap between experience and self-concept
increases. This occurs in an atmosphere of acceptance fos-
tered by the empathy, genuineness, and unconditional positive regard of a caring significant other. For the person
with a perfectionistic self-concept, an atmosphere of
unconditional acceptance becomes an invitation to examine
her own highly conditional acceptance of herself and others.
This process cultivates a more flexible self-concept. Empathic understanding of the perfectionistic client's feelings can lead to her own awareness of the feelings she sup-
pressed because they did not fit her perfectionistic self-
image. In short, unconditional acceptance can reverse
introjected conditions of worth and lead to a more flexible
self-concept and a recovery of feeling and vitality. This
is the state of congruence which Oden refers to by the term
"authenticity."

Oden's notion of guilt as the failure to be one's
authentic self substantially differs from the idea of guilt
as moral transgression. From a psychoanalytic view, Oden's
"guilt" is more akin to shame. "Shame," technically defined,
is the failure to reach an ideal. It is experienced as a
"falling short" of an ego ideal rather than as "cutting
across," or violating superego restrictions. In Erik
Erikson's developmental terms, shame is part of a child's
second stage of development (autonomy vs. shame and doubt)
while guilt is part of the third (initiative vs. guilt).
Developmentally "sin" in terms of guilt would result from
an excess or lack of initiative, whereas "sin" at stage
two would result from an excess or lack of autonomy. Oden
attributes "guilt" to deficient autonomy--the failure to
become one's true self. The moral transgression view sees
guilt in terms of excessive initiative. The two notions
of "guilt" are clearly different. The moral transgression
view clearly presumes a conflict psychology. Oden instead
presumes a fulfillment psychology.

Oden's choice of the fulfillment rather than the conflict approach to personality affects his choice of approach
to Christian theology and practice. We have noted that
while conflict psychologies have affinities to a cultic
theology, fulfillment psychologies have a logical connection
with ecstatic theologies. Oden's implications for the
Christian practice of penance differ substantially from
those of cultic theories. explained earlier in this chapter.
First of all, the cultic-conflict notion of penance presumes a common moral order to which believers have an internal commitment. This is why they experience guilt when they
break that order. However, for Oden the believer's commitment is primarily to his own inner strivings toward

self-actualization, not to a moral community. Oden has been influenced in this regard by Heidegger's notion of the call of conscience. By conscience Heidegger means the inner calling of one's true self. The moral basis for both Heidegger and for Oden is thus not a moral community outside the self, but an inner "real" self. This individualistic basis of morality has a basic affinity with an ecstatic theological approach, in which individual experience is the divine.

Secondly, it is important to ask which practices flow from Oden's fulfillment notion of guilt. One implication is that in the sacrament of penance the penitent would not be "forgiven" for transgressing commonly held moral bonds, but instead would be "accepted" in spite of his refusal to accept God's love for him. This sacrament technically would involve no penance then, for there would be no debt or repayment required of the sinner by the moral community. Furthermore, there would be no communal sanction such as exclusion from the sacraments in Oden's view, as one is primarily responsible to oneself for his sin. Oden would support highly therapeutic practices of confession and penance because therapy seeks to help the client get in touch with his own inner strivings, and to create an atmosphere in which he accepts those strivings.

Such an orientation to individual uniqueness would be quite appropriate in a pluralistic culture characterized by diverse values and attitudes. Indeed, Oden might well suggest that small group therapy or encounter groups be the new form for the ecclesial handling of sin and guilt. In The Intensive Group Experience: The New Pietism, he notes the striking parallels between the current encounter group movement and 17th and 18th century Protestant and Jewish pietism. In that book he also suggests some "transverbal" liturgical innovations. He notes that the arrangement of pews in most churches locks people into relationships that establish a distance between superior and subordinate, that militate against dialogue, and keep people physically separate. This is in contrast with Oden's recommendations:

> to touch, to embrace warmly, to experience many of the interpersonally involving liturgical acts which have been so important in the history of Christian celebration (such as the laying on of hands, the passing of the peace, the bathing of feet, the pagentry of feast days, etc.).[4]

Oden's advocacy for such transverbal experiences in Christian liturgy identifies clearly his preference for fulfillment practices. His concern for democracy and dialogue in the Church gives hints of a pluralistic social theory which we shall deal with later. First we shall look at Oden's theological commitments to see whether in fact he does operate out of the ecstatic position as his fulfill- ment choice would lead us to expect.

2. Oden's Ecstatic Commitment

Two theological loyalties form the basis of Oden's response to the behavioral sciences--revelation and kerygma. We first will examine his highly ecstatic notion of revela- tion, and then explore some of the tensions in his thought pertaining to his understanding of kerygma.

a. Revelation

To understand what Oden means by "revelation," it first will be helpful to identify what he does <u>not</u> mean by the term. Revelation is not dogma or doctrine <u>authorized</u> by ecclesiastical authority. Neither is revelation God's will communicated in Scripture. Oden does say that "authority for speaking of revelation in Christianity is fourfold: <u>Scriptural</u> truth <u>experienced</u> in life and illuminated by <u>reason and tradition.</u>"[5] Oden acknowledges that none of the <u>four</u> authorities can claim exclusive priority. Yet Oden himself stresses Scripture and experience. From Scripture he takes the historically unique event of Jesus Christ. In experience he stresses the reception of God's love and com- fort mediated through human relationships. Together these form the basis of his theology. They also form the ongoing polarities of Oden's theological reflection. The revelation of God's love through Jesus Christ and the experience of divine love are theologically united in the Pauline affirma- tion, "God's love has been poured into our hearts through the Holy Spirit which has been given to us" (Rom. 5:4-5). This is the basis by which Oden relates kerygma and psycho- therapy. The <u>proclamation</u> of divine love is <u>experienced</u> in the therapeutic situation.

For Oden, revelation is thus primarily revelation to the individual. Oden does not develop a doctrine of the Holy Spirit; yet this clearly is the direction of his thought. Of course Oden holds that what is revealed is God's love and that historically this love was mediated through the event of Jesus Christ. Yet he primarily empha- sizes the <u>experience</u> of this love. From a trinitarian standpoint, this puts primacy on the Holy Spirit.

Oden's notion of grace is also quite ecstatic. Grace is related to authentic existence. Grace is divine love experienced by the self. Grace is mediated not by a sacra- mental cult nor by the Word, but by persons. Oden says, "If from time to time this grace cries out to be articulated, it most of all asks to be inconspicuously mediated through

192

concrete empathetic relationships."[6] God's call is to
accept His love. For Oden this may just as well occur in a
religionless fashion--in the psychotherapeutic interview,
for instance--as in religious life or community. Oden does
not point to any particular cultic or biblical form through
which God's grace is ordinarily mediated. His theological
base is clearly ecstatic.

Were Oden to emphasize the second person of the Trinity, he might stress the Word of God and its demand for
obedience to the Will it reveals. This is the way the
Swiss theologian, Eduard Thurneysen, interprets pastoral
care.[7] Thurneysen advocates that at some time in the pastoral counseling session, the minister should bring God's
Word to bear on the believer's dilemma. The Word thus becomes a "breech" in the conversation. It puts the believer's
idolatrous assumptions under divine judgment. This calls
the believer to a decision for or against God. While some
might see this as a harsh notion of pastoral care, Thurneysen would claim that divine judgment is rooted in divine
love. And without judgment there can be no reconciliation
with God.

Obviously Oden does not ground his theology of pastoral care in the Word like Thurneysen. His commitment to
individual autonomy and inner fulfillment does not fit with
Thurneysen's implicit equilibrium assumptions about obedience and conformity. More importantly, Oden does not view
Christ as judgmental or as demanding the either-or decision
essential to the biblical-prophetic perspective. Rather
Oden takes Bultmann's approach and views Christ's call of
"for or against" in terms of one's own selfhood--for or
against one's own authenticity--not in terms of behavioral
conformity to the Word.

At first sight Oden's theology does not seem to be
based in the first person of the Trinity either. If it were,
he would likely have some notion of natural law or of the
natural order created by God, the Creator and Governor of
the universe. In that tradition, the notion of Creation has
implied some set of moral standards that are "given" with
the natural order. While Oden appreciates Teilhard de
Chardin's affirmation of the goodness of the world and of
the divine presence within creation, he does not perceive
any particular natural moral order within creation. What
is "natural" for Oden is self-actualization.

Oden has been strongly influenced by Karl Barth, however. Oden often refers to his own work as a "covenant
ontology." By this he means that "the historical [and] the
natural order exists in covenant. All creation is covenant
creation."[8] Oden agrees with Barth that the being of God
is love, and that God exists in covenant fellowship with man.

Along with Hartshorne, Oden sees that inorganic as well as organic reality exists "in an unending continuum of responsive interaction with every other part of cosmic history."[9] Man is thus called to honor the covenant of being in which he lives and moves and has his own being.

In his later thought Oden stresses nature as a part of his covenant ontology. In his earlier work he primarily stresses the interpersonal focus of the covenant. This later natural trend could lessen his orientation to interpersonal experience as the vehicle of the sacred, and thus affect his initial ecstatic commitment. In terms of ecclesial practices, however, it is difficult to tell where Oden's stress on covenant ontology might take him. Certainly he would not go in the biblical-prophetic direction since in that approach nature and the self both are seen as basically "fallen." Neither is imbued with grace in the way Oden's covenant ontology seems to imply. This leaves a cultic direction for Oden's theology. Before we consider this implication, however, we first will deal with his theological notion of kerygma.

b. Kerygma

One of the puzzling aspects of Oden's work is the emphasis he places on the kerygma. He defines kerygma as the proclamation of God's eschatological reign. The final end-time that the kerygma announces is not universal judgment or condemnation as prophetic voices would claim. Rather the kerygma announces "God's caring service to humanity."[10] The idea of caring service draws together theology and psychology. Oden defines "therapeia" to be attentive, caring, and intimate service rendered by a skilled and careful servant. He claims that in the New Testament Jesus Christ is the prototype of the "therapon" or servant. His healing service mediates divine love. Kerygma is the announcement of this significant event in history. "Kerygma complements therapeia by witnessing overtly to the hidden source of healing, the God of all comfort."[11]

One of the challenges that Oden makes to psychotherapists is to acknowledge the ultimate Christian ground of their work. Oden claims that implicit in all theories of effective psychotherapy is the assumption that God loves man. Because God loves man, each individual is lovable. Thus therapists have an ultimate ground for accepting their clients as worthy individuals. Moreover because God revealed Himself uniquely in the historical event of Jesus Christ, it is important that therapists know the historical basis of the love and care they communicate to their clients. This does not mean that therapists are to proclaim Christ to their clients, but it does permit Oden to proclaim Christ to the therapists.

Thus there exists a tension in Oden's thought between proclamation of the kerygma and the communication of divine love at an experiential level. If proclamation is as important as Oden seems to believe it is, then why does he not see it as a mandatory part of the counseling interview? He does not even suggest, strange as it may seem, that proclamation should be the distinguishing mark of pastoral--as opposed to secular--counseling. In practice, they both appear to be the same in that all effective counseling communicates unconditional acceptance to the client. But if proclamation is not a part of counseling practice, why does Oden take such pains to identify the ontological basis of counseling theory? Why does he not let counselors go their unconditionally accepting ways without translating their work into abstruse theological dicta?

The weakness of Oden's kerygmatic claim lies in the fact that there can be ontological bases for the worth of the individual that are not Christian bases. Oden does not acknowledge possibilities in Jewish or Buddhist thought for such a positive regard for the individual. Nor does he acknowledge humanistic claims that see the world as basically benevolent. Nor does he entertain any pragmatic notion that merely believing in individual worth is itself therapeutically effecitve. Moreover, Oden's stress on divine benevolence puts the uniqueness of Christian revelation of ultimate love on shaky grounds. He needs some theological rationale for Anselm's question, "Why did God become man?"

This betrays Oden's notion of sin. If indeed, it is written into the universe that every individual is acceptable, then Christian revelation of this universal truth is not necessary. The implication of Oden's emphasis on kerygma, however, is that somehow this truth does need to be proclaimed. This implies a notion of sin in which man somehow needs the explicit proclamation of divine love in order to operationalize it. [12] Otherwise there would be no necessity of a concrete Christian revelation. Were Oden to develop a Christological rationale for the kerygma, he likely would also develop a rationale for preaching the kerygma. He does not do this, yet there are openings in his work for such a move, particularly in his social theory, to which we now turn.

3. Oden's Societal Choice

Oden explains his social theory in Beyond Revolution: A Response to the Underground Church. [13] Given Oden's previous ecstatic and fulfillment choices, we would logically expect him to select a pluralistic social theory to complete the ecstatic triad. Logically he might move to an understanding of how certain power arrangements in society foster conditions of worth, and conclude that concerned

Christians should form power groupings and voluntary associations to counteract idolatrous societal powers that
suppress individual self-actualization. While the title,
"Beyond Revolution..." indicates that Oden probably is not
employing a dualistic social theory, we get a clue to his
societal inclinations by examining his theory of organization.

. Oden speaks of the Church as an organism. He acknowledges that the contemporary institutional church deserves
much of the criticism it has received for irrelevance and
ineffectiveness. Yet he claims that certain cells of the
ecclesiastical organism can die without the death of the
entire body. He calls for the task of corporate reconstruction of "creating authentic Christian community in our time."[14]

Oden's organismic imagery is a clue that he has taken
a systemic approach to society. Our assessment is supported
when he stresses the importance of the Church as the visible
embodiment of Christ. Oden also turns down dualistic and
pluralistic notions of the Church. He accuses the underground church of pursuing sectarian and separatist practices.
And he criticizes ecstatic ecclesiologies of "the invisible
church" in his concern for some institutional embodiment of
Christian tradition and life. He claims that Christians
cannot rely on "sheer, spontaneous, unstructured, sporadic
charisma without any deliberate concern for historic continuity."[15]

Oden's concern for historic continuity and for a "con-
serving radicalism" of "the living tradition of the apostles,
prophets, and martyrs"[16] suggests a commitment to the systemic notion of culture. He goes on to criticize the calls
for revolutionary destruction of the Church. Yet he nevertheless affirms Marxist criticisms of church practice as
part of the overall dialectical historical process. Oden
does not embrace anything about revolution except its moti-
vational intensity. He claims that Christians cannot truly
conserve traditional values unless they are "willing to wake
up to the revolutionary character of history."[17]

Oden's practical recommendation for church renewal is
the establishment of centers for church experimentation
which would be "living communities of reconciliation" such
as the Ecumenical Institute in Chicago. Oden does not see
these communities as replacements of mainline denominations
however, but rather as catalysts for new forms of church
life. Thus Oden does not take a pluralistic view of these
centers as alternatives to predominant ecclesial patterns in
contemporary culture. Rather these communities would function to enliven existing parts of the church organism.
Though he never elaborates this, his assumptions impel him
toward a basically systemic view of society.

From a trilateral standpoint what is more surprising than Oden's systemic choice for an ecclesiology is some of the conflict assumptions that accompany his ecclesiology. These stand in stark contrast with his previous fulfillment commitments. For instance he says:

> It is by means of institutions that we
> learn to reshape our subjective impulses
> and individual energies into socially
> acceptable forms of behavior. [18]

Oden goes on to affirm how institutions can channel and program individual behavior from generation to generation such that each individual is saved from the "painful and hazardous trial and error process" of learning to live in society. These statements exist in tension with Oden's earlier fulfillment assumptions that the basic personality instincts are pro-social; they are not anti-social impulses that need shaping or programming. Also Oden for the first time mentions human sexuality, an important concern for conflict psychologies, but a secondary concern for most fulfillment theorists.

> Far from being against all instinctual or
> biological urges or drives, institutions
> provide structured means of satisfying
> erotic drives in ways that are not des-
> tructive to the larger social organism. [19]

Thus Oden has made a shift in his psychological theory at the same time he adopts a systemic social theory. Clearly the conflict psychology fits better into a systemic perspective for him. Yet now he emphasizes the needs of the social organism rather than the needs of the individual. In fulfillment psychologies the latter are primary.

Our trilateral analysis has uncovered an important tension in Oden's thought. His choice of societal approaches does not fit with prior psychological choices. One practical implication for Oden involves ecclesiastical practice. Would he change his notion of guilt from moral imperfection to that of moral transgression in order to match his systemic-conflict assumptions? Or is he so committed to individual autonomy and worth that they become prior to the needs of any social organism, including the Church as the embodiment of Christ?

The trilateral tension in Oden's thought also pertains to the tension treated earlier between the proclamation of the kerygma and its concrete communication. From a systemic standpoint, the proclamation of the kerygma is important. Proclamation would be the specifically religious function in a secular society. This would be part of the Church's

mission. In his discussion of the welfare state in America,
Oden, using a typical systemic conception, sees the federal
government as having taken over many church functions. In
many ways, he claims, the government can serve the poor
better than the Church can. What then is the function of
the Church in the welfare state? It is to be a Christian
witness and to become a model of genuine human community.
This notion of witness has a systemic thrust in that the
Church has a particularly religious function in society
that no other institutional body possesses. This fits with
Oden's concern for proclamation of God's love that we mentioned earlier.

Oden's concern for the history and tradition of the
Church can also be connected with his notion of God as
radically for man. However, the systemic concern for culture and tradition would have to be matched by the historical dimension of Oden's covenant ontology. We have seen
how he stresses the interpersonal and natural dimensions of
covenant. To maintain his systemic ecclesiology he would
have to take these systemic elements more seriously than
he does.

4. A Final Assessment

Our trialteral analysis of Thomas Oden's work shows a
fascinating tension between two quite different trilateral
packages. On the one hand he seems to pursue an ecstatic-
fulfillment-pluralistic triad. Here his commitment to
fulfillment psychology is strongest. On the other hand,
Oden is also drawn to a systemic-conflict connection, with
its usual implications for a cultic approach to Christianity.
He does not develop the cultic motif in any depth, yet his
commitment to a systemic ecclesiology is clear.

We have noted Oden's treatment of guilt as moral imperfection. Yet his conflict assumptions move toward the moral
transgression notion of guilt that fits so well into a systemic ecclesiology. Our judgment is that the key to Oden's
theology lies in his Christology, specifically his doctrine
of the atonement. That doctrine brings theories of sin,
guilt, church, and God into a synthesis. Were Oden to pursue the systemic-conflict connection he would need to take
Anselm's atonement theory into account. He does acknowledge the penal-substitutionary theory as the center of all
atonement theories.[20] Yet he does not fully integrate this
insight into the structure of his theology, nor realize its
implications for his choice of psychologies. On the other
hand, were Oden to retain his fulfillment commitment as a
priority, he might pursue what Aulen calls the moral influence theory of the atonement. Christ would then be the
moral exemplar of authenticity.[21]

The tensions in Oden's thought are representative of those in many other contemporary theologians. However he moves subsequently in his theological development, his work stands as a creative synthesis arising from the interchange between theology and the behavioral sciences.

CHAPTER ELEVEN

CHRISTIANITY AND SOCIETY IN TRANSFORMATION:

GUSTAVO GUTIERREZ

We now turn to a theologian whose primary concern is
society rather than personality. Gustavo Gutierrez has been
a central figure in the construction of Christian thought
and practice relevant to Latin America. Well versed in the
classical theological disciplines, Gutierrez has taken
seriously the experiences of the Church in his native Peru
and in the rest of South and Central America. Chief among
these experiences has been the increasing radicalization of
the Church as many of its priests and laity side with the
poor against the centralized powers of business, government,
and the military. This radicalization reached its clearest
articulation in the movement known as Christians for Socialism, which rose during the presidency of Salvador Allende
in Chile in 1971-73. Gutierrez was a major contributor to
the thought of that movement. A Theology of Liberation
has been its chief theoretical exposition.1*

In the course of building an indigenous theology
Gutierrez has engaged the behavioral sciences. We are concerned here with elucidating how he has done this, what his
trilateral choices have been, and how these have raised
certain important critical questions.

A. The Prophetic Starting Point

Gutierrez' loyalties and theory are dominated by a
prophetic thrust drawn from Scripture. The final appeal for
any theological claim is "the Gospel message" (50) or
"Biblical theology" (152). The Kingdom of God (13) appears
constantly as a focus for Christian thought and action. His
central discourse on salvation appeals directly to the notion
of historical action. "The history of salvation is the very
heart of human history" (153). "The prophetic perspective
(in which the Kingdom takes on the present life, transforming it) is vindicated before the sapiential outlook (which

---

*Notes for this chapter begin on page 257.

stresses the life beyond)" (152). God desires justice, not sacrifices (196). The Exodus event emerges repeatedly as the well from which to draw fundamental Christian theology (159).

This prophetic outlook leads him directly to this societal concerns. The Kingdom motif is essentially "political" in the most general sense. Since there is a continuity between the existing creation in history and the future state of redemption, the examination of contemporary political experience and theory is intrinsic to the search for this future Kingdom of God (153-57). Salvation is first of all a political event (though here political is not yet construed in any particular way). Though salvation transcends politics in any usual sense we still must affirm that the political sphere is the door to the kind of salvation portrayed in the Bible.

This search for the political currents leading to salvation is heightened by the realization that all of life is a "yes or a no to the Lord." The choice for the Kingdom is a radical and total choice. While Gutierrez rejects any kind of dualistic choice between the temporal and the spiritual, the flesh and the spirit (166), he repeatedly emphasizes the radical nature of this faith decision. That decision is a deep conversion that breaks with the sin of the past (163).

B. The Societal Choice: Marxism

These commitments and concepts lead Gutierrez directly to the kind of approach to society taken by many Marxists. He takes this direction for a number of reasons. First, the Marxists (and he acknowledges that there is a variety of Marxisms) offer us the clearest and most accurate description of society, especially in Latin America. "Only a class analysis will enable us to see what is really involved in the opposition between oppressed countries and dominant peoples" (37). In other words, Marxism offers us the best "science" of society and history (273). It is therefore the human science closest to the channel of revelation.[2] Secondly, the key distinction of oppressor-oppressed fits well with the sharp oppositions present in the prophets' attack on injustice throughout biblical history. They inveigh against the rich, the powerful and those who "lay field to field" and destroy people's basis for livelihood. Thirdly, only the Marxists offer a vision of the task of the future which accords well with the radical notion of salvation in history. They provide a concrete program for responding to God's promise of a just society. Gutierrez himself does not, except in the first instance, explain why he chooses Marx, but the logic of his choice is clear and understandable.

Having selected Marx he now picks up a number of concepts explicating his theology. Alienation emerges as the foremost "manifestation" of sin (156-57, 173-75, 269). We shall see momentarily why he does not reduce the concept of sin to alienation, but finds that "sin" underlies all alienation. The concept of ideology becomes fundamental for Gutierrez' understanding of theology and mission. No theory or concept can be understood apart from its function in the struggle between the classes. Our eyes must search out right and wrong action rather than right or wrong thoughts, for it is righteousness that is to be achieved.

C. Transforming Christianity with Marxist Categories

Upon return to a Christian context Gutierrez uses the Marxist theory of knowledge to emphasize right doing (orthopraxy) over right thinking (orthodoxy). God's judgment observes the righteousness of our practices rather than the elegance of our thoughts (10,203). The emphasis on right action already indicates an affinity for an equilibrium approach to personality, which we will pick up later. The focus on practice within the Marxist approach to society amplifies his theological conviction and gives a special meaning to the phrase, "critical reflection on praxis." For Gutierrez, all of theology is really a reflection on prior events, actions, and experiences. It is not a sophisticated plan of action or a series of moral objectives thought out ahead of action. Action, like history, is prior to thought. For Gutierrez, "criticism" is not merely a search for consistency or even for congruence of thought and practice. To be critical means to see things from the standpoint of the oppressed and their efforts at liberation (214). It implies the choice of particular societal loyalties, specifically those found in a dualist approach.

Because of his espousal of Marxist loyalties, "revolution" and "socialism" (111) become key symbols for the coming of the Kingdom of God. The extent to which they become complete translations of that Christian symbol is unclear. While he never spells out the meaning of these terms (perhaps because of the very real political and military constraints within which he has had to write and work) they stand as important correctives to any ameliorist notions of redemption or any purely interior redemption of the heart wihtout a radical change away from all forms of capitalism.

In solidifying this connection between a prophetic theology and a dualist social theory Gutierrez is implicitly subordinating or excluding cultic and ecstatic approaches. On the face of it he will be unlikely to emphasize inspired movement over ethical rigor or symbolic anticipation over systematic practical action to overthrow the oppressor.

D. Formal Critical Questions

At this point we must ask to what degree Gutierrez is willing to follow Marx. Might he reduce Christian theology to Marxist theory? Will he reduce Christianity to revolutionary political practice? Does he take on only Marx's theories but not his practices? Will he take on only his practices as the proper mode of Christian action? Or is he merely adding Marxist symbols, theories and practices to his Christianity in an eclectic way?

A close examination of Gutierrez reveals he is not engaged in simple eclecticism. Neither is he going to reduce Christianity to Marxism. Rather, he is engaged in transforming Christianity while respecting its integrity and, to a small extent, transforming the societal perceptions and programs of Marxists around him. How, then, are these purposes evidenced in his work?

E. Gutierrez' Formal Achievement: Sin and Salvation

Gutierrez places very careful constraints around his uses of Marxist concepts at a number of points. When he is construcing his theology he retains traditional Christian terminology in a way that seems to claim that the Christian terms point to something other or more than the Marxist ones. This is especially obvious in his discussion of sin and salvation.

Alienation is not simply equated with sin. Nor is sin simply reduced to alienation. If anything Gutierrez' work suffers from a theological reduction of alienation to sin. The notion of alienation in a general sense leads us into the deeper reality called sin--"the absence of brotherhood and love in relationships among men, the breach of friendship with God and with other men, and, therefore an interior, personal fracture" (175). At the root of all injustice, exploitation, and alienation is the rupturing of "communion" with God and with neighbor (227, 231). It is selfishness, the negation of love (177, 198, 300). In short, Christian theology pushes the notion of alienation to its full conclusion to produce a more extensive notion of human wickedness.

Here we see how his loyalty to the symbols of love and communion leads him to transform the Marxist concept of alienation. The symbol "communion," which we associate generally with cultic motifs, arouses questions about the degree to which Gutierrez will stay within a strictly prophetic and dualistic program. Alienation as unlove and broken communion is different from Marx's original theory of work and productivity, where alienation meant a violation of human capacity to produce expressions of the self. This major change in the meaning of alienation signals an openness to alternative approaches to personality and society.

In parallel fashion Gutierrez can offer a more expansive notion of liberation to match his notion of sin. Liberation occurs at three mutually interpenetrating levels in history--the level of the class struggle for political liberation, the level of the general liberation of man throughout history, and liberation from sin and admission to communion with God (36, 176).

This complex notion of sin and liberation is the fulcrum of Gutierrez' critical appropriation of Marx. On the one hand he wants to lead Christians to practices which engage radical movements for political, social, and economic change. On the other hand, without undercutting that commitment he wants to point to the necessity for dealing with the whole person and with ultimate forms of broken communion (150-52, 205). His intent seems to be however, not merely to add radical action onto traditional forms of Christian piety, but to present new kinds of spirituality which integrate personality with a political commitment (203-8). That is, he is concerned with reconstructing both the personal and societal aspects of Christian faith.

F. Gutierrez' Transformation of Christianity
via the Three Levels

Gutierrez is trying to reform Christian theology. He is neither reducing Marxism to Christianity nor is he simply translating Christianity into Marxist terminology and practice. The division of sin and salvation into three levels of salvation history is the means for this delicate interchange.

By presenting us with three levels of liberation he can adopt Marxism in a more selective, less reductionistic way. He seems to use the word "level" in the sense of "dimension," for the three levels occur simultaneously rather than successively. The Marxist categories relate first of all to the first level. At that point Gutierrez warmly embraces some auxiliary themes in Marxist theory. Salvation in this sense is very much a matter of man's self-creation in history (173). Here he strongly rejects traditional ideas of God's total initiative in saving humanity. The political kingdom is not a gift but the result of human struggle. To say otherwise is an ideological ploy to create passivity in the masses.

The second level of liberation accents the utopian dimension in Marxism. However, by lifting up the picture of "the whole man in history" it begins to move beyond any strictly economic or political change and emphasizes a

205

change in culture and personality. This effort is still
very much a matter of human initiative and action, however.

     With regard to the third level, however, the Kingdom
of God is very much a gift (153, 159, 177, 205, 227, cf.
218). Gutierrez does not carefully distinguish his earlier
appropriation of the idea of self-creation from that of
receiving a gift. This unclarity is not resolved by a more
systematic transformation of theological categories by
behavioral ones. (For instance, the Marxist notion of the
transpersonal inevitability of revolution could corroborate
or explicate the idea of Kingdom as gift.) In fact, at this
point he seems to turn to personality concerns to explicate
his theology.

     Close reading indicates that this redemptive gift
involves primarily psychological dynamics. The specifically
Christian motifs which have not undergone Marxist translation are now implicity directed to psychological theories.
The third level redemption offered by Christ otherwise
stand in a rather lofty abstraction in comparison with his
more practically related notions of liberation. Here
Gutierrez must also seek to tell us practically how we
encounter Christ or how he redeems us, at least in some
preliminary way. The dynamics here demand psychological
examination. Gutierrez' Christian expansion of Marxism
leads him to personality concerns.

G. The Personality Option:
The Meaning of "Conversion"

     One of the principal symbols of personal transforma-
tion is, for Gutierrez, "conversion" (194-208).

> Conversion means a radical transformation
> of ourselves; it means thinking, feeling,
> and living as Christ--present in exploited
> and alienated man. To be converted is
> to commit oneself to the process of the
> liberation of the poor and oppressed, to
> commit oneself lucidly, realistically, and
> concretely. It means to commit oneself
> not only generously, but also with an
> analysis of the situation and a strategy
> of action (205).

This focus on transformed behavior evinces an equilibrium
bias. The equilibrium approach focuses on a change in external behavior first. This behavioral change then creates
whatever other changes may arise in the thought and motivation of the self. These changes result from the presence
of new and different external stimuli. In Gutierrez' framework they are the preached word of God as well as the real

demands of the poor and the horrors perpetrated by the ruling class in order to defend its wealth. In conversion we change our social location in the class structure so that objectively we experience solidarity with the oppressed. We enter into their environment. Under the impact of that condition our minds are transformed and we meet the Lord in the oppressed. Indeed, in a very firm sense the oppressed are the channel of God's grace and presence among men (210-12).

The biblical anchor for Gutierrez' understanding of God's presence and man's conversion and liberation is Matthew 25:31-46, in which Jesus tells the parable concerning God's basis for judging us. We will be justified or condemned on the basis of our treatment of "the least of these," for in helping or hurting them we have helped or hurt Christ. This emphasis on specific actions toward the oppressed implies that conversion can never be merely a solitary act of the mind, a purely personal experience. It is simply the outcome of being placed in a particular social location. As we have shown earlier, this equilibrium move is typical of those who adopt prophetic and dualist orientations.

However, Gutierrez himself specifically mentions Freud, the major conflict theorist, when he turns to personality. Where and how does he carry out this thrust? This conflict interpretation of salvation seems to operate most effectively with regard to the third level of liberation--that from sin itself and from estrangement from God.

The first manifestation of sin is selfishness. Selfishness is the motivation behind all misery, exploitation, and injustice. This already begins to depart from the Marxist preoccupation with the objective, trans-moral forces producing human misery. The dualism in society is rooted in a deeper conflict within the self. The militant Marxist is simply not interested in selfishness, other than in terms of pleasure-pain response familiar to the equilibriumist. But for Gutierrez the curbing of selfishness is crucial to human liberation (110). But how is this to be done?

Gutierrez' own tantalizingly brief efforts in this direction yield little, partly because he has not explored this realm and partly because his previous commitments pull him back from pursuing a conflict approach on its own terms. Either he is pulled back into an equilibrium approach, which implies that one's selfish interests would synchronize with those of the oppressed, or he takes a fulfillment tack, in which God's gratuitous offer of His presence draws out our latent love for all people. In the first our selfishness is justified by being seen as the instrument of God to liberate the oppressed and righteous class in conflict over

against the evil oppressors. In the second our selfishness
as an evil is eradicated by meeting the legitimate needs we
all have for support and self-expression. Neither of these
explorations are taken very far. From a trilateral perspective this is a deficiency in his work.

It is difficult to sort these matters out, however,
because of the ambiguous use of the term "man" throughout
the book. The generic term "man" is a basic flaw from a
trilateral perspective, since it does not distinguish
between individuals and societies (46-8, 57, 218). We do
not know whether "man" (as in mankind) is a collective en-
tity (perhaps having some representative in the chief
officer of some government or association) or is merely a
cover term pointing to certain psychological characteristics
held in common by everyone. A more careful distinction
between his psychological and societal referents would have
prevented Gutierrez from making this confusion, which,
apart from its sexist connotations, seems so harmless in the
context of theological discourse.

Even these few invitations to psychological explorations can, however, be tentatively related to Gutierrez'
three levels of liberation. The psychological options can
possibly be related to each of these levels. Equilibrium
approaches seem to be tied to the first level, fulfillment
views to the second and conflict perspectives to the third.
However, we have also seen that a fulfillment assumption
underlies his notion of our conversion-response to God's
free gift on the third level.

Another way he may be using these personality options
is to match them with different social classes. At some
points his Marxist theory makes him differentiate between
oppressor and oppressed classes (214, 273). Sometimes it
seems as if selfishness (a conflict analysis on the surface)
describes the sin of the ruling class, while dependence,
a negative self-image and lack of self-worth (a fulfillment
analysis), characterizes the oppressed class. The upper
class needs liberation from their selfishness (a conflict
view) while the lower class need liberation from external
blockage (a fulfillment approach). The practices for
converting from this situation seem to revolve around the
equilibrium practice of changing the conditions that
produce these two responses. This kind of synthesis would
make sense within Gutierrez' general framework.

The distinction between classes is, at two points,
seemingly reduced to the categories of Freudian analysis
(30, 96). The opposed forces in society are seen as repli-
cations of the opposed forces of the psyche--a crucial shift
in reference characteristic of Freudian Marxists like
Herbert Marcuse.[3] That is to say, the concept of repression

in Freud is selected because it fits nicely Marx's concept
of oppression. The over-class, by oppressing the under-
class, represses its natural drives, thus creating all kinds
of deviancies. But this is definitely not what Freud meant,
since it was society as a whole, not a ruling class, which
stood over against the primitive drives of the self.

In holding that the ruling class represses the natural
drives of the oppressed, Gutierrez moves in a fulfillment
direction, in which our natural feelings, far from being
potential tyrants over us, are in need of liberation. Thus
Gutierrez, far from being a Freudian, moves back and forth
between equilibrium and fulfillment choices. In practice,
however, we are caused to wonder how it comes about that a
member of the ruling class would choose to convert to the
oppressed class. Marx tended to choose a deterministic
answer (the evolution of the forces of production), but
Gutierrez has none other than to appeal to the impact of
Christian preaching and teaching within the environment of
the Church.

H. Societal Implications of Psychological Options

From a tri-lateral standpoint the inadequate exploration of these differences implies an inadequate consideration of the parallel differences in the societal and Christian realms. Not only is his psychological practice still
unclear with regard to appropriate "client" (the oppressor
or the oppressed), but his way of combining perspectives
within a discipline and of linking them with perspectives
from other fields is unclear as well.

For instance, let us assume that Gutierrez basically
oscillates between fulfillment and equilibrium approaches.
According to trilateral logic, he would correlatively move
betwen pluralist and dualist societal approaches. Having
raised awareness of this possibility we find evidence of it
in numerous places. In combatting rigid dualism he opposes
reducing the gospel to a "revolutionary ideology" that would
"distort reality" (a societal concern) and "oversimplify
the Gospel" (a Christian one) (271). Though he understands
the repressive situation which forces revolutionary groups
to suppress internal debate, he still opposes such restrictions on free expression (103). He tempers his loyalty to
revolutionary resistance with a different loyalty to openness, expression, and pluralism. Simultaneously he is very
concerned, however, that criticisms of church solidarity
with the oppressed not become merely another excuse for
continued oppression. The choice posed by dualistic analysis must always be prior to any criticism (271).

While this tension seems to be a manageable one, it
does not adequately deal with the pluralistic claim that

209

some social plurality is necessary in order to ensure an order of justice for minorities. The Christian symbol of communion, which is central for Gutierrez, links up easily with those of solidarity, brotherhood, and even equality (259, 263, 268). In giving these symbols societal form he tends to find himself among the radical dualists rather than the pluralists, for they are more congenial to this recovery of solidarity and communion. The power evidenced in the clash of interest groups is to be replaced by loving service (98, 198-200). The manifold ways in which persons and groups determine the action of others is to be transcended in mutual empathy. As a political formula this utopian vision has almost universally been impossible to fulfill. Either it demands a radical change of personality or it demands the application of force. In the former case it demands a very small city of the elite, such as the Greek polis. In the latter the means contradict the very vision of communion and love.

Therefore, in practice dualistic analysis with a commitment to love usually moves to a systemic or pluralist program. In the former, practitioners and theorists find a way to fit everyone into a functional network of relationships that takes account of each persons' unalterable attributes (their "talents"). In the second, they search for a way of letting powers seek their own expression within a framework of minimum consensus and law--balancing power against power rather than trying to eliminate it. Pluralists and systemics alike criticize dualist practices because they inevitably lead to the use of force in order to "liberate oppressors from themselves" (276).

We must not be led here, and Gutierrez is not, to discussion of non-violence from a purely inter-personal perspective. In recognizing "the autonomy of the political realm" Gutierrez wants to deal with human affairs as they are in order to transform them. The question concerns the ends for which force is to be used, not the inherent value of force. "Love," when interpreted dualistically, entails the use of force to secure the best interests, the true good, of others. The criterion of justice is love. Justice is brotherhood, equality and, ultimately, communion. Love, when taken pluralistically, could entail the use of force to defend the publicly acknowledged rights of others, regardless of whether protection of rights guarantees the good, much less the ideals of brotherhood, equality and communion.

The question facing Gutierrez as he tries to take in some pluralistic motifs is how, in a class war, to legitimate law and secure its benefits for all. Clarity about the desirability of achieving such pluralist values would help Gutierrez discriminate more precisely between acceptable and unacceptable revolutionary actions.

In general Gutierrez has launched his criticism of dualist practices on the basis of his Christian loyalties and theology. He affirms that the Kingdom of God always transcends and advances ahead of particular fulfillments within history. The Kingdom of God is fulfilled only in a final communion with the Lord--an affirmation which tends to oppose a personality loyalty to a societal one rather than to clarify in societal terms what the symbol of "kingdom" demands.

Secondly Gutierrez has preserved a critical view by picking up a central (often called a revisionist) theme of Marx; namely, that practice is not the wooden application of a dogma but has its own autonomy in order to deal with changing circumstances effectively. Thus, Marx takes on a methodological priority--a commitment to flexible and objective analyses of present situations. Gutierrez uses self-corrective theories within Marxism.

What he does not do is to entertain with seriousness alternative societal theories to critique his Marxist choice. Affirmation of the class struggle as a scientific "fact" deters him from flexibility at the level of theory. We are trying to show here that critique from a wider range of societal options would in fact enhance the precision of his analysis and selection of practices, even within his dualist commitment.

I.   System, Sacrament and Liberation:
The Christian Synthesis

While Gutierrez is reluctant to endorse any specific program of church action, he does endorse a strategy flowing in reality from a systemic analysis of the relation of church and society in Latin America (224-25). Because the Church exercises the entire function of social integration and in most part socialization and education, the Church's message and symbolic acts are very powerful and necessary parts of social change (106, 122). While he neither desires nor foresees the Church maintaining its special and privileged position in Latin America, he is willing to use its present powers to further the advance of the oppressed class. His book could be read, however, as a plea for the Church to permeate the whole society with its true essence. The criticism of the Church in the past is that it restricted Christian mission to a few priestly and religious elites and pursued only an otherworldly purpose. Thus, while the cultural practices of the Church in this systemically perceived situation might be apparent, the practices after this interim situation are much less so.

At the least, however, Gutierrez sets forth two societal principles for·the Church of the future. It will be
clearly separated from the state (115) and will clearly
be affiliated with the poor and the oppressed (114-116). It
is not clear of course how far he wants to take the plural-
ization and consequent secularization this separation of
Church and state implies. At what point would his plea for
the goal of solidarity, equality, brotherhood and communion
offset pluralism and freedom? His pluralist commitments do
not produce an answer to such questions. They function
first of all to temper the practical implications of his
dualistic preferences.

His dualist emphasis leads him to take the cultural
function of the Church away from the legitimizing of the
state or dominant powers and attach it to the promotion of
the work and aspirations of the oppressed. The Church can
then play the cultural function of legitimizing the "system" of the under-class or oppressed culture. This appears
to be the meaning of the Church's participation in the
"cultural revolution" which must undergird the political-
economic one. Without this broader revolution and the
personality change it entails the political battle will
become ineffective or narrowly totalitarian.

The practices flowing from this change of referent
for the Church's cultural function appear to be analogous
to those the Church has played within the previous system--
freeing individuals from false guilt, anxiety, and other
impediments to their proper socialization, while also providing the common themes, loyalties and symbols uniting
them with one another in a common historical project. This
notion of the Church's mission, so familiar to systemic
theorists, implies that Gutierrez here is finally picking
up some cultic motifs. Indeed, chapter twelve of A Theology
of Liberation is devoted to the Church as "the sacrament of
history." What does this phrase mean theoretically and
practically?

Some readers, knowing that Gutierrez is a Roman
Catholic priest, might have expected him to take a cultic
direction, but we have tried to show that the prophetic
orientation firmly directs his thought and action. The
prophetic motifs take up and give meaning to themes usually
found in the other approaches to Christianity. In this case
the prophetic orientation seizes upon two key themes usually
associated with a cultic one--communion and sacrament. The
tie between the two is the concept of Eucharist. The Eucharist is the central sacrament. Moreover, the essence of
the Eucharist is the communion celebrated there among people
and between them and God.

Sacrament takes a peculiar turn of interpretation here

212

because Gutierrez has already expressed the idea that the
oppressed class is the mediator with the divine in history.
We find Christ in the oppressed (201). We receive the grace
of conversion in solidarity with the oppressed (159, 200).
The theme of sacrifice so familiar in cultic approaches
to Eucharist is also seen at a different angle. The Eucharist is a feast of remembrance in which we experience the
joy arising in our conversion toward solidarity with the
oppressed. It is truly a pass-over meal. The dualist and
prophetic perspectives give Eucharist a meaning rarely
seen in traditional cultic approaches.

In all of this the oppressed emerge in effect as
channels of grace. Through them and their efforts at self-
liberation the fullness of liberation takes place in the
world. They are, to pick up Marxist themes, the leading
edge of historical transformation. The Church should be in
the very vanguard of this movement. We border here on
saying that the oppressed are the invisible, true Church.
But Gutierrez does not quite say that. Christianity, including its institutions, still has its own integrity,
perhaps we could even say its own essence. However, it is
not clear what legitimacy is left for an ecclesiastical
organization apart from the organizations of the oppressed.
To say this would raise the possibility of the Church
criticizing or opposing the organizations of that class.
For tactical reasons alone (keep in mind the political
nature of his book) Gutierrez does not say this. We are
led to ask, however, what would he want to say on this
point?

The Church is the sacrament of history in the sense,
then, that it is the Church of the oppressed. It is the
oppressed who are the Church and the Church as institution
functions within that oppressed group in the same way that
we normally think of the sacraments functioning in the
Church--to nourish, strengthen, and give ultimate vision
to the members. In short, the oppressed, through their
struggle, make the grace that exists in the Church visible
and manifest (259-62).

By seeing communion as the goal of liberation Gutierrez has been able to introduce allied cultic themes. But
he has tried to avoid the usual systemic social implications
of a cultic approach by seeing the oppressed class as the
proper social partner for the Church. Thus the cultic
themes are integrated into a dominantly prophetic approach.
The basic prophetic-dualist connection remains intact but
enriched by attention to cultic and systemic claims.

J. Concluding Remarks

We have tried to open up the work of Gustavo Gutierrez

as a set of choices within and among the three disciplinary realms. In some respects we have seen stark and clear commitments which permeate his method for handling a wide range of considerations, especially in ecclesiology and theology. In other respects we have found that he has not clarified his progress, especially in the realm of personality. In yet other cases we have suggested some moves by which he might improve the pursuit of his primary triad.

Even within this brief but careful examination, A Theology of Liberation ranks as a sophisticated and challenging effort to transform theological and societal theories and practices. He has acknowledged the integrity of the disciplines and yet pursued some very daring transformations. The balance and the complexity of the moves (as with the notion of three levels of liberation) by which he tries to hold together various elements without departing markedly from a primary triad indicate that it will have an enduring validity and usefulness as a major trilateral interchange. We look forward especially to a further development of the personality implications of his present position.

PART V

TRILATERAL ANALYSIS

We began this journey into the theology-behavioral science interchange with a brief overview of its history and with a proposal for critical interdisciplinary thinking. From there we singled out two influential figures in current theology-behavioral science conversations--Carl Rogers and Saul Alinsky. We identified critical problems in the way theologians have engaged their practices, loyalties, and theories.

In Part II we systematically organized the three disciplines dealing with Christianity, personality, and society as they appear in relation to one another. In the resulting typology of approaches we identified certain ongoing motifs and patterns that characterize interdisciplinary exchanges.

In Part III we set forth a formal trilateral schema by which we could better understand and evaluate the work of theologians and behavioral scientists. In proposing hypotheses about the primary and secondary patterns of interdisciplinary relations, we laid the basis for critical analysis. This was then combined with various ways of approaching the problem of congruence among the dimensions of loyalty, theory, and practice.

In Part IV we exposed the formal values intrinsic to our method--integrity, comprehensiveness, congruence, and reciprocal transformation. We also pointed out the importance of clarifying the substantive commitments with which one enters the complex process of analysis, critique, and transformation. We then analyzed certain critical issues in the work of Thomas Oden and Gustavo Gutierrez in order to bring out the nature of critical trilateral analysis more clearly.

In Part V we explore some uses of trilateral analysis and its implications for the theological concept of faith, catholicity, and incarnation.

CHAPTER TWELVE

TRILATERAL ANALYSIS: RETROSPECT AND PROSPECT

A. Trilateral Analysis: The Retrospect

Through our trilateral schema we have sought to lay
the basis for an imaginative and fruitful exploration of the
vistas that have been opening in recent years for participants on both theological and behavioral sides. This book
provides an entree to the interchange, sets forth some directions for   analysis and criticism, and indicates tasks yet
to be accomplished by participants' efforts at reciprocal
transformation. All of these steps have been an effort to
consolidate and advance interdisciplinary interchange. We
have been especially concerned about advancing the conversation along two lines--from bilateral to trilateral engagement, and from precritical to critical engagement.

1. From Bilateral to Trilateral Interchange

The very structure of our presentation calls for
participants to move from a bilateral relation between theology and behavioral science to a trilateral one that recognizes the two distinct realms of personality and society.
It can also be interpreted as an invitation to behavioral
scientists to move beyond their own disciplinary boundaries
to take up the challenges of the other two disciplines.

While for the psychological and sociological participants this is an invitation, for the theologians it is a
demand, since, as we believe, no Christian can long escape
the societal implications of God's law and Kingdom or the
personality implications of sanctification and love. Under
the conditions of the world as we know it, these implications require an engagement with the behavioral sciences.
The only question concerns the degree of critical awareness
and comprehension with which it is entered.

Trilateralism may appear to some as an attempt to
water down traditional Christian theories and practices. It
is meant, however, to enrich and revitalize them through an
engagement with contemporary thought and practice. It may
appear to others as an attempt to fragment theology by
diverting concern to behavioral science. However, it is an

217

attempt to show how many of the arguments and debates that
divide Christians actually involve choices and commitments
within the realms of society and personality. Theological
conversation can be advanced only by clarifying and resolving these polarities. The arguments between "evangelical"
and "liberal" Christians in the United States has surely
been intensified and confused by these implicit behavioral
choices.

Our call to trilateralism reflects one of our basic
formal values, that of comprehensiveness. It goes hand in
hand with our effort to move the conversation to a more
critical level.

2.   From Precritical to Critical Interchange

Earlier we described a number of exchanges between
theology and the behavioral sciences. In particular we
pointed out some of the diverse ways psychotherapy and
community organizing have offered stimulating ideas, practices, and even symbols to ministers and theologians. In
many cases these interdisciplinary exchanges occur at an
intuitive or common sense level. Our perspective, by
contrast, operates on a formal, critical level.

In Chapter One we identified the three steps necessary
to such a critical approach. Within each step we located
some major critical pitfalls. We emphasized the importance
of making interdisciplinary distinction, of drawing accurate
relations among dimensions and approaches, and of creating
changes through a process of interdisciplinary transformation. In moving through these three steps we tried to advance the interchange from a posture of reductionism to one
of reciprocal transformation. We presented ways it could
move from eclecticism to systematization. We showed the
range of concerns it would have to embrace in order to move
from isolation to comprehensiveness.

In this way formal analysis can refine, complement,
and expand the inspirations of intuitive interdisciplinary
exchanges. In effect, we have presented a kind of grammar
for interdisciplinary conversation. Precritical analysis
is similar to the intuitive acquisition and use of our
mother tongue. Critical analysis is like the formal gram-
matical concepts and rules we acquire only through conscious
education.

Furthermore, trilateral grammar is not only descriptive of how people are conversing. It is a norm for how
they ought to speak. For instance, our description of
perennial primary and secondary triads implies that certain
interdisciplinary logics are stronger than others. Depar-
tures from these triads evidence either inconsistencies

218

or novel syntheses. Yet these risks of inconsistency, irrelevance, and novelty must be taken in order to honor the values of comprehensiveness within and among the three disciplines.

We tried to expose some of the dynamics of this necessary tension in the work of Oden and Gutierrez. We found that Oden did not follow the ecstatic and fulfillment implications of his thought with a pluralistic social theory, but instead chose a more systemic approach. Having picked up certain conflict strains in his personality approach as well, he fell into tension with his earlier client-centered assumptions about personality and with his earlier recommendations for ecstatic liturgical practices.

Similarly, Gutierrez' attempt to pursue all three personality orientations requires that he define more specifically in practice the meaning of these choices, both within and outside the Church. His preference for Marxist approaches to society resonates with his prophetic theological choice and supports the equilibrium strains in his thought. But the dualistic motifs in this Marxist choice stand in tension with fulfillment notions of personality and also with the cultic thrusts in his theology. These tensions identify the key points of necessary development in his own work.

Such critical analyses rest on the earlier descriptive work in the book. The metaphor of grammar directs our attention to the two kinds of critique we have presented--a formal description and a normative challenge.

B. The Prospect: Uses of the Trilateral Scheme

We have found our trialteral scheme to be useful in five ways--as a general mode of critical analysis, as a guide for theological construction, as a pedagogical tool, as a means of comparative religious study, and as a framework for church consultation.

1. As a General Mode of Critical Analysis

Our general intent to present a mode of analysis should be clear. We need to add two remarks concerning the way it is to be used. First, we have tried to stress that we are not presenting a taxonomy but an ideal typology. Some readers may be tempted to use these categories, especially the identification of approaches, as boxes into which reality must be crammed, even with danger to intellectual life and limb. The problem with a taxonomic approach is not merely that of Procrusteanism, however. More importantly, it deflects our attention from the tensions, alternatives, implications, and decisions among

219

various emphases. When applied taxonomically to any profound author, the scheme might seem trivial because he or
she might seem to fit in every category. But, used as a
device for asking questions in an ideal-typical way, it
becomes a means for locating the tensions and issues in
that person's thought and practice.

Secondly, it should be clear that these analytical
tools--the concepts, the scheme, the logic--are "second-
order" language. They are not the immediate "first order"
language of simple description. These terms, such as
dualist, systemic, or fulfillment, are not necessarily used,
or used in these particular ways, by participants in these
interchanges. Rather, they are a means for examining the
general emphases and patterns of relationships they pursue.

People using the scheme should be careful to distinguish their own way of understanding or acting from the
viewpoints of others. For instance, I may see a situation
as being, on the basis of empirical observations, best
described from a dualist societal position. However, the
participants may see it as being systemic. Or similarly,
I may, in reading an author, see basically fulfillment and
cultic patterns. However, the author, while giving lip
service to the symbols usually associated with these
approaches, may actually be using them in a conflict and
ecstatic way. In short, people utilizing the scheme must
distinguish clearly between their own viewpoint and that of
others. Moreover, they must be careful to see key symbols,
concepts, and practices in the context of an overall
approach in order to identify accurately what is going on.

2. As a Guide for Theological Construction

The scheme can also function as a guide or checklist
for putting together a trilateral combination of thought,
loyalty and practice. Thus, whether people are assessing
the work of others, as we have with Oden and Gutierrez, or
developing their own position, the scheme is a helpful map
of pitfalls to avoid and of possible avenues to pursue.
Certainly the scheme is not a recipe for instant promul-
gations. It challenges us to go beyond simple acknowledg-
ments of alternatives or curt rejections of opponents. It
is a scheme grounded in and committed to interdisciplinary
dialogue.

3. As a Pedagogical Tool

The trilateral scheme has an important teaching use.
Like any pedagogical tool, it should not be confused with
the end product of substantive thought. For instance, just
as a therapist has a theory about a client's behavior and
may use that theory in treating a client without divulging

220

it to him, so teachers can use the trilateral scheme in a parallel way. Ascertaining students' interests in the theological realm, we often suggest they read authors is the behavioral fields who would complement their theological commitments. We have also suggested that students famili- arize themselves with positions that are quite contrary to their own so that they may more adequately articulate the reasons for their basic personality, societal, or Christian convictions. Teachers may use the trilateral scheme in such ways without directly exposing students to the formal scheme. We have found in addition, however, the exposure to it enables students to gain a wider grasp of interdisciplinary dialogue and be more critical of their own substantive commitments.

4. As a Basis for Comparative Religious Studies

The trilateral map can also be helpful in ordering the interchanges between other religious standpoints and behav- ioral sciences. We have restricted our focus to Christianity, but we see no reason why materials from Judaism, Islam, or Hinduism could not be handled in a similar way. especially to the degree that they are dealing with Western behavioral science. However, we suspect that the more an interchange departs from this Christian or North Atlantic context the more general and abstract the contributions of the scheme might become. However, our selection of a Christian focus has not been intended to imply an antipathy toward this kind of critical effort in other religious and cultural contexts. Quite the contrary, we welcome and encourage it.

The scheme could also provide a basis for comparing the behavioral affinities of various religions along with Christianity. Do the same kinds of affinities exist in Hinduism? What crucial connections or lacunae dictate different patterns of relating personality and society to the religious life? How have each of these other religions constructed their psychologies and sociologies? How might they be responding in different and unique ways to the impact of Western behavioral science?

Judaism would probably provide the easiest alternative case for the use of trilateral analysis. David Bakan has already examined the relation of Freud's conflict psychology with Jewish mysticism. Since we would expect a more cultic companion for Freud, Bakan's claims would raise the question of the relation between Christian sacramentalism and Jewish mysticism. Other studies have shown the deep connection between Karl Marx and the tradition of biblical prophecy. The scheme might provide a way to discriminate among the varieties of prophetic religion in Judaism and Christianity and how these have affected their interchange with Marx. Finally, the works of major figures such as Martin Buber and Abraham Heschel could be examined for the interplay of personality and social theory in their own expositions.

In Hinduism we find numerous analogs to our Christian typology. An ecstatic emphasis is expressed in various forms of mysticism, such as Vedanta, Buddhism, and devotionalism (Bhakti). Hinduism manifests a variety of cultic tendencies stemming from Vedic and Tantric traditions. The prophetic orientation is, however, muted, appearing only occasionally in millenialistic-like movements. The cultic tradition clearly follows a set of affinities similar to that in the West, taking in the caste system and various kinds of asceticism.

On the other hand, the development of alternative Indic psychologies, such as the notions of "no-self" and non-duality, can be seen as the result of pressures from more ecstatic adherents, especially those influenced by Buddhism. Buddhism itself developed a more pluralistic thrust in the practice of assembling monks in self-sufficient congregations (samgha). The dynamics of the prophetic triad might help interpret India's seeming ideological resistance to Communism as well as the rise of various forms of Marxism in Kerala, the one area traditionally influenced by "religions of the Word."

Even these brief speculations indicate that the spirit of trilateral analysis could be applied in other arenas. It invites a more critical and comparative analysis of these materials and provides a way of entering into a comparison with Western and Christian developments.

5. As a Framework for Church Consultation

The scheme can also be used as a framework for consultation with decision makers. In this case we have in mind especially officers in church organizations. It is a way for charting the considerations that need to be taken into account in a decision. It provides some categories for ordering the immense amount of data present in any decision that seeks to be theoretically as well as practically appropriate to the loyalties of the organization.

For example, denominational bodies are frequently confronted in recent times with the necessity for evaluating and reorganizing their social service projects and agencies. Churches, inasmuch as they seek to set forth some kind of message before the world, should not make these judgments simply on the basis of success values present in organizations or in therapeutic practices. The priest needs to inquire into the relation of sacrament to community organizing. Ministers ask whether self-acceptance or forgiveness is the final word about guilt and reconciliation. These are theological questions. They require us to identify the values and loyalties present in a particular sociological or psychological description and evaluation. They move us to trace the theological grounds of behavioral claims. Is this agency's pattern of operation, the way the staff is organized, the way clients relate to professionals, and the way the operation is funded express the basic loyalties and values of the Church? Is the pattern of the agency congruent with the ecclesiology of the denomination? Are therapeutic practices congruent with the societal practices sponsored by the denomination? Where are the points of actual or possible conflict?

The discussion of triads and congruence offers a way into this labyrinth of questions and connections. It enables a denomination to spell out the connection between its pastoral counseling programs and its community organizing projects. Then it can trace the possible connections or disjunctions between these and the actual claims and loyalties of the Church.

As a tool in decision making the scheme can help church leaders and officials bring greater coherence and theological rigor to their organizational and pastoral efforts. It can help identify their mainstream commitments and the possible ways subordinate themes can be related to them. Finally, it can help interdenominational bodies find an appropriate complementarity among efforts springing from different theologies and organizational emphases. It can help identify ways that ecumenical efforts can divide up societal and personal ministries in order to express the strengths of the respective traditions, rather than having each denomination carry a thin commitment to every possible approach.

C. Trilateral Criticism: Some Theological Implications

At this point we can look back at some methodological and theological assumptions that have emerged in the course of our work. In this concluding section we want to point out three areas of fruitful theological reflection raised by our methodology. It is always tempting in such an enterprise to inflate the theological grounds or significance of things. We are tempted to overuse analogy so that all the components of trilateral analysis fit classical theological categories, such as divinity and humanity, grace and nature, sin and salvation. Or, in the way of theological apologia, we are tempted to "proof text" our work with appeals to traditional formulations. Conversely, we are tempted to reconstruct theology completely by filling it with the new meanings offered by trilateral method. All

223

of this would constitute a premature closure indeed. In
the spirit of our own method we must pursue a more modest
course. We will show in a preliminary fashion how our
methodological position might engage three classic motifs
in Christianity--faith, catholicity, and incarnation.

1. Behavioral Science Partners and the Meaning of Faith

We have selected the behavioral sciences as the primary partners for theology and ministry. This decision is
not meant as an exclusion of other possible partners, such
as philosophy, literature, or the arts. But it does mean
that the behavioral sciences stand at the center. The
spotlight falls on them.

For those grounded in traditional and contemporary
philosophy, our effort might be interpreted as an excursion
in ontology. It is an effort to get at the nature of
things. It attempts to interpret "being." That it is.
But it is also a rejection to a large degree of the discourse, concepts, and methods associated with philosophies
of "being," such as we find in Tillich, Heidegger, or
Sartre. It is not merely a matter of their claims, whatever they might mean. It is a matter of their frame of
reference. To be precise, it is a matter of their distance
from practice, practical theory and the issues of congruence
created by values. The language of "being" (or equally the
language of "freedom") tends toward an idealism that masks
over matters of practice and loyalty. It tends inevitably
to be ideological. Therefore, our avoidance of ontological
discourse is a systematic one grounded in our formal critical values.

Similarly, our choice of the behavioral sciences for
a theological partner also implies a choice of epistemology.
It assumes a certain approach to the process of knowing.
Theologians have, for many centuries, used a model of knowing that is based on a model drawn from the physical sciences. It assumes that language and thought are efforts to
point to something else that stands beyond human affairs,
practically in a spatial sense. To be sure, subordinate
groups within Christianity have tried to emphasize a different approach to knowing and speaking. Under the impact of
interchange with the behavioral sciences, however, these
undercurrents are now gaining the ascendancy. They emphasize knowing as a dimenion of action and valuation. In
Gutierrez' words, it is "reflection of praxis." Jürgen
Habermas points in the same direction with his concept of
interested knowledge. Our own effort here flows in the
same stream.

This kind of method takes very seriously the significance of persons, institutions, and practices as bearers

of thought, symbol, and value. The meaning of these arises
in the pattern of congruence (or incongruence) articulated
by practice, theory and loyalty. This view of knowledge
is a systematic assumption of the trilateral scheme.

All of these methodological choices and emphases stand
in a mutually reinforcing position with a central understanding of faith. Common to all three approaches in Christianity is the understanding that faith is intimately bound
up with action. How those two dimensions are related of
course varies, as we have seen. But the concept of faith
first of all points to the need for some kind of congruence
among the three dimensions of loyalty, theory, and practice.
Faith is an effort at Christian congruence. Faith and
righteousness are intimately bound together.

In bringing the formal critical value of congruence
into relation with faith, we are reminded of Carl Rogers,
for whom the term "congruence" has explicit theoretical
and practical meaning. Indeed, he would most probably
applaud this conjunction. If we were to reduce faith to
congruence in this respect it would become that kind of
knowing which grasps both our personal experience and our
loyalty to God.

But of course congruence has a more general meaning.
We have already pointed out its importance, in the sense
of "praxis," for Marxist sociologists. Here faith means
that kind of congruence which enables persons and even
institutions to go beyond ideological forms of knowledge.
Indeed, a number of Christian theologians have turned to
the concept of de-ideologization to spell out the contemporary meaning of faith. Faith therefore becomes an
institutional quality as well as a personal one. It is a
quality which could be assigned to the church as such. It
would denote its pattern of institutional congruence.

Faith points not only to an institutional quality, but
also to a historical and traditional qualification of our
present life. Or, to put it differently, in being institutional it is historical. We have tried to speak as much
of Christianity as of theology. We have tried to recall
that the religious partner here is bound up in a whole complex of practice, theory and loyalty. Each of the partners
has a practical, institutional base. Each of them has a
history. The present pattern of congruence (or incongruence) has its history, its memory, its precedents. Faith
as congruence therefore, is always part of this history
and memory. The struggle for faithfulness always arises in
this relation of received patterns and present possibilities.

Congruence always means a struggle to relate valu-
ative, theoretical, and practical dimensions. This

225

congruence is often explored by Christians in terms of the
relations of faith and righteousness, rectitude, or sanctification. It should be clear, however, that the pattern
of congruence varies with each approach, though all approaches maintain that faith is tied to practice. The practices may be primarily cultic, primarily social or
primarily individualistic. In all of these cases, however,
persons will face the gap between their loyalties and their
practices. They will find ways of living in the Pauline
tension between commitment and practice. Faith in this
situation of incongruence means the stubborn refusal to let
go of the three dimensions. It means a continual consciousness of the strain toward congruence. Personal motivation
in these situations may be maintained by symbolic participation in the eschatological resolution of this tension.
It may mean reliance on the pure justifying grace of God.
Or it may be a continual reaffirmation of the indwelling
spirit which works for its own good pleasure. Faith in any
event points to the personal strain toward a Christian
congruence.

Congruence in the trilateral engagement arises out of
a complex pattern of reciprocal critique. So, indeed, does
faith. Faith arises in the interchange. It is not something given by the Christian partner to the others. What
the Christian partner gives is the Christian past and memory.
But faith as such arises in the present engagement and
encounter. It is here that congruence is tested and new
patterns developed.

This view of faith applies to many different forms of
interchange. It is manifested in the encounters between
churches and the many kinds of Marxist socialism around the
world. Faith is manifested and transformed in the encounter.
Faith is similarly generated and transformed in the therapeutic encounter. Some old forms of seeming faithfulness
are revealed to be idolatrous. Old forms of satisfactory
functioning are transcended with more profound patterns of
health.

In this sense faith itself has a revelatory quality.
It is not so much a proposition (this would be belief at
its coldest) brought to the interchange. It is a revelatory
transformation in the interchange. It is a new way of knowing, doing, and valuing that arises in deep and mutually
critical encounter.

2.   Dialectical Method and Catholicity

a.   Dialectics

The term "dialectics" has been seized upon by many who
want to avoid any simplistic or static resolution of the

complexity of human affairs. It has therefore lost much of its particular meanings, leaving us in as much of a haze as appeals to "process." Yet it remains an important term, and we too have availed ourselves of it.

We have not been using it in the Hegelian sense of the dialectics of opposites. In that view polarizations and contradictions lead to new syntheses which in turn fall into self-contradiction. We do not conceive the disciplines nor the approaches in such terms, nor is their mutual engagement dialectical in that sense.

The dialectical interaction is shaped more by the ideal-typical method we assumed earlier. In this case the ideal types are asymptotes which shape a field of interaction. The typical poles are perennial tendencies rather than evolutionary protagonists. The process engendered by these tendencies does indeed consist of negations or reduction and rejection. But it also consists of "positives" such as corroboration, translation, and addition. All of these processes lead to that synthetic activity we call reciprocal transformation. In this sense, then, the interchange is dialectical.

At this point many might claim that pluralistic assumptions have shaped our method to an excessive point. We can at least say this. We do not means to elevate societal pluralism as a normative choice, for such choices always depend on a number of empirical and systematic assessments. Neither, by any means is societal pluralism a preferred descriptive approach, for the same reasons. However, there is indeed a kind of methodological and somewhat formal pluralism dictated by the critical commitment to integrity of the disciplines and to comprehensiveness of interchange within and among the disciplines.

b. Catholicity

This methodological orientation offers up a particular approach to the concept of catholicity--one of the four historic characteristics of the Church. It has indeed been interpreted in a variety of ways. Sometimes it has meant that the Church should embrace all peoples. Others have taken it to mean that Christianity should engage or penetrate every facet of life, especially in a sympathetic way.

The patterns of engagement we have delineated are one way of spelling out the process of engagement implied by this second meaning of catholicity. Catholicity does mean engagement, especially with the sciences of self and society, with their attendant practices and values. The method we have set forth here, then, can be taken as a kind of program for achieving authentic catholicity in this regard.

227

Catholicity means not only the openness to so called "secular" disciplines and a dialectical engagement with them. It also means in some sense Christian ecumenicity. It means engagement with the whole variety of professedly Christian movements, organizations, and theologians. Catholicity as ecumenicity consists in the challenge of seeing the relative integrity of each participant in this global variety. It means the legitimation of this plurality.

It also means a steady awareness of the alternatives pursued by Christians over the past two millenia. They, too, are special partners in a catholic engagement. They are not ecclesiastical dinosaurs superceded in Christian evolution. To some extent they stand as perennial alternatives. They have challenges to offer to us today, tomorrow, and in the future we cannot envision.

However, neither trilateral method nor ecumenicity can stop with a sheer justification of plurality. Ecumenical catholicity challenges us to critical mutual engagement. It challenges us to reciprocal transformation. Ecumenicity ought not to be the vision of a static "representation" of eternal ecclesiastical interests. It is a call to transformations.

The trilateral view of this process of reciprocal transformation affirms, moreover, that this transformative interaction among the churches can occur and indeed is occurring through their common engagement with the behavioral sciences. They are engaging each other in issues of personality development as it applies to Christian education. They are transforming each other as they deal with the challenges of Marxian socialisms and revolution. They are changing each other as they assess and adopt various patterns of ecclesiastical organization which are drawn from contemporary social sciences and practices. The trilateral interchange is also the basis for transformative exchange among the churches. It is a crucial context for genuinely catholic ecumenicity.

3. Reciprocal Transformation and the
    Meaning of Incarnation

In Chapter Nine we presented the concept of reciprocal transformation as a kind of summary critical value. It emerged on the basis of a formal analysis of the patterns of change in the trilateral interchange. While it has this formal characteristic it also clearly betrays some substantive commitments as well. Two of these substantive commitments have already emerged in terms of faith and catholicity. To conclude this sketch of theological ramifications of trilateral analysis we turn directly to the concept of reciprocal transformation and the way it is grounded in, and in turn transforms, the Christian concept of incarnation.

Let us recall a few salient points about reciprocal transformation. First of all it depends on the assumption that all three partners to the exchange contain all three dimensions. The behavioral sciences are value-laden, just as Christian theologians are not without definite practices. This fact enables the partners to engage each other on all three dimensions.

Second, the summary outcome of reciprocal transformation arises in a process characterized by attempts to reduce one partner or component to another, to add them, reject them corroborate them and to achieve congruence among them. No one of these steps or attempts can be final, since the call for comprehensiveness and integrity never allows us to settle for these isolated steps. The dialectical process we have described presses toward reciprocal transformation.

While there are many theological concepts and values with affinities to this process, that of incarnation stands at the forefront. Here we must be even more cautious and modest however. Some quick analogies must be immediately rejected. The co-presence of divinity and humanity indicated by incarnation cannot be translated into an analog in which "divinity" indicates Christianity and "humanity" the behavioral sciences. This would deny the humanity of the Church as well as the work of God in the created order and the reasonable efforts of human beings to understand it.

It would be more tempting and perhaps closer to the mark to identify divinity with the dimensions of loyalty and humanity with that of theory and practice. Incarnation in this sense would reinforce theologically the necessity for congruence. It would be closely tied to the notion of faith. The incarnational work of redemption would then be occurring in all partners in the search for congruence, in the pursuit of values, and the effort to improve the human condition.

Here, however, we immediately realize that not all values and loyalties are divine. Idolatry is ever with us, and, speaking prophetically, the demonic stands ever present to entice us. Yet each of these defective analogies contains some truth. At the least incarnation has generally meant that the redemptive process carried out by God involves more than an escape from the present order. It has meant that salvation is in some sense the perfection and completion of that order. It has meant that divine purposes are realized through that order rather than by removing individuals from it in some gnostic, "spiritual" way.

If this doctrinal minimum is accepted, then some

process of engagement with processes of worldly change are legitimated and encouraged. The degree to which we accept this invitation and demand, however, probably depends quite heavily on the extent (at least symbolically and theoretically) to which we accept some kind of identification between Christ and the Church or between Christ and ourselves. For the incarnational formula as it was finally established at Chalcedon refers to the person of Christ. Only by analogy does it then refer to the Church's "nature" and its involvement in human affairs. Only by analogy and symbolic identification is it then transferred to believers who are "in Christ."

As difficult and problematical as these moves may be, they point to some crucial tasks and choices for Christians. The question of incarnation, in the trilateral context, becomes the question of the degree to which we will embrace the value of comprehensiveness and engage in the processes leading to reciprocal transformation. This reciprocal transformation is a leading way by which churches and individual Christians in our time can articulate the meaning of an incarnate center of redemption, of a church which is loyal to an incarnate God, of Christians who are one with this incarnate bringer of salvation. To pursue this incarnate mission involves ambiguity, incompleteness and the danger of losing personal and institutional integrity in the clash of perspectives and practices. But it also can mean renewal and transformation.

NOTES

CHAPTER ONE
STEPS IN TRILATERAL ANALYSIS

1.   See the articles in Slant Manifesto: Catholics and
the Left, by Adrian Cunningham, et al. (Templegate, 1968).

2.   Abraham Maslow, Toward a Psychology of Being (Van
Nostrand Reinhold, 1968), pp. 71-102.

3.   I. L. Horowitz, ed., The Rise and Fall of Project
Camelot (MIT Press, 1967).

4.   The Catholic Priest in the United States: Sociological Investigations, ed. Andrew Greeley (United States
Catholic Conference, 1972).

5.   Lawrence Kohlberg, "Education for Justice: A Modern
Statement of the Platonic View," in James Gustafson, et
al., Moral Education: Five Lectures, with an introduction by Nancy F. and Theodore R. Sizer (Harvard
University Press, 1970), pp. 57-83.

6.   Max Stackhouse, Ethics and the Urban Ethos (Beacon,
1972), esp. pp. 23-32, 108, 141.

7.   Adrian van Kaam, C.S.S.Sp., Religion and Personality
(Prentice-Hall, 1964); Charles Curran, Psychological
Dynamics in Religious Living (Herder and Herder, 1971).

8.   Seward Hiltner, Theological Dynamics (Abingdon, 1972),
pp. 108-24. Psychologist of religion, Paul Pruyser,
touches what we mean at one point in his A Dynamic
Psychology of Religion (Harper and Row, 1968), pp.
262-67.

9.   Reinhold Niebuhr incorporates Marxist perspectives in
Moral Man and Immoral Society (Scribner's, 1960), written in 1932. His incorporation of Freud resonates
through his later work, The Self and the Dramas of History (Scribner's, 1955). Gregory Baum's work, Religion
and Alienation (Paulist, 1975) is an excellent introduction to the theology-sociology interchange.

231

CHAPTER TWO
     CARL ROGERS AND PASTORAL CARE

1.   Carl R. Rogers, "Niebuhr on the Nature of Man," in
The Nature of Man in Theological and Psychological
Perspective, ed. Simon Doniger (Harper, 1962), p. 70.

2.   Carl R. Rogers, Client-centered Therapy (Houghton
Mifflin, 1965), p. 35.

3.   Charles A. Curran, Psychological Dynamics in Religious Living (Herder and Herder, 1971), pp. 70-124.

4.   Cf. Thomas C. Oden, Kerygma and Counseling (Westminster, 1966), p. 171, note 2.

5.   Oden, Kerygma.

6.   Don S. Browning, Atonement and Psychotherapy (Westminster, 1966).

7.   William E. Hulme, Pastoral Care Come of Age (Abingdon, 1970), p. 15.

8.   Ian F. McIntosh, Pastoral Care and Pastoral Theology
(Westminster, 1972).

9.   Curran, Psychological Dynamics; Andre Godin, S.J.,
The Pastor as Counselor, tr. B. Phillips (Holt, Rinehart and Winston, 1965), pp. 28-30; Raymond Hostie,
S.J., Pastoral Counseling, tr. G. Barth, T.O.R. (Sheed
and Ward, 1966). Michael J. O'Brien, C.S.V., also makes
extensive use of Rogers in An Introduction to Pastoral
Counseling (Alba House, 1968), pp. 75-93.

10.   Seward Hiltner, Pastoral Counseling (Abingdon,
1949). Hiltner makes specific references to Rogers in
his discussion of interview material on pp. 253-60. Paul
E. Johnson, Psychology of Pastoral Care: The Pastoral
Ministry in Theory and Practice (Abingdon, 1953), pp.
98-100.

11.   Howard J. Clinebell, Mental Health through Christian
Community: The Local Church's Ministry of Growth and
Healing (Abingdon, 1965), pp. 217-41.

12.   Ian F. McIntosh, Pastoral Care and Pastoral Theology
(Westminster, 1972), pp. 102-08.

13.   Don S. Browning, The Moral Context of Pastoral Care
(Westminster, 1976).

14.   Rogers, "Niebuhr on the Nature of Man," pp. 53-71.

232

CHAPTER THREE
SAUL ALINSKY AND SOCIETAL MINISTRY

1.   For a typical case see Lyle Schaller, Community Organization: Conflict and Reconciliation (Abingdon, 1966). An extensive bibliography is available from the Institute on the Church and Urban Industrial Society, Chicago, especially Issues in Community Organization, L. Witmer, ed. (1968).

2.   For the varieties of theories and practices see W. Bloomberg, "Community Organization," in R. Kramer, H. Specht, eds., Readings in Community Organization Practice (Prentice-Hall, 1969), pp. 91-127; J. Rothman, "Three Models of Community Organization Practice," in F. Cox, et al., eds., Strategies of Community Organization (F. E. Peacock, 1970), pp. 20-36; R. Pruger, and H. Specht, "Assessing Theoretical Models of Community Organization Practice," Social Service Review, 4:32 (1969), 123-35.

3.   Robert Lee and Russell Galloway, The Schizophrenic Church: Conflict over Community Organization (Westminster, 1969).

4.   These points are drawn from Alinsky's two popular books, Reveille for Radicals (University of Chicago Press, 1946), and Rules for Radicals (Random House-Vintage, 1972).

5.   Alinsky, Rules for Radicals, p. 3.

6.   Dan Dodson, "The Church, Power, and Saul Alinsky," Religion in Life, 36 (1967), 108-118; Karl Hertz, "Community Organization and Conflict," Lutheran Quarterly, 19:4 (1967), 397-407; Gibson Winter, "The Churches and Community Organization," Christianity and Crisis, (May 31, 1965), 119-22.

7.   James L. Adams, "Blessed are the Powerful, Christian Century (June 18, 1969), 838-41.

8.   Ethics and the Urban Ethos (Beacon, 1972), p. 143.

9.   Charles A. Curran, Psychological Dynamics in Religious Living (Herder and Herder, 1971), pp. 90-124; Carl Rogers, Client-centered Therapy, (Houghton Mifflin, 1951), pp. 26-30.

10.   J. H. Fish, Black Power and White Control: The Struggle of the Woodlawn Organization in Chicago (Princeton University Press, 1973): Charles Grosser, New Directions in Community Organization (Praeger, 1972);

I. A. Spergel, Community Organization: Studies in Constraint (Russell Sage, 1972); D. Thurz, "Community Participation: Should the Past be Prologue?" American Behavioral Scientist, 15 (1972), 733-48.

11.   Saul Alinsky, "Of Means and Ends," Union Seminary Quarterly Review 22:2 (1967), 107-24; responses by H. D. White, D. R. Steinle, and R. Stone in the same issue, pp. 125-37.

CHAPTER FOUR
CHRISTIANITY

1.   For a basic survey of Christian symbols see George Ferguson, Signs and Symbols in Christian Art (Oxford University Press, 1966). See also F. W. Dillistone, Christianity and Symbolism (Westminster, 1955).

2.   Among the extensive number of introductions to theology or encyclopedias of theology, perhaps the most accessible is Sacramentum Mundi, ed. K. Rahner, C. Ernst, K. Smyth, 6 vols. (Herder and Herder, 1968-1970). For short introductions by single authors see Joseph Ratzinger, Introduction to Christianity, tr. J. R. Foster (Herder and Herder, 1970), and John MacQuarrie, Principles of Christian Theology (London: SCM Press, 1966).

3.   For some other typologies see Avery Dulles, Models of the Church (Doubleday, 1974), (Church as Institution, Mystical Communion, Sacrament, Herald, Servant); H. R. Niebuhr, Christ and Culture (Harper and Row, 1951) (Christ against, above, of, in paradox with, and transforming culture); Gustave Aulen, Christus Victor, tr. A. G. Herbert (Macmillan, 1969), (Classic, Latin, and Moral atonement theories); and Carl Braaten, Christ and Counter-Christ: Apocalyptic Theories in Theology and Culture (Fortress, 1972), Past-, Now-, and Future-oriented).
      From a psychological viewpoint we have William James' distinction between "once-born" and "twice-born" personalities in The Varieties of Religious Experience (Macmillan, 1961).
      From the sociology of religion see the excellent discussion by Roland Robertson, The Sociological Interpretation of Religion (Schocken, 1970).

4.   Calvin's Institutes of the Christian Religion, ed. J. McNeil (Westminster, 1960) is still the best source for Calvin's thought. For a balanced commentary see Francois Wendel, Calvin, tr. P. Mairet (Harper and Row, 1963).
      George H. Williams gives us the sweep of the "radical" reformation in The Radical Reformation (Westminster,

1962). For the revolutionary Thomas Münzer, see Eric
Gitsch, Reformer without a Church: The Life and Thought
of Thomas Münzer (Fortress, 1967).

For Luther see John Dillenberger, ed., Martin Luther:
Selections from his Writings (Doubleday-Anchor, 1961).
See also Gerhard Ebeling, Luther: An Introduction to his
Thought (Fortress, 1970). For a more ecstatic inter-
pretation see Jaroslav Pelikan, Spirit vs. Structure:
Luther and the Institutions of the Church (Harper and
Row, 1968).

We will deal extensively with Gutierrez in Chapter
11. For Cone, who is only one of dozens of theologians
in the recent movements of liberation theology, see
A Black Theology of Liberation (Seabury, 1969). For
Mary Daly see Beyond God the Father (Beacon, 1973).

P. T. Forsyth is a noted exponent of the Reformed
tradition among English speaking peoples. See his
Positive Preaching and the Modern Mind (Eerdmans,
1964). See also John H. Rodgers, The Theology of
P. T. Forsyth (London: Independent Press, 1965), esp.
p. 255.

The American theologian Carl Henry has been widely
influential. See for example, The God Who Shows Himself
(World Books, 1966).

The Mennonite tradition is amply represented in John
H. Yoder, The Politics of Jesus (Eerdmans, 1972) and The
Original Revolution (Herald, 1972).

Prophetic emphases have also played an important
role in the post-Tridentine Catholicism shaped by Robert
Bellarmine and Ignatius Loyola. The base of this prophetic stance tended to be the Church rather than
Scripture as such. The persecution experience of
immigrant Catholicism in America also produced a prophetic orientation. See Mark Schoof, A Survey of
Catholic Theology, 1800-1970, tr. N. D. Smith (Paulist
Newman, 1970), esp. pp. 146-51.

For Barth see his The Word of God and The Word of
Man, tr. D. Horton (Harper and Row, 1958). For Barth's
resonance within the Reformed tradition see Gerrit
Berkouwer, The Triumph of Grace in the Theology of Karl
Barth, tr. H. R. Boer (Eerdmans, 1956). For his impact
among Catholics see Hans Küng, Justification: The Doc-
trine of Karl Barth and a Catholic Reflection, tr. T.
Collins, et al. (Nelson, 1964).

Prophetic themes figure prominently in the work of
Reinhold Niebuhr. See his two early works, Moral Man
and Immoral Society (Scribners, 1960), and The Children
of Light and the Children of Darkness (Scribners, 1960).
These prophetic themes are somewhat transformed under
the impact of depth psychology in The Nature and Destiny
of Man, (Scribners, 1949).

5.   Protestants generally speak of the former as

235

justifying grace and the latter as sanctifying grace.
Catholic theology generally uses various other cate-
gories. See <u>Sacramentum Mundi</u>, ed. K. Rahner, et al.
(Herder and Herder, 1969), vol. 2, "Grace," pp. 414-24.

6.   Dietrich Bonhoeffer, letter of April 30, 1944, in
<u>Letters and Papers from Prison</u>, enl. ed., E. Bethge, ed.
(Macmillan, 1972), pp. 278-81.
     For a classic short statement on the American side
see Harvey Cox, <u>The Secular City</u> (Macmillan, 1966).

7.   Jerome Hamer, <u>The Church is a Communion</u>, tr. R.
Mattheus (Sheed and Ward, 1965).

8.   For a contemporary presentation of this idea see
Edward Schillebeeckx, <u>Christ The Sacrament of the
Encounter with God.</u>, tr. P. Barrett (Sheed and Ward,
1963).

9.   Karl Rahner, <u>The Church and the Sacraments</u>, tr. W. J.
O'Hara (Herder and Herder, 1963).   Schillebeeckx takes
up Jürgen Habermas' critical theory as he engages the
behavioral sciences in <u>The Understanding of Faith</u>,
tr. N. D. Smith, (Seabury, 1974).

10.   Emile Mersch, <u>The Theology of the Mystical Body of
Christ</u>, tr. C. Vollert (Herder, 1958).   Eric L. Mascall,
<u>Corpus Christi: Essays on the Church and the Eucharist</u>,
2nd ed., rev. enl. (London: Longmans, 1965).

11.   For Thomas Aquinas, see <u>Summa Theologica</u>, I, Q. 5,
art. 3, 4; and <u>Summa Contra Gentiles</u>, Bk. III, chaps.
3, 4, 17.   This tradition finds contemporary, somewhat
transformed, expression in the work of Bernard Lonergan.
See David Tracy, <u>The Achievement of Bernard Lonergan</u>
(Seabury, 1970).

12.   B. R. Brinkman, "On Sacramental Man," <u>Heythrop Jour-
nal</u> 13 (1972), 371-401, and <u>Heythrop Journal</u> 14 (1973),
5-34, 162-189, 280-306, and 396-416.   We are indebted
to Fr. Kenneth Smits and Fr. Thomas Fait for bringing
Brinkman to our attention.

13.   See Troeltsch's analysis in <u>The Social Teaching of
the Christian Churches</u>, tr. O. Wyon (Harper, 1960), and
H. R. Niebuhr's discussion of "Christ above Culture"
in <u>Christ and Culture</u>.

14.   One of the best introductions to contemporary charismatic movements is Walter Hollenwegger, <u>Pentecostals:
The Charismatic Movement in the Churches</u>, tr. R. A.
Wilson (Augsburg, 1972).   Hollenwegger has also inves-
tigated their relationship to the more prophetically

oriented realities of racism in <u>Pentecost between Black and White</u> (Belfast: Christian Journals Ltd., 1974).
For a sociological-historical exploration of this type of religion see I. M. Lewis, <u>Ecstatic Religion</u> (London: Penguin, 1973). William G. McLoughlin seeks to give shape to "movement Christianity" in "Is There a Third Force in Christendom?" in W. G. McLoughlin and R. Bellah, <u>Religion in America</u> (Houghton Mifflin, 1968), 45-72.

15.   For Tillich, "the personal encounter with God and the reunion with him are the heart of all genuine religion." <u>Systematic Theology</u> (University of Chicago Press, 1967), vol. 2, p. 86. See also vol. 2, pp. 125-29, and vol. 3, pp. 107-110. For a discussion of ecstasy in Tillich, see J. L. Adams, <u>Paul Tillich's Philosophy of Culture, Science, and Religion</u> (Harper and Row, 1965), pp. 48-51.

16.   Rufus Jones, <u>Studies in Mystical Religion</u> (Russell and Russell, 1970) and <u>Mysticism and Democracy in the English Commonwealth</u> (Octagon, 1965). For the mystical tradition see also Dean William Inge, <u>Mysticism in Religion</u> (University of Chicago Press, 1948).

17.   John Wesley, <u>A Representative Collection of His Writings</u>, ed. Albert C. Outler (Oxford University Press, 1964). See also below, Chapter 7, note 20.

18.   For an example see Harvey Cox, <u>Seduction of the Spirit</u> (Simon and Schuster, 1973).

19.   For some historical studies see R. A. Knox, <u>Enthusiasm: A Chapter in the History of Religion with Special Reference to the 17th and 18th Centuries</u> (Oxford University Press, 1950) and Arthur D. Nock, <u>Conversion: The Old and the New in Religion from Alexander the Great to Augustine of Hippo</u> (Oxford University Press, 1961).

20.   The best example of a comparative study of ministerial practice is Peter Rudge, <u>Ministry and Management: The Study of Ecclesiastical Administration</u> (London: Tavistock Publications, 1968). Rudge uses the categories of classical, traditional, charismatic, human relations, and systemic theories of management. Using the concept of "Body of Christ" as a norm he chooses a systemic ministerial practice.

CHAPTER FIVE
PERSONALITY

1.   The division of contemporary psychology into three broad fields represents the historical development of

psychotherapy. We are not so directly concerned with developments, for instance, in cognitive, experimental, or testing psychologies except as they bear on the differences among psychoanalysis, behaviorism, and humanistic psychology.

Carl Rogers, Abraham Maslow and others agree with our division of contemporary psychology into these three approaches. Some differ with us on the basis on which the divisions are made. Rogers' typology is rooted in differing epistemological modes, and he does not distinguish respective theories, practices, or loyalties. Cf. Carl R. Rogers, "Toward a Science of the Person," in Behaviorism and Phenomenology: Contrasting Bases for Modern Psychology, ed. T. W. Wann (University of Chicago Press, 1964), pp. 109-40.

Psychologist Salvatore Maddi also makes a triadic division of current psychology. He uses the terms conflict and fulfillment similarly to the way we do. We are indebted to his thinking in this regard. His difference for the third approach is that he covers mainly cognitive, not behavioral, theories, in what he calls the "consistency" model. Also Maddi's emphasis is on theory, and he generally excludes practice and loyalty dimensions. See his Personality Theories: A Comparative Analysis (Dorsey, 1968).

Psychologist Perry London divides current psychotherapy into "insight" and "action" therapies. London prefers behaviorist (action) therapies and does not make the distinctions among insight therapies that we feel deserve careful attention. Differing conceptions of the "good personality," for instance, separate conflict from fulfillment orientations in ways that London does not acknowledge. London does identify theoretical, practical, and loyalty components of psychological systems, however, and clarifies the interrelation of these in many current theorists and clinicians. His excellent book is Modes and Morals of Psychotherapy (Holt, Rinehart and Winston, 1964).

The Protestant pastoral theologian William B. Oglesby, Jr., also divides current psychologies into three approaches. The basis of his typology is the modes of knowing, being, and doing. He associates the knowing mode with the insight emphasis in psychoanalysis, the being mode with the focus on the inner state of the organism or self in phenomenology, and the doing mode with the action emphasis in behaviorism. Cf., "Pastoral Care and Counseling in Biblical Perspective," Interpretation, 27:3 (1973), 307-26.

For a detailed, historical summary of psychoanalysis, behaviorism, and of the roots of humanistic psychology, see Benjamin B. Wolman, Contemporary Theories and Systems in Psychology (Harper and Row, 1960). Raymond Corsini supplies a broad selection of approaches in

Current Psychotherapies, Raymond Corsini, ed. (F. E. Peacock, 1973).

2. Freud's own writing and that of his interpreters is voluminous. Calvin S. Hall's A Primer of Freudian Psychology (New American Library, 1954) is a concise, readable introduction, and it is available in paperback. Freud's original work can be found in The Standard Edition of the Complete Works of Sigmund Freud (London: Hogarth Press, 1962). His essays on religion include "Totem and Taboo," "Moses and Monotheism," and "The Future of an Illusion." Freud's polemical defense of psychoanalysis is found in A General Introduction to Psychoanalysis, tr. Joan Riviere (Washington Square Press, 1960). David Shakow and David Rapaport attempt sympathetically to put Freud in historical perspective in The Influence of Freud on American Psychology (World, 1964). Other helpful summaries of Freud are found in Perry London, Modes, and Salvatore Maddi, Personality Theories.
Erik Erikson's contribution has been to stress the positive influence of culture on personality--compared with Freud's notion of culture as primarily restrictive. Erikson's Childhood and Society, 2nd ed., rev. and enl. (Norton, 1963) is a classic in the field of personality and culture. His interest in religion emerges in two studies: Young Man Luther: A Study in Psychoanalysis and History (Norton, 1962), and Gandhi's Truth: On the Origins of Militant Non-violence (Norton, 1969). Erikson sees identity diffusion as the prime personal malady accompanying our technological culture. He details his ideas on identity in "Identity and the Life Cycle," Psychological Issues, Vol. 1, No. 1 (International Universities Press, 1959), and Identity: Youth and Crisis (Norton, 1968). For interpretations of Erikson's work, see Robert Coles, Erik H. Erikson: The Growth of His Work (Little, Brown, 1970), and Don S. Browning, Generative Man: Psychoanalytic Perspectives (Westminster, 1973).

3. Cf. Perry London, "Psychotherapy Boom: Trend Away from Cure toward Self-fulfillment," Psychology Today, 8:1 (June, 1974), 62-68. Of the "smorgasbord" of therapies offered in Southern California, he cites "re-evaluation therapy, the food sexperience, journey into consciousness, sexual-awakening exercises, hypnosis, Reichian sensitivity, actualization, psychocybernetics, job therapy, Esalen love massage, bio-energetics, Transactional Analysis, existential analysis, Rolfing, Primal therapy, and psychodrama." He might have supplemented his list with other brands of human potential as well, such as Transcendental Meditation, and Mind Control. The human potentials boom has seen numerous

239

growth centers springing up in major cities across the country. Accompanying these are diverse growth manuals with specific techniques for expanding human potential: Some of these are William Schutz, Here Comes Everybody (Harper, 1972); Muriel James and Dorothy Jongeward, Born to Win: Transactional Analysis with Gestalt Experiments (Addison-Wesley, 1971); John O. Stevens, Awareness: Exploring, Experimenting, Experiencing (Real People Press, 1971); Howard R. Lewis and Dr. Harold S. Streitfeld, Growth Games: How to Tune in Yourself, Your Family, Your Friends (Harcourt, Brace, Jovanovich, 1970); Alexander Lowen, M.D., Pleasure (Lancer Books, 1970).

4.   The humanistic approach to personality is not as clearly delineated as that of psychoanalysis or behaviorism. A helpful book putting this approach in perspective is Frank T. Severin, Humanistic Viewpoints in Psychology (McGraw-Hill, 1965).

Carl Rogers' writing spans forty-five years. His major contributions are: Counseling and Psychotherapy (Houghton Mifflin, 1942), Client-centered Therapy (Houghton Mifflin, 1951), On Becoming a Person (Houghton Mifflin, 1961), "A Theory of Therapy, Personality, and Interpersonal Relationships as Developed in the Client-centered Framework," in S. Koch, ed., Psychology: A Study of Science, Vol. III, Formulations of the Person and the Social Context (McGraw-Hill, 1959), pp. 184-256, and "Toward a Modern Approach to Values: The Valuing Process in the Mature Person," Journal of Abnormal Social Psychology, 68 (February, 1964), 160ff. Rogers has many subsequent writings on education, marriage and encounter groups. We see these as applications of his earlier theoretical formulations, and do not believe he makes significant changes from earlier work as some hold.

Gordon Allport preceded Rogers as a lone humanistic voice in a field dominated by behaviorists and psychoanalysts, particularly in the 1930's and 1940's. While not read extensively today, Allport's work has both historical and contemporary relevance. Pattern and Growth in Personality (Holt, Rinehart, and Winston, 1961).

Abraham Maslow's work became popular, especially with those interested in religion and interpersonal relationships, in the late 1960's and the 1970's. His major works include: Motivation and Personality (Harper, 1954), Toward a Psychology of Being, 2nd ed. (Van Nostrand and Reinhold, 1968), Religions, Values and Peak-experiences (Viking, 1971), The Farther Reaches of Human Nature (Viking, 1972). An overview of Maslow's work is Richard J. Lowry. ed., Dominance, Self-esteem, Self-actualization: Germinal Papers of A. H. Maslow (Brooks Cole, 1973).

The basic reference for Carl Jung is <u>Collected Works</u>, Herbert Read, Michael Fordham, and Gerhard Adler, eds. ("Bollingen Series," 20 vols.; Pantheon, 1953-). An early disciple of Freud, Jung disagreed with him about the influence of sexuality on behavior and the nature of the unconscious. He ultimately broke from Freud and began his own analytic therapy. Highly versed in primitive cultures, both East and West, Jung was knowledgeable about early Christian culture as well. Jung's interest in symbols and rites has drawn an avid Christian readership. For a briefer introduction, see <u>Basic Writings</u>, edited with an introduction by Violet Staub de Laszlo (Modern Library, 1959).

Victor Frankl brings an existentialist blend to his psychotherapy. A survivor of a concentration camp during World War II, he writes about the will to meaning as essential for survival. His works include: <u>Man's Search for Meaning: An Introduction to Logotherapy</u>, tr. Ilse Lasch (Beacon, 1963), <u>The Doctor and the Soul: From Psychotherapy to Logotherapy</u>, 2nd exp. edn. (Bantam 1967), <u>The Will to Meaning: Foundations and Applications of Logotherapy</u> (World, 1969), and <u>The Unconscious God: Psychotherapy and Theology</u> (Simon and Schuster, 1975).

Frederick (Fritz) Perls has influenced the practices of American psychotherapy probably more than any other single humanistic psychologist. Practitioners from conflict and equilibrium orientations have used his approaches to dream work. Increasing numbers of transactional analysts are blending Gestalt Therapy into their practices. His writings include: <u>Ego, Hunger, and Aggression: The Beginning of Gestalt Therapy</u> (Random House, 1969), <u>In and Out of the Garbage Pail</u> (Bantam, 1972), <u>The Gestalt Approach and Eyewitness to Therapy</u> (Science and Behavior Books, 1973), and <u>Gestalt Therapy Verbatim</u>, comp. and ed. John O. Stevens (Bantam, 1972).

5.   For an extensive and excellent bibliography on behaviorism, see London, <u>Modes</u>. The references we list here are the ones we have found especially helpful.

B. F. Skinner is the best-known behaviorist in America. He is an experimentalist par excellance, and uses as little theory as he thinks necessary. His writing style occasionally is polemical and his terminology at times stretches conventional usage. <u>Science and Human Behavior</u> (Macmillan, 1953), <u>Walden Two</u> (Macmillan, 1948), "Some Issues Concerning the Control of Human Behavior," (symposium with Carl Rogers), <u>Science</u>, 124:3231 (November, 1956), 1057-66. James G. Holland and B. F. Skinner, <u>The Analysis of Behavior: A Program of Self-Instruction</u> (McGraw-Hill, 1961), "Behaiorism at Fifty," <u>Science</u>, 140 (1963), 951-58. <u>About Behaviorism</u>, (Knopf, 1974), and <u>Beyond Freedom and</u>

<u>Dignity</u> (Knopf, 1971).

Albert Bandura is the most careful and refined behaviorist with whom we are familiar. In addition his ethical reflection and concern for client autonomy is notable. Our perspective on the field has been shaped by his <u>Principles of Behavior Modification</u> (Holt, Rinehart, and Winston, 1969). Also see his <u>Social Learning and Personality Development</u>, co-authored with Richard H. Waters (Holt, Rinehart, and Winston, 1963).

Joseph Wolpe describes his work in the readable and interesting <u>The Practice of Behavior Therapy</u> (Pergamon, 1969).

O. Hobart Mowrer is an experimental psychologist whose early work was a significant development in learning theory. <u>Learning Theory and Behavior</u> (Wiley, 1960), <u>Learning Theory and the Symbolic Processes</u> (Wiley, 1960). Then Mowrer's focus shifted to wider interdisciplinary issues among psychiatry and religion. His polemical and incisive analyses are found in <u>The Crisis in Psychiatry and Religion</u> (Van Nostrand, 1961), and <u>The New Group Therapy</u> (Van Nostrand, 1964).

John Dollard and Neal E. Miller contributed a significant book from the standpoint of learning and behavior, <u>Personality and Psychotherapy: An Analysis in Terms of Learning Thinking, and Culture</u> (McGraw-Hill 1950).

For a useful summary of Thomas Stampfl's work, see London, <u>Modes</u>.

Albert Ellis has written extensively, particularly on sexual issues. References to his rational-emotive therapy include: <u>Handbook of Rational-emotive Therapy</u> by Albert Ellis and Russell Grieger (Springer, 1977), <u>A New Guide to Rational Living</u>, by Albert Ellis and Robert A. Harper (Prentice-Hall, 1975), <u>Growth through Reason</u> (Science and Behavior Books, 1971), and <u>Reason and Emotion in Psychotherapy</u> (Stuart, 1963).

Lawrence Kohlberg has written numerous articles on moral judgment and cognitive development. An excellent summary of his work can be found in "Stage and Sequence: The Cognitive-Developmental Approach to Socialization," in David A. Goslin, ed., <u>Handbook of Socialization Theory and Research</u> (Rand McNally, 1969), pp. 347-480. Cf. also T. J. Bachmeyer, "Ethics and the Psychology of Moral Judgment," <u>Zygon</u> 8:2 (1973), 82-95.

6.   Joseph Wolpe makes one of the clearest statements about the essential equilibrium motif in behavioristic practice. "The behavior therapist takes it for granted that human behavior is subject to causal determination no less than the behavior of falling bodies or growing plants. For example, a man pauses at the cross-roads, undecided along which of two routes to proceed. The route that he eventually takes is the inevitable one,

being the resultant of a balancing out (emphasis ours) of conflicting action-tendencies." (The Practice Behavior Therapy, p. 55.) The conflicting action tendencies are the old habit and the new response. The inevitable route taken is the new equilibrium resulting from an applied stimulus.

7.   Albert Bandura, Principles.

8.   Carole Wade Offir, "Their Fingers Do the Talking," Psychology Today (June, 1976), 72-78.

9.   James Rest, "Hierarchies of Comprehension and Preference in a Developmental-Stage Model of Moral Thinking," (unpublished Ph.D. dissertation, University of Chicago, 1969).

10.   The role of values in personality assessment is an old debate. It goes back to Freud in at least two ways. One is his assigning to the ego the function of "reality testing." This raises the problem of who defines what is real, for whom, and in behalf of whose interests. The second is his depiction of belief in God as a universal obsessive neurosis. This clearly raises ontological issues in a polemical fashion.
      The value debate continues to this day. One portion concerns the values of the psychotherapist and/or her supposedly neutral or scientific therapeutic stance. Thomas Szasz renews this issue with his book The Myth of Mental Illness: Foundations of a Theory of Personal Conduct (Hoeber-Harper, 1961). Seymour Halleck's The Politics of Therapy (Science House, 1971) assumes all psychiatric intervention has political consequences. Halleck builds philosophical and ethical guidelines for therapists who share his orientation.
      The radical therapists have taken Szasz and Halleck a step further. They see psychiatry as directly oppressive--of women, of ethnicity, even of personal dignity. An excellent collection of readings in the radical perspective is Radical Psychology, edited by Phil Brown (Harper and Row, 1973).
      The more moderate discussion of the value dimension in personality issues deals with the values that make therapy effective. The focus here is on the distorted values (or superego) of certain client populations (addicts, delinquents, scrupulous people) and how therapists can treat such values. O. Hobart Mowrer is a vociferous critic of Freud's "permissive" stance toward restrictive superego values. He believes instead in personal confession of moral "sins" and therapeutic restitution. Cf. Mowrer, Crisis. Mowrer draws a wide religious readership for obvious reasons. He also has edited a collection of articles on how values and

religion relate to therapy, <u>Morality and Mental Health</u>
(Rand McNally, 1967). William Glasser stresses the role
of responsibility in his <u>Reality Therapy: A New Approach</u>
<u>to Psychiatry</u> (Harper and Row, 1965). He defines
responsibility as the ability to get one's own needs
met without depriving others of ways to get their needs
met. He finds responsibility a helpful value especially
in dealing with delinquent populations.

Finally, there is a cultural perspective on values
and therapy that puts moral issues in a broad context.
Jerome Frank's <u>Persuasion and Healing</u> (Schocken, 1963)
is an excellent cross-cultural comparison of psychotherapy with primitive religious healing, revivalism,
thought reform, and medical treatment.

11. The "Eclectic" school of psychotherapy uses treatment
techniques from all available approaches. Their fundamental explanation of why a technique works in a
particular case, however, rests on an equilibrium
model. See Frederick C. Thorne, "Eclectic Psychotherapy," in R. Corsini, <u>Current Psychotherapies</u>, pp.
445-486; Robert R. Carkhuff, <u>Helping and Human Relations:</u>
<u>A Primer for Lay and Professional Helpers</u> (Holt, Rine-
hart, and Winston, 1969); and Gerard Egan, <u>The Skilled</u>
<u>Helper</u> (Brooks Cole, 1975).

CHAPTER SIX
SOCIETY

1. Howard Becker and Harry E. Barnes have assembled a
compendious survey of the rise of social theory in
<u>Social Thought: From Lore to Science</u>, 3 vols., 3rd
ed. (Dover, 1961). Robert Nisbet, in <u>The Sociological</u>
<u>Tradition</u> (Basic Books, 1966), draws attention to some
key factors in the rise of modern sociology.

2. For a fuller discussion of these problems see May
Brodbeck, ed. <u>Readings in the Philosophy of the Social</u>
<u>Sciences</u> (Macmillan, 1968), esp. chaps. 13-16, 28; and
T. B. Bottomore, <u>Sociology: A Guide to Problems and</u>
<u>Literature</u> (Pantheon, 1971), pp. 49-51.

3. For Weber's normative side see Arthur Mitzman, <u>The</u>
<u>Iron Cage: An Historical Interpretation of Max Weber</u>
(Knopf, 1970), and Weber's own essay, "Politics as a
Vocation" in <u>From Max Weber</u>, ed. Hans Gerth and C.
Wright Mills (Oxford University Press, 1958), pp. 77-128.
The struggle to root action in "objective social
reality" runs through all schools of sociology. See
Emile Durkheim, <u>The Division of Labor</u>, tr. G. Simpson
(Free Press, 1964), pp. 45, 408-9, 411-35. See also
Karl Marx, "Theses on Feuerbach," in Robert Tucker, ed.,
<u>The Marx-Engels Reader</u> (Norton, 1972), pp. 107-9. For a

contemporary statement see Norman Denzin, The Values
of Social Science (Aldine, 1970).
The belief in a "value free social science" originally pursued by Weber has drowned in a deluge of criticism exposing the commitments of sociologists and of
sociology. For the attack see Alvin Gouldner, "Anti-
Minotaur: The Myth of a Value Free Sociology," in
I. L. Horowitz, ed., The New Sociology: Essays for C.
Wright Mills (Oxford University Press, 1965), pp. 196-
217. For the defense see Reinhard Bendix, Embattled
Reason: Essays on Social Knowledge (Oxford University
Press, 1970), pp. 62-94, and Jürgen Habermas, "Knowledge and Interest," in D. Emmet and A. MacIntyre
eds., Sociological Theory and Philosophical Analysis
(Macmillan, 1970), pp. 36-54.

4.   We have expanded on the normal division of social
theories into "order" and "conflict" schools, since all
theories try to account for order and conflict. The
question is, what dynamic accounts for these features
of social life? The concept of "system" and "pluralism"
are drawn directly from popular vocabulary, while "dualism" is a term combining various forms of Marxism
with other approaches sharing their basic model of the
social structure.
        The following authors offer some alternative typo-
logies:
        John Horton, "Order and Conflict Theories of Social
Problems," American Journal of Sociology, 71 (1966),
701-13;
        Amitai Etzioni, The Active Society (Free Press,
1968), pp. 60-69 (categories of atomistic-aggregate,
collectivist-systemic, and voluntaristic);
        Earl Rubington and Martin Weinberg, The Study of
Social Problems; Five Perspectives (Oxford University,
Press, 1971) (categories of pathology, disorganization,
value conflict, deviant behavior, and labelling as
theoretical bases for practices);
        Werner Stark, The Fundamental Forms of Social
Thought (Fordham University Press, 1963) (organic,
mechanical, and processual or cultural, each view having
a positive and normative usage);
        Don Martindale, The Nature and Types of Sociological
Theory (Houghton Mifflin, 1960) (positivistic organi-
cism, conflict theory, formalism, social behaviorism,
sociological functionalism).

5.   The founder of modern systemic views is Emile Durkheim, The Division of Labor in Society, tr. G. Simpson
(Free Press, 1964), Suicide, tr. J. A. Spaulding, G.
Simpson (Free Press, 1951), and The Elementary Forms of
the Religious Life, tr. J. F. Swain (Free Press, 1965).
        The key contemporary figures in a systemic approach

245

are: Talcott Parsons, The Social System (Free Press, 1951), and Sociological Theory and Modern Society (Free Press, 1963), which includes a bibliography of Parsons' writings; Robert Merton, Social Theory and Social Structure (Free Press, 1963); Walter Buckley, Sociology and Modern Systems Theory (Prentice-Hall, 1967); F. Kenneth Berrien, General and Social Systems Rutgers University Press, 1968); Karl Deutsch, The Nerves of Government: Models of Political Communication and Control (Free Press, 1966); Kenneth Boulding, The Organizational Revolution (Quadrangle, 1963), and A Primer on Social Dynamics (Free Press, 1970).

For the structuralist school of social thought, which is closely related to these approaches, see Claude Levi-Strauss, Structural Anthropology, tr. C. Jacobson and B. G. Schoep (Doubleday, 1969) and Jacques Ehrmann, Structuralism (Doubleday, 1970), which has an excellent bibliography.

6.   For expositions of evolutionary views see T. Parsons, Societies: Evolutionary and Comparative Perspectives (Prentice-Hall, 1966), T. Parsons, "Christianity and Modern Industrial Society," in Sociological Theory and Modern Society, pp. 385-421; and Robert Bellah, "Religious Evolution," American Sociological Review, 29 (1964), 357-74. For a critique see Robert Nisbet, Social Change and History (Oxford University Press, 1964).

7.   This move from description to prescription is set forth clearly in Durkheim's work, at least as a program. Kenneth Boulding and Karl Deutsch have both given attention to this in their works cited above.

8.   For the classic presentation see Robert Merton, "Manifest and Latent Functions," Social Theory and Social Structure, pp. 73-138. In anthropology, where it has had a near monopoly, see A. R. Radcliffe-Brown, Structure and Function in Primitive Society: Essays and Addresses (Free Press, 1965), esp. chaps. 8, 9, 10. For its use in meeting social problems see Robert Merton and Robert Nisbet, Contemporary Social Problems (Harcourt, Brace, and World, 1961), esp. pp. 697-738.

For critical assessments of structural-functionalism see the collection of articles in N. J. Demerath and R. A. Peterson, System, Change, and Conflict (Free Press, 1967).

9.   David Aberle, et al., have tried to set forth the functional prerequisites for any society in "The Functional Prerequisites of a Society," in Demerath and Peterson, System, Change and Conflict, pp. 317-22.

10.   On the American side this idea received its classic

formulation by C. H. Cooley, Social Organization (Free Press, 1956).

11. F. Toennies, Community and Society, tr. C. P. Loomis (Michigan State University Press, 1957). For other discussions of this theme see Robert Nisbet, The Sociological Tradition, ch. 3, and The Social Philosophers: Community and Conflict in Western Thought (Crowell, 1973).

12. For the definition of culture and its relation to society see Parsons, The Social System, pp. 3-23; and Louis Schneider and Charles Bonjean, eds. The Idea of Culture in the Social Sciences (Cambridge University Press, 1973).
     The concept of symbols is crucial to that of culture and to the relation of systemic social theory to theology. See Lyman Bryson, ed., Symbols and Society (Harper, 1955); Hugh D. Duncan, Communication and Social Order (Bedminster, 1962), and Symbols and Social Theory (Oxford University Press, 1969); and Raymond Firth, Symbols: Public and Private (Cornell University Press, 1973). For some connections with religion see Mary Douglas, Natural Symbols: Explorations in Cosmology (Pantheon, 1970); Thomas Fawcett, The Symbolic Language of Religion (Augsburg, 1971); Paul Tillich, "The Religious Symbol," in Fred Dillistone, ed., Myth and Symbol, "Theological Collections," No. 7 (London: SPCK Press, 1966), pp. 15-34.

13. On legitimacy and authority from a systemic perspective see Talcott Parsons, "Authority, Legitimation, and Political Action," in Structures and Process in Modern Societies, pp. 170-98. See also Carl J. Friedrich, "Law, Authority, and Legitimacy," in The Philosophy of Law in Historical Perspective (University of Chicago Press, 1963), ch. 21; and Hannah Arendt, "What is Authority?" Between Past and Future (World, 1961), ch. 3.

14. Durkheim, The Division of Labor, pp. 353-73; Suicide, pp. 241-76. See also, R. Merton, Social Theory and Social Structure, chaps. 5, 6, and Marshall B. Clinard, ed., Anomie and Deviant Behavior (Free Press, 1964).

15. For some specific attempts to define a pluralist approach see Robert Presthus, "The Pluralist Framework," in H. Kariel, ed., Frontiers of Democratic Theory (Random, 1970), pp. 274-304; Nelson Polsby, Community Power and Political Theory (Yale University Press, 1963), ch. 6; Hannah Arendt, On Revolution (Viking, 1966); Pierre van den Berghe, Race and Racism: A Comparative Perspective (Wiley, 1967); William Newman, American Pluralism: A Study of Minority Groups and Social Theory

(Harper and Row, 1973); and Andrew Greeley, The American
Catholic: A Social Portrait (Basic, 1977).
     For some critiques see Theodore Lowi, The End of
Liberalism (Norton, 1969), and William Connolly., ed.,
The Bias of Pluralism (Atherton, 1969).

16.   For a sampling of the extensive literature on power
see Marvin Olsen, ed., Power in Societies (Macmillan,
1970); Michael Aiken and Paul E. Mott, eds., The
Structure of Community Power (Random, 1970); and Willis
D. Hawley and Frederick Wirt, eds., The Search for
Community Power (Prentice-Hall, 1968).

17.   For a good presentation of Weber's view see Martin
E. Spencer, "Weber on Legitimate Norms and Authority,"
British Journal of Sociology, 21 (1970), 123-34. For
expositions emphasizing the dimension of power in authority see Robert Bierstedt, "The Problem of Authority,"
in Morroe Berger, et al., eds., Freedom and Control in
Modern Society (Octagon, 1954), pp. 67-81, and I. L.
Horowitz, "The Norm of Illegitimacy: The Political So-
ciology of Latin America," in Horowitz, ed., Latin Amer-
ican Radicalism (Randon House-Vintage, 1969), pp. 3-28.
     For two analyses in this tradition see James M.
Gustafson, "Authority in a Pluralistic Society," The
Church as Moral Decision Maker (United Church Press,
1970), pp. 47-61, and Jürgen Habermas, "What Does a
Crisis Mean Today? Legitimation Problems in Late
Capitalism," Social Research, 40:4 (1973), 643-67.

18.   For rationalization and routinization in Weber see
Julien Freund, The Sociology of Weber, tr. M. Ilford
(Pantheon, 1968), pp. 17-24, 229-45. Glen C. Dealy
explores rationalization and routinization in the Latin
countries in The Public Man (University of Massachusetts
Press, 1977).

19.   Peter Berger and Richard Neuhaus present a brief but
lucid pluralist proposal in To Empower People: The Role
of Mediating Structures in Public Policy (American
Enterprise Institute, 1977).

20.   For examples of prescriptive pluralism see Henry
Kariel, The Promise of Politics (Prentice-Hall, 1966);
Bernard Crick, In Defence of Politics (University of
Chicago Press, 1962), and Paul T. Heyne, Private Keepers
of the Public Interest (McGraw-Hill, 1968).

21.   For a presentation of Marx's thought see David McLel-
lan, The Thought of Karl Marx (Harper and Row, 1972).
The best contemporary American expression of this
tradition is Paul Baran and Paul Sweezey, Monopoly
Capital: An Essay on the American Economic and Social

Order (Monthly Review Press, 1968). For the European
side see Ralf Dahrendorf, Class and Class Conflict in
Industrial Society (Stanford University Press, 1959).
The more populist version is presented and critiqued
in G. W. Domhoff and H. B. Ballard, eds., C. Wright
Mills and the Power Elite (Beacon Press, 1968).
     For some reactionary as well as progressive and
radical forms see A. James Gregor, ed., Contemporary
Radical Ideologies (Random, 1967). Ortego y Gasset's
famous work, The Revolt of the Masses (Norton, 1932)
represents the conservative position.
     Dualist themes run through most Black American social
thought. See the collections in Howard Brotz, ed.,
Negro Social and Political Thought (Basic, 1966) and
August Meier and Francis Broderick, eds., Negro Protest
Thought in the 20th Century (Bobbs-Merrill, 1966).

22.   A typical study on equality is Arthur Shostak, J. Van
Til, S. B. Van Til, Privilege in America: An End to
Inequality? (Prentice-Hall, 1973). For Marxist ethics
see Eugene Kamenka, Marxism and Ethics (London: Macmillan, 1970) for a beginning. The anarchist route is
spelled out by April Carter, The Political Theory of
Anarchism (London: Routledge and Kegan Paul, 1971).

23.   See James H. Meisel, The Myth of the Ruling Class
(University of Michigan Press, 1962) for discussion of
elite theories of Mosca, Pareto, and Michels. For a
general overview see T. B. Bottomore, Elites and Society (Basic, 1964).

24.   For excellent surveys of the problem of class theory
and analysis see T. B. Bottomore, Classes in Modern
Society (Random, 1968); Leonard Reissman, Class in
American Society (Free Press, 1965); and M. Tumin, ed.,
Readings on Social Stratification (Prentice-Hall, 1970).

25.   Bertil Ollman presents Marx's theory in Alienation:
Marx's Concept of Man in Capitalist Society (Cambridge:
Cambridge University Press, 1971). Contemporary con-
fusions are discussed by John Horton in "The Dehumani-
zation of Anomie and Alienation," British Journal of
Sociology, 15 (1964), 283-300.

26.   Karl Mannheim, Ideology and Utopia, tr. L. Wirth, E.
Shils (Harcourt, Brace, and World, 1936). George
Lichtheim provides a wide-ranging historical introduc-
tion to the problem in The Concept of Ideology and Other
Essays (Random, 1967). For Habermas, see Theory and
Practice (Beacon, 1973) and note 3 of this chapter.

27.   Marx's view can be found in The Communist Manifesto
(1848), Pt. I. Mao Tse-Tung's perspective is found in

his 1937 essay, "On Contradiction," <u>Selected Readings from the Works of Mao Tse-Tung</u> (Peking: Foreign Language Press, 1971), pp. 85-133. Franz Schurmann presents an American analysis in "System, Contradictions, and Revolution in America, in R. Aya and N. Miller, eds., <u>The New American Revolution</u> (Free Press, 1970), pp. 18-96.

28.   This problem is reflected in Eastern Europe through Milovan Djilas' <u>The New Class: An Analysis of the Communist System</u> (Praeger, 1957) and in China with the cultural revolution under Mao's Red Guards in the late 1960's. Latin American radicals focus attention on the global contradiction between the "center" and the "periphery" regions of the world.

29.   V. I. Lenin represents the elitist and activist tradition, classically expressed in <u>What Is To Be Done? Burning Questions of Our Movement</u>, tr. Fineburg and Hanna (International Publishers, 1969). For an approach to education in the general dualist vein see P. Freire, <u>Pedagogy of the Oppressed</u> (Herder and Herder, 1972).

30.   For the violent end of the spectrum see Carl Leiden and Karl Schmitt, <u>The Politics of Violence: Revolution in the Modern World</u> (Prentice-Hall, 1968). A more pluralistic and political approach finds popular expression in Michael P. Lerner, <u>The New Socialist Revolution: An Introduction to its Theory and Strategy</u> (Delacourte, 1973). Most of the long revolutionists turn to cultural changes. See Raymond Williams, <u>The Long Revolution</u> (Columbia University Press, 1961), or Theodore Roszak, <u>The Making of a Counter Culture</u> (Doubleday, 1969).

CHAPTER SEVEN
INTERDISCIPLINARY TRIADS

1.   Ernst Troeltsch, <u>The Social Teaching of the Christian Churches</u>, 2 vols., tr. O. Wyon (Harper Brothers, 1960), pp. 331-42, 477-94, 515-20, 993.

2.   Emile Durkheim, <u>Moral Education</u> (Free Press, 1961), and the volume of Durkheim's essays edited by Robert Bellah, <u>On Morality and Society</u> (University of Chicago Press, 1973).

3.   Talcott Parsons, <u>Social Structure and Personality</u> (Free Press, 1964).

4.   B. R. Brinkman, "On Sacramental Man," <u>Heythrop Journal</u>, 13 (1972), 371-401, and <u>Heythrop Journal</u>, 14 (1973), 5-34, 162-189, 280-306, and 396-416.

5.   Urban T. Holmes III, The Future Shape of Ministry
(Seabury, 1971), and "Liminality and Liturgy," Worship,
47 (1973), 386-97.

6.   See James Cone, A Black Theology of Liberation
(Seabury, 1969). For an overview of the Latin American
developments see Philip Berryman," Latin American
Theology of Liberation," Theological Studies, 34 (1973),
357-95. For a blend of Marxist and populist theories
in a theological position see William Coats, God in
Public: Political Theology Beyond Niebuhr (Eerdmans,
1974).

7.   See the essay by James Luther Adams, "Is Marx's
Thought Relevant to the Christian?" in N. Lobkowicz,
ed., Marx and the Western World (Notre Dame University
Press, 1967), pp. 371-88.

8.   See the notes on Gutierrez in Chapter 11. For Bonino
see Christians and Marxists: The Mutual Challenge to
Revolution (London and Toronto: Hodder and Stoughton,
1976). See also Jose Miranda, Marx and the Bible (Orbis,
1974).

9.   For the social impact of Calvinism see R. Kingdon and
R. Lindner, eds., Calvinism and Democracy (Heath, 1970)
and R. W. Green, ed., Protestantism, Capitalism, and
Social Science: The Weber Thesis Controversy, 2d ed.
(Heath, 1973).

10.   See above, Chapter 1, note 9. Also, The Nature and
Destiny of Man: A Christian Interpretation (Scribner's,
1949).

11.   In Christ and Culture H. Richard Niebuhr points out
the dualistic strands in Luther's theology and sociology
along with the paradoxical elements that divert it from
our primary triad.

12.   For a compendious interpretation of the historical
sources of the two-kingdom notion see Ulrich Duchrow,
Christenheit and Weltverantwortung (Stuttgart: Klett,
1970). Two Kingdoms and One World, Karl Hertz, ed.
(Augsburg, 1976) provides a wide-ranging selection of
views as well as a more liberal or radical use of the
two-kingdoms tradition.

13.   Erik Erikson, Young Man Luther: A Study in Psychoanalysis and History (Norton, 1962).

14.   For a lively and penetrating example of this thrust
see James Luther Adams, On Being Human Religiously:
Selected Essays in Religion and Society, ed. Max L.

Stackhouse (Beacon, 1976). The Introduction by Stack-
house traces a number of these themes in Adams' writings.
See also the Adams Festschrift, <u>Voluntary Associations:</u>
<u>A Study of Groups in Free Societies</u>, ed. D. B. Robertson
(John Knox, 1966).

15.   Thomas C. Oden, <u>The Intensive Group Experience: The</u>
<u>New Pietism</u> (Westminster, 1972), pp. 69-77.

16.   Frank Goble, <u>The Third Force: The Psychology of</u>
<u>Abraham Maslow</u> (Pocket Books, 1971).

17.   For the theological roots of this liberal economics
see the articles in R. W. Green, <u>Protestantism, Capital-</u>
<u>ism, and Social Science</u>, and for the political side,
Winthrop S. Hudson, "John Locke: Heir of Puritan Political Theorists," in George L. Hunt, ed., <u>Calvinism and</u>
<u>the Political Order</u> (Westminster, 1965), pp. 108-29.

18.   Thomas C. Oden, <u>Kerygma and Counseling: Toward a</u>
<u>Covenant Ontology for Secular Psychotherapy</u> (Westminster,
1966).

19.   John Wesley, <u>A Representative Collection of His</u>
<u>Writings</u>, ed. Albert C. Outler (Oxford University Press,
1964).

20.   Donald G. Bloesch defends Wesley and other pietists
from the charge that they were not socially concerned
and that they did not promote social change.
       "Both social service and political action have been
prominent in later Pietism (Evangelicalism). The
Clapham sect in England, which was composed of wealthy
Evangelical laymen, was instrumental in the abolition
of the slave traffic...
       "John Wesley, who preached the gospel of regeneration,
sought to demonstrate the fruits of new birth in his
daily life. Besides working for the abolition of
slavery he instituted clinics and credit unions. He
held that the increase of personal wealth is the most
subtle foe to a life of consecration." <u>The Evangelical</u>
<u>Renaissance</u> (Eerdmans, 1973).
       Our statement that Wesley never sought to change
wider political or economic structures of his time is
not a charge that he had no social responsibility or
that his social theory was inadequate. His emphasis on
individual transformation through voluntary association
is typical of a pluralistic social theory in contrast
to other theories that would emphasize more immediate
comprehensive change of social structures.

CHAPTER EIGHT
CONGRUENCE

1.   Cf. Edward C. F. A. Schillebeeckx, <u>Christ the Sacrament of the Encounter with God</u>, tr. P. Barrett (Sheed and Ward, 1963).

2.   Cf. David P. O'Neill, <u>The Priest in Crisis: A Study in Role Change</u> (Pflaum, 1968).

3.   Thomas C. Oden, <u>The Structure of Awareness</u> (Abingdon, 1969).

4.   Lowell Colston, <u>Judgment in Pastoral Counseling</u> (Abingdon, 1969).

5.   Eduard Turneyson, <u>A Theology of Pastoral Care</u> (John Knox, 1963).

6.   Erik Erikson, <u>Childhood and Society</u>, 2d. ed. (Norton, 1963).

7.   See discussion of Mannheim's concept of ideology in Chapter 6 above, and note 26 of that chapter.

8.   Eric Berne, M.D., <u>Games People Play</u> (Grove, 1964).

9.   Bernard E. Meland, ed., <u>The Future of Empirical Theology</u> ("Essays in Divinity," vol. 7), ed. Jerald C. Brauer (University of Chicago Press, 1969); and also Robert W. Bretall, ed., <u>The Empirical Theology of Henry Nelson Wieman</u> (Southern Illinois University Press, 1969).

CHAPTER NINE
TRILATERAL CRITIQUE AND TRANSFORMATION

1.   Bernard Lonergan, <u>Method in Theology</u> (Herder and Herder, 1972), ch. 2.

2.   Paul Tillich, "You Are Accepted," <u>The Shaking of the Foundations</u> (Scribner's, 1948), pp. 153-63.

3.   Carl Jung, "A Psychological Approach to the Dogma of the Trinity," <u>Psychology and Religion: West and East</u>, 2d. ed., tr. R. F. C. Hull ("Bollingen Series," vol. 20; Princeton University Press, 1969), pp. 107-200.

4.   John Rawls, <u>A Theory of Justice</u> (Harvard University Press, 1971), p. 20.

5.   Paul Tillich, "The Protestant Principle and the Proletarian Situation," <u>The Protestant Era</u>, tr. J. L. Adams (University of Chicago Press, 1957), pp. 161-81;

6.	In the cases of Marxism and Freudianism considerable
effort had to be devoted to identifying the "classical"
or "authentic" thrust of the thinker. For Marx, was it
the "orthodoxy" running through Engels-Lenin-Stalin (and
perhaps Mao) or was it the "young Marx" and the humanistic strands that emerged in Eastern Europe in the
1960's? For Freud, was it the cautious and conservative
defender of self-consciousness and cultural sublimation
or was it the defender of libidinal interests against
the claims of culture?
	For penetrating appropriation of Marxist positions
see, for Europe, Helmut Gollwitzer, The Christian Faith
and the Marxist Criticism of Religion, tr. D. Cairns
(Scribner's, 1970).
	For the reappropriation of Hegel see Wolf-Dieter
Marsch, Die Gegenwart Christi in der Gesellschaft: Eine
Studie zu Hegels Dialektik (München: Chr. Kaiser, 1965).
	On the American scene see John Raines and Thomas
Dean, eds., Marxism and Radical Religion: Essays Toward
a Revolutionary Humanism (Temple University Press, 1970);
Thomas Dean, Post-Theistic Thinking: The Marxist-
Christian Dialogue in Radical Perspective (Temple Uni-
versity Press, 1975). Rosemary Ruether, The Radical
Kingdom: The Western Experience of Messianic Hope
(Harper and Row, 1970); as well as the survey, Radical
Christianity and Its Sources, by John C. Cooper (West-
minster, 1968). See also the journal Radical Religion
(Berkeley, California).

7.	Martin Jay provides a helpful history of the Institut
in The Dialectical Imagination: A History of the Frank-
furt School and the Institute of Social Research 1923-50
(Little, Brown, 1973). See also Albrecht Wellmer,
Critical Theory of Society, tr. J. Cumming (Herder and
Herder, 1971). For a representative writing see Max
Horkheimer and Theodore W. Adorno, Dialectic of
Enlightenment, tr. J. Cumming (Seabury, 1972).

8.	Johannes Metz, Theology of the World, tr. W. Glen
Doepel (Herder and Herder, 1969). See also "The Church's
Social Function in the Light of a Political Theology,"
in J. D. Metz, ed., Faith and the World of Politics
(Concilium, vol. 36; Paulist, 1968). See also Wolfhardt
Pannenberg, Theology and the Kingdom of God (Westminster,
1969) and What is Man?, tr. D. A. Priebe (Fortress,
1970). Peter Berger, The Sacred Canopy: Elements of a
Sociological Theory of Religion (Doubleday, 1967), and
A Rumor of Angels: Modern Society and the Rediscovery
of the Supernatural (Doubleday, 1969). Gregory Baum,
Religion and Alienation: A Theological Reading of Sociology (Paulist, 1975). For further elaboration of the
impact in Germany see J. B. Metz, J. Moltmann, Willi
Oelmüller, Kirche im Prozess der Aufklärung: Aspekte

einer neuen politischen Theologie (München: Chr. Kaiser, 1970) and J. B. Metz, Trutz Rendtorff, eds., Die Theologie in der interdisziplinären Forschung (Düsseldorf: Bertelsmann Universitätsverlag, 1971).

9.   For some motifs in psychology see Jerome Agel, producer, Rough Times (Ballantine, 1973); Phil Brown (1971); Jerome Agel, Radical Therapist (Ballantine, 1971); and the journal, Issues in Radical Therapy (Oakland, California). See also above, Chapter 5, note 10. Robert Coles' most impressive contribution has been the three volume Children of Crisis (Little, Brown, 1967, 1972).

10.   In sociology see Alvin Gouldner, The Coming Crisis in Western Sociology (Basic, 1970). Franz Fanon, Wretched of the Earth, tr. C. Farrington (Grove, 1968); James Robert Ross, comp., The War Within: Violence or Non Violence in the Black Revolution (Sheed and Ward, 1971); Albert Cleage, Black Christian Nationalism: New Directions for the Black Church (Morrow, 1972); Joseph Washington, Jr., Politics of God: The Future of the Black Churches (Beacon, 1967); James Cone, A Black Theology of Liberation (Lippincott, 1970) and God of the Oppressed (Seabury, 1975).

11.   Shulamith Firestone, Dialectic of Sex: The Case for Feminist Revolution (Morrow, 1974). For a thoroughgoing theological appropriation of these themes see Mary Daly, Beyond God the Father: Toward a Philosophy of Women's Liberation (Beacon, 1973). See also Letty M. Russell, Human Liberation in a Feminist Perspective: A Theology (Westminster, 1974).

12.   Ivan Illich, Deschooling Society (Harper and Row, 1972); Christopher Jencks, et al., Inequality (Basic, 1972); and Harold W. Sobel and Arthur Salz, Radical Papers: Readings in Education (Harper and Row, 1972); Herbert Marcuse, One Dimensional Man (Beacon, 1964).

13.   The movement of radical evangelicals arose in the 1960's especially in the mid West and gave rise to a paper titled The Post American (now, Sojourners). See Richard Quebedeaux, The Young Evangelicals (Harper and Row, 1974) for an introduction.

14.   For an example of this effort see William Everett, "Liturgy and American Society: An Invocation for Ethical Analysis" Anglican Theological Review, 51 (1974), 16-34.

CHAPTER TEN
CHRISTIANITY AND PERSONALITY IN TRANSFORMATION:
THOMAS C. ODEN

1.   Thomas C. Oden, Kerygma and Counseling (Westminster, 1966).

2.   Thomas C. Oden, The Structure of Awareness (Abingdon, 1969).

3.   Carl R. Robers, Client-centered Therapy, pp. 524-530.

4.   Thomas C. Oden, The Intensive Group Experience: The New Pietism (Westminster, 1972).

5.   Oden, Kerygma, p. 33.

6.   Ibid., p. 162.

7.   Eduard Thurneysen, A Theology of Pastoral Care (John Knox, 1962).

8.   Oden, Structure, p. 267.

9.   Ibid., p. 268.

10.   Oden, Kerygma, p. 147.

11.   Ibid., p. 153.

12.   Don S. Browning uses Dorothy Emmet's epistemology to handle this problem in his Atonement and Psychotherapy, (Westminster, 1966), pp. 161-73.

13.   Thomas C. Oden, Beyond Revolution: A Response to the Underground Church (Westminster, 1970).

14.   Ibid., p. 17.

15.   Ibid., p. 46.

16.   Ibid., p. 16.

17.   Oden, Structure, p. 67.

18.   Oden, Beyond Revolution, p. 29.

19.   Ibid.,

20.   Oden, Structure, p. 93.

21.   Browning, Atonement, pp. 31-50, 214-57. Following Browning we also note a third atonement option in

Christian history, Irenaeus' ransom theory, in which
Christ is the ransom God pays to the devil for man's
salvation. This has certain affinities with Oden's
conception of the bondage of the will and with conflict
motifs in Rogers' own thought.

CHAPTER ELEVEN
   CHRISTIANITY AND SOCIETY IN TRANSFORMATION:
   GUSTAVO GUTIERREZ

1.   We are using the English translation by Sister
      Caridad Inda and John Eagleson (Orbis, 1973). Hence-
      forth cited by page number within the text.
          For the important practical expression of Gutierrez'
      kind of thinking within the Chilean movement, Christians
      for Socialism, see "First Latin American Encounter of
      Christians for Socialism: Final Document," I-DOC,
      November, 1972; and John Eagleson, ed., Christians and
      Socialism, tr. J. Drury (Orbis, 1975).

2.   Helder Camara, Archbishop of Olinda and Recife,
      Brazil, has proposed that Karl Marx is the new Aristotle
      in the dialogue between Christian theology and culture
      in "What Would St. Thomas Aquinas, the Aristotle Commen-
      tator, Do If Faced with Karl Marx?" Journal of Religion,
      Supplement, vol. 58 (December, 1978).

3.   Herbert Marcuse, One Dimensional Man (Beacon, 1964).
      For a less obviously Marxist exploration see Norman O.
      Brown, Life Against Death (Random, 1959).

ABOUT THE AUTHORS

WILLIAM W. EVERETT has taught Theology and Social
Science at St. Francis Seminary, Milwaukee, since 1969. He
is a graduate of Wesleyan University (B.A.), Yale Divinity
School (B.D.), and Harvard University (Ph.D.). He has also
taught at the Johann-Wolfgang Goethe Universität, Berea
College, and St. Mary of the Lake Seminary, Mundelein,
Illinois. He is active in the American Baptist Churches and
has engaged in extensive consultation with the Lutheran
World Federation. In addition he has participated deeply
in ecumenical work among local churches. A member of
several scholarly societies, his articles have appeared in
Zygon, Anglican Theological Review, Encounter, and the
Journal of Religious Ethics.

T. J. (TIM) BACHMEYER is a psychotherapist and human
relations consultant in private practice in Milwaukee. He
taught Theology and Personality at St. Francis Seminary in
Milwaukee from 1970-75. Since 1977 he has been instructor
in psychology, Holy Redeemer College, Waterford, Wisconsin.
He has also taught at St. Mary of the Lake Seminary,
Mundelein, Illinois. He is a graduate of Yale University
(B.A.) and the University of Chicago Divinity School (B.D.,
M.A., Ph.D.). He has published in Zygon, Religious
Education, and The Living Light. A Clinical Member of the
International Transactional Analysis Association, he
conducts workshops in human sexuality as well as in
comparative psychotherapy.